Have a
New
Teenager
by Friday

Do you know this person?

- He eats cereal out of a large mixing bowl.
- Her bedroom looks like a garbage dump . . . on a good day.
- She changes outfits three times before breakfast.
- If there was an Academy Award for eye-rolling, he'd win.
- Her favorite sport is talking back.
- His earbuds are permanently glued to his ears.
- She can text like a mad woodpecker while watching *The Bachelor*, listening to her favorite music, and doing her homework.
- Some days he thinks that you, his parent, are the dumbest creature who ever walked this earth.

Congratulations! You have a teenager in your home.

Life will never quite be the same again (you already know that). But it can be *better than you've ever dreamed.*

I guarantee it.

Have a New Teenager by Friday

From Mouthy and Moody to Respectful and Responsible in **5 Days**

Dr. Kevin Leman

Revell

a division of Baker Publishing Group
Grand Rapids, Michigan

© 2011 by Dr. Kevin Leman

Published by Revell
a division of Baker Publishing Group
P.O. Box 6287, Grand Rapids, MI 49516-6287
www.revellbooks.com

Printed in the United States of America

Paperback editon published 2013
ISBN 978-0-8007-2215-9

The Library of Congress has cataloged the hardcover edition as follows:
Leman, Kevin.
    Have a new teenager by Friday : from mouthy and moody to respectful and
responsible in 5 days / Kevin Leman.
      p.   cm.
    Includes bibliographical references and index.
    ISBN 978-0-8007-2021-6 (cloth) — ISBN 978-0-8007-2110-7 (pbk.)
    1. Parent and teenager. 2. Parenting. 3. Parenting—Religious aspects—
Christianity. I. Title.
HQ799.15.L463 2011
306.874—dc22   2011016899

Scripture quotations are from *The Living Bible*, copyright © 1971. Used by permission of Tyndale House Publishers, Inc., Wheaton, Illinois 60189. All rights reserved.

To protect the privacy of those who have shared their stories with the author, some
details and names have been changed.

14   15   16   17   18   19   7 6 5 4 3 2

To my little muffin,
aka Lauren, LB, Lorney, Lorney Beth,
the last Leman child to leave the nest

May your best dreams come true. I really can't wait to see what you accomplish in life.

Your compassion for others, your work ethic, and your friendly, outgoing nature—not to mention your downright loveliness—will take you to great heights. So fly, my sweet angel, fly!

I love you,

Dad (and Mom too)

Contents

Acknowledgments   9

Introduction

I'm Telling You, They'll Get Weirder than Weird   11

You've just entered the Great Metamorphosis.

Monday

He Used to Be Normal. What Happened?   17

This alien creature didn't just morph overnight. How to make adjustments for your new life together.

Tuesday

Talking to the "Whatever" Generation   47

Getting beyond the crossed arms, the grunt, the staring out the car window, and the "whatever" comments to reach your child's heart.

Wednesday

Belonging Matters More than You Think   65

How to keep your teenager in your world while traveling through his or her world.

Thursday

"You're Grounded!" (I Hope So)   81

Are your teenagers grounded for what they do . . . or grounded in who they are? How to raise a street-smart kid.

Friday

Ka-ching, Ka-ching, Dividends on the Way   99

No more pull-ups. No more sippy cups. How to take advantage of these free 'n' easy years.

Ask Dr. Leman

A to Z Game Plans That Really Work   123

The 75 hottest topics parents have asked Dr. Leman about in his seminars across the country—and his time-tested advice that really works. Plus more "It Worked for Me" stories of parents who tried Dr. Leman's tips—and are now smiling all over.

Epilogue   299
The Top 10 Countdown to Having a New Teenager by
    Friday   305
Notes   307
Index of A to Z Topics   309
About Dr. Kevin Leman   311
Resources by Dr. Kevin Leman   313

Acknowledgments

To my editor, Ramona Cramer Tucker, whose passion to grow a healthy relationship between parents and teenagers is as deep as mine, and who is the best mom to one of my favorite teenagers, Kayla.

To my Revell editor, Lonnie Hull DuPont, who always entertains the creative ideas of this baby-of-the-family author. She does a great job of making me "behave" myself.

And to Jessica Miles, my spot-on project editor, who doesn't miss a flaw.

Introduction

I'm Telling You, They'll Get Weirder than Weird

You've just entered the Great Metamorphosis.

I was in the airport recently, taking off my shoes, belt, and just about everything except my Skivvies to stash in one of those rubber bins to go through the security checkpoint. I happened to be carrying a copy of my books *Have a New Kid by Friday* and *Have a New Husband by Friday*—rubber-banded together—so I placed those in the bin too. After I'd been "wanded" and cleared through security, I was gathering up my earthly possessions and still shoeless when a woman behind me exclaimed, "Oh, Dr. Kevin Leman! I *love* him!"

I swiveled to look at her. She was pointing to *Have a New Kid by Friday* in my bin.

"He's so practical," she said enthusiastically. "He helped me raise all my kids."

I smiled. "Well, I love him too."

I was going to let it go at that . . . until she frowned a bit, adding, "He's been around a long time. In fact, I wonder if he's still alive."

I figured then that I'd better pony up. I pointed to the book. "Well, 'him' is me."

Her face morphed into shock. "You're kidding."

"No."

"Oh my goodness!"

"And I still have one teenager at home," I told her. "A senior in high school. In fact, we had one child when my wife was 42 and I was 44, and another when my wife was 48 and I was 50."

"Oops." She nodded sagely. "Mistakes."

"No," I said. "Two great kids."

I meant every word.

Even better, I *have* been around a long time, and the good news is I'm still alive! Even with weathering the teenage years five times with my kids!

If you picked up this book, you've just entered the Great Metamorphosis—those weirder-than-weird, critical years when your child is between the ages of 11 and 19. I call them the *critical years* because what your child does during these years can affect the rest of his or her life, and you, Mom or Dad, won't always be there to look over your child's shoulder.

> **Top 5 Requirements to Parenting Teenagers**
>
> - A healthy sense of humor
> - Long-term perspective
> - The good sense God gave you
> - The ability to say it once, walk away, and then let the chips fall where they may
> - Some Excedrin . . . and a long nap

Not that you would probably *want* to know all the things your teenager does. If you don't believe that to be true, think for a moment. What stories do you swap with friends now about the crazy things you did as a teenager? The dumb antics you pulled that would make your mom break out in hives or your dad gain a few more gray hairs? Things your parents had no idea you did until years later, when the crises had passed, and you could all laugh about them?

But no one needs to tell you these are years of great change, do they? The proof is right in front of your eyes. Your precious babies are growing up faster than you ever could have imagined. Suddenly pant legs are too short, appetites are never-ending, shoes are too small, and mouths are too large. Some of your kids will let you hug them until they get married; others, who used to be warm and cuddly toddlers, will give you a straight-arm like an NFL running back if you even attempt a hug in front of their friends. And don't forget "the look" that says it's now your role to walk 10 feet *behind* your teenager, if you even have to walk on the same sidewalk at all. And heaven forbid if you drop her off at the front door at school, where all her peers can see your less-than-new SUV.

> *In a teenager's world, every zit is the size of Mount Vesuvius.*

Every teenager is different—it comes with the territory. One night he'll hate chicken, the next night he'll hate tacos. Realize that, for a teenager, no dinner you'll make will ever be perfect . . . even if it's the exact one he requested an hour ago. That's because his likes and dislikes change as rapidly as the direction of the wind.

Think back on your own teenage years—the clothes you used to wear, the hairstyles, the things you used to say. I can picture myself right now as I was as a teenager: greased-back hair, attitude with a capital *A*, and a cigarette hanging from the corner of my mouth. Yeah, I was cooler than cool, and I knew it. At least that's what I told myself.

Picturing yourself when you were 11 to 19 will give you perspective and a sense of humor about that boy of yours who is wearing his pants halfway down his tail. In light of such fashion, just make sure your son has some good-lookin' boxer shorts, because they're certainly going to be on display for a lot of folks to see.

Someday your teenager will laugh at herself in pictures, just as you snicker at yourself "back then." She'll be showing her own children the stupid styles and ideas she fell prey to. But right now, she takes everything about her world seriously. Life, to teenagers, is not a laughing matter. So when you do need to laugh about their predicaments, I suggest you do it in private or at least around the corner of the kitchen. In a teenager's world, every zit is the size of Mount Vesuvius. Every embarrassing comment is doubly, even triply, embarrassing. Each sideways look or eye-roll from a peer means "I hate you" or "you're a loser" and can ruin even the best of days. Lows are lower than low, and emotions run as high as hormones. That's why most teenagers live a roller-coaster existence.

> *This time will disappear faster than sand in an hourglass, so why not take advantage of it?*

The greatest thing you can do for yourself and for your teenagers is to have a healthy sense of humor because, in these years, their development will resemble a seismography during an earthquake—all wavy, crisscrossing lines. You need to be the semi-straight line—note I didn't say a *perfect* straight line—knowing where you're heading as a family. You're that steady guide who keeps them walking along the path, not the helicopter parent who hovers over their every move. In fact, the more you hover during these hormone-group years, the more likely you are to push your teenagers into rebelling against you and everything you stand for.

Have a New Teenager by Friday will help you stand by your kids and stand up to them, and will assist you in packing their bags full of what they need for life (things like integrity, doing the right thing, and respecting people) at home, at school, and in the adult world. Your child may be 11. If so, you have a good six-plus years before you're standing in front of her dorm at college crying and saying good-bye to her. If your child is 14, you have a few less years. This time will disappear faster than sand in an hourglass, so why not take advantage of it? These are the great years, the best and most fun years with your kids . . . if you understand the mission you're on and maintain your balance along the way.

And oh, the fun you'll have! Trust me. I've not only survived but thoroughly enjoyed *all five* of my children's teenage years—and with Lauren, the last in the nest, I'm still in the midst of these exciting years. In fact, I was sitting at the kitchen table a few minutes ago, working on this book, when Lauren walked in.

"What are you doing, Dad?" she asked.

"Oh, thinking through my new book, *Have a New Teenager by Friday.*"

Lauren eyed me and said calmly, "Hey, I want to get a piercing in my nose and have it connect to my mouth."

"Oh, good, honey," I said. "We're having spaghetti tonight."

Lauren turned to me with a twinkle in her eye. "Oh, Dad, that is *good.*"

The point is, parent, you don't have to react to everything. Maintain your sense of humor. Don't make a mountain out of a molehill. Then you too can enjoy these years and give yourself many memories to reflect on and laugh about as a family.

If you think that once your kids become teenagers, you don't have any influence over them anymore, you're dead wrong. You're still in the game. Even more, you're the coach calling the shots. Yes, the clock is ticking and the game might get intense from time to time, but it isn't over yet. You're only in the third quarter of life with your kids, and how the game ends has everything to do with you. If you follow the principles in this book, you'll establish authority, gain their respect, provide direction for them, and know what to do and when to do it.

The secret is all in how you play your parental cards.

I also guarantee that you'll have a new teenager in five days (or even less). Attitudes will change, behaviors will change, and a character you'll really like will be formed—one that will last a lifetime. Your teenager will have integrity, do the right thing, and be a respectful, contributing member of your home.

The secret is all in how you play your parental cards. You hold the aces, because you count far more in your teenager's life than you'll ever know or he'll ever admit (at least until he's in college and wants to know how to do the laundry).

For some additional encouragement to stick to your guns—the rewards are worth it!—I'm including some "It Worked for Me" stories I've gathered from in-the-trenches parents who have tried these time-tested principles I've talked about at seminars, on the radio, on television, in my video series, and now in this book. These parents are now smiling all over, and soon you will be too.

If you have a kid who is moody and mouthy on Monday, in less than five days that same kid is going to come into your living room and say to you, "What can I do to help, Mom?"

Brace yourself for the fall.

Just make sure you're positioned over a soft chair.

Monday

He Used to Be Normal. What Happened?

This alien creature didn't just morph overnight. How to make adjustments for your new life together.

Have you seen those T-shirts women wear when they're pregnant? The ones that say "Baby under Construction"? They always make me smile because they're right on the money. After all, that baby is being constructed and growing even though you haven't been able to see his little cherub face yet. Then that baby comes into the world, and you spend the first 10 years of life interacting with him, teaching him, loving him, and disciplining him.

Then what I call the *hormone-group years*—ages 11 to 19—hit, and you're blindsided by the metamorphosis from child to teenager.

What has happened to your sweet child to transform him or her into the alien creature you're now interacting with each day? The son whose language skills have dwindled to the occasional grunt? The naive daughter whose complexion was so perfect that she could have been a model for an Irish Spring commercial—"Aye, yes, I love it too!"—but whose skin is now best suited for a Pizza Hut commercial? A son who no longer wants kisses and hugs from you in front of his buddies and wants you to walk a block behind him? A daughter who calls you from the city jail because she's been arrested for shoplifting? A son who tells you to go to h-e-double-hockey-sticks when you tell him he can't use the car? A daughter who's a professional at texting, door slamming, and fighting with her sister? A son who refuses to help out around the house anymore and gets mouthy when you remind him to—or, worse, ignores you? A daughter who used to be outgoing but now seems sad, cries a lot, and wants to be alone? A son who got a DUI when you didn't even know he was drinking? A daughter who sleeps until 3:00 p.m. every Saturday and then wants to go out with her friends for the evening?

It's easy to react. All it takes is opening your mouth and letting something spew out before you think. Things like:

- "You are *never* going to drive again . . . ever." But can you fulfill that promise? What about the next time you're in a bind and you need your son to pick up his little brother from soccer practice?
- "Talk to me!" That demand just about guarantees a teenager's mouth clamping shut.
- "Young man, you will never talk to me that way again! You're grounded for life!" But are you really ready to take that statement to the mat . . . for a lifetime? What about when he's 40 and still hanging around the house, burping and leaving pizza crusts by your couch?
- "It's about time you got out of bed. No way are you going out with your friends. You've got a list of chores as big as a mountain to do at home first." But then who gets to deal with the sulky, door-slamming, if-looks-could-kill personality for the rest of the afternoon and evening? You do. So did you win after all?

- "So you've got a few zits. No big deal. I did too, and I lived through the experience." Think back a moment, parent, to when your parent said that same thing to you. Was the first thought that came to your head, *Well, that was certainly helpful. I can't wait to follow through on that advice.* Or was your thought more like, *Wow, they really don't get it, do they? Talk about being on a completely different planet!*

It's Not Your Grandma's World

Today's children are growing up faster than ever before. Their world is not the world you grew up in, and it's certainly not your grandma's world. Your teenager is facing issues like cutting, drugs, depression, suicide, terrorism threats, an uncertain economic future, and anorexia, on top of all the things teenagers have traditionally faced for generations: peer pressure, hormone changes, mounting homework, life stresses, preparation for their life's work, worry about getting into college or serving in the military, etc. The growing rate of deaths of 11- to 19-year-olds—through suicide, drunk driving, and drug overdose—is a sober reminder that many of today's hormone group are simply overwhelmed, and they don't know where to turn.

It's easy to react. All it takes is opening your mouth.

Here's a scary thought: a 17-year-old kid can do anything she wants. She can drive a car legally. That means she can get to a lot of places you might not want her to go. She can hang out with kids you don't know. Can she drink? Of course. All she needs is a fake ID saying she's over 21, and she can easily get that online. Can she do drugs? Obviously. But my question is, if teenagers *can* do all these things, then why do so many kids *not* do them?

Why do so many teenagers choose *not* to drink, *not* to do drugs, *not* to sleep around, and *not* to stay out later than their agreed-upon curfew?

The answer to that question is what this book is all about. You see, attitudes don't happen overnight; they build up over time.

What Kind of Construction Work Do You Need?

Parent, you already know you have a job to do in these hormone-group years, or you wouldn't have picked up this book. Evidently you want to see some things change around your house. But the first thing you need to evaluate is the work to be done.

Whenever a contractor gives you a quote to do some work on your house, he'll first need to know the nature of the job. Is he going to be completely rebuilding the house? Remodeling the house? Changing one room in the house? Repairing a crack in the foundation? Painting a wall or replacing the tile in your bathroom?

Let's say you want to turn a bedroom in your basement into a rec room. The contractor comes in, is in the middle of doing the estimate for what you think will be a fairly simple job, and then notices that there's a crack in the foundation wall. Suddenly that simple job is looking much bigger than you could ever have guessed it could be. Why? Because the foundation—the underpinning of your house—is in trouble. And before anything else gets done, you have to fix that.

> **Signs of a Teenager in the House**
>
> - Your TiVo is overloaded with reality shows.
> - Your grocery bill shot up 30 percent this month.
> - It's 2:30 on a Saturday afternoon, and you've already heard the word *whatever* 59 times.
> - Vocabulary is abbreviated to OMG, LOL, BFF, IDK, ROFL.
> - Likes and dislikes are as changeable as a lightbulb.
> - The word *like* is used as a conjunction, preposition, noun, verb, adverb, and adjective.

Some of you are reading this book because you know the foundation is off. Your teenager is headed for, or is already in, real trouble. Others of you need a room or two rearranged or some walls torn down. Some of you merely need a little touch-up—a coat of paint to freshen things up.

What do you want to accomplish in the next five days? Are you doing a total reconstruction, a partial replacement, or just a paint job? If your teenager is telling you where to go and using the F-word to relate to you, I'd say you need to go for the total reconstruction because his attitude is saying it all—loudly. If your kid has turned lazy and doesn't want to do his chores or "forgets" to do them, a partial replacement might be in order. Or maybe your kid is just entering her teenage years, starting to get mouthy, and becoming Miss Know-It-All, and you don't like it. A good paint job at this stage will probably do the trick—and will last for years if you do it right.

> *Are you doing a total reconstruction, a partial replacement, or just a paint job?*

To have a new teenager by Friday, you need to know first what you have to start with. Then you need to know where you want to end up. As internationally respected leader Stephen Covey says, "Begin with the end in mind."[1] What do you want your son or daughter to be like five days from now? Do you want a kid with character who isn't a character? Do you want her to be respectful and obedient? Do you want him to choose his friends more wisely? Do you need to get him off drugs? Do you want to motivate her to do her schoolwork—on time?

If you know what you want to accomplish, you're more likely to accomplish it. Also, if you just have a little paint job to do, you might have a new teenager by Wednesday if you stick to the principles in this book. But then, if you're doing a total reconstruction, you'll definitely need until Friday—and maybe then some, especially if your teenager has been involved in cutting, anorexia, bulimia, a cult, alcohol, or drugs, and needs professional help.

Some of you also need to call in the exterminator. Sometimes you get these little creatures called bugs in your house. The fact that you have them isn't a castigation of you as a housekeeper; they can get in anybody's house, and they frequently do. But the sooner you get rid of them, the happier you'll be.

I've done 13 commercials for a local pest control in Tucson called 5-Star Termite & Pest Control. When these commercials run, people who see them laugh hysterically.

> *"Begin with the end in mind." What do you want your son or daughter to be like five days from now?*

"I'm Dr. Kevin Leman," I say, "and I've got one wife, five kids, and cockroaches. I was just in the garage yesterday and saw a cockroach on his back—just where I like to see him, by the way. And right before he kicked off, he looked up at me and said, 'The 5-Star guy got me!'"

But the truth is, for those of you who have undesirable cockroaches infesting your home (the friends your kid is hanging out with who aren't good for him or her), it's far from a laughing matter. You, parent, need to rid yourself of the problem immediately. It doesn't mean you won't have more problems down the line, but the undesirables have to go. Right now. Sometimes that might mean driving your son or daughter to and from school, sitting at school events to monitor what's happening, saying no to outings with that group of friends, stashing the car keys somewhere where they can't be found, or even moving your son or daughter to a different school. Yes, all these things are emotionally difficult and time consuming, but the alternative is frightening. There is far too much at stake for you not to act now.

So what kind of help do you need? A little guidance on a paint job? A contractor who could remodel one room? A whole new construction crew? Or a referral to the 5-Star Termite & Pest Control or the Orkin man?

It Worked for Me

Anne has always been a follower, and that has gotten her into big trouble. When she was 13, she fell in with a group of older girls who smoked dope. These girls would come into our house all jacked up and hang out for hours, making a mess. I didn't know what to do because I couldn't stop her from using (I used to smoke weed when I was a teenager too, so I thought, *Who am I to say she can't?*), but I didn't want her to be recovering from "the haze" anywhere else but home. Then I heard your advice on a local radio show and decided to try it out.

The next day, when Anne came home with her friends, I was prepared. I had asked our neighbor Kenny—a big guy who can look scary if you don't know him—to help me out since I'm a single mom. After Anne walked through the kitchen door, he blocked it so the other girls couldn't get in, then locked it and stood there. Anne was furious and started screaming.

I told her calmly, "Your friends are no longer welcome here." Then I turned and walked away into another room. She followed, screaming and cussing, but I went into my bedroom and locked the door. I could hear her trying to wheedle Kenny into letting the girls in. But he had agreed with me to stand firm.

The next day after school, Anne came home by herself, very grumpy. Four hours later, she barked out, "You ruined my life! Now they won't talk to me anymore."

I didn't reply, but inwardly I smiled. I'd gotten rid of the undesirable pests from my home.

A month later, Anne came home alone and holed up in her bedroom for two hours. Some hard news had hit home. One of the girls in her old group had just gotten her learner's permit and was driving the other three girls around. Jacked up on weed, she'd rammed into a concrete median at full speed. All four girls were hospitalized with multiple injuries; one was paralyzed.

I didn't need to say anything. I just held Anne while she cried.

Anne just turned 15 last week. She hasn't smoked dope since the day her old friends were injured. When she brought up that event again yesterday, I finally shared with her some of the awful things that had happened to me when I smoked dope as a teenager. "I don't want to see those things happen to you either," I told her.

Then my daughter did something I never could have expected. She hugged me. Thanks, Dr. Leman, for encouraging me to stick with it. It was far from easy, but wow, the results!

Angela, New Jersey

Developmental Carnality

How your teenager will respond has everything to do with respect—your kid's respect for you, and your respect for your kid. Respect begins from the earliest of stages and builds up over your years of relationship together.

The battles between wills—what I call *developmental carnality*—usually start when your child is about 18 months old, figures out he has a will of his own, and realizes he can exert it. What happens after that point has everything to do with you, parent, because your child's attitude and behavior were created within the space of your home.

From this early stage, it's crucial that you parents pick your battles carefully, and that as situations come up, you don't *react* but *act*. *Reacting* takes you out of the driver's seat and flings you right onto the moment-by-moment emotional roller coaster with your child. *Acting* allows you to sit back, relax, say things once and hold firm, and remain calmly in control, letting the chips fall where they may.

> *Your child's attitude and behavior were created within the space of your home.*

So when your two-year-old spouted off, how did you respond?

- You said, "Oh, Johnny, you shouldn't talk that way. It's not nice. I'm going to give you one more chance to be nice."
- You said, "Young man, you've just earned yourself a time-out. Get in the corner for the rest of the morning."
- You turned, walked into another room, and ignored him. Later, when he wanted to play with his favorite toy, you said, "No, you may not play with that toy today. Mommy doesn't like the way you talked to her." No amount of blue-eyed pleading changed your mind either.

Which scene played out over and over in your house? Your child didn't morph overnight into this alien teenage creature. Guess whom he had help from? How you've acted as a parent and how you've run your home has everything to do with the person your teenager is now.

Take three-year-old firstborn Shannon. When she was being stubborn and disrespectful about eating her lunch, her mother put her in a time-out. She calmly picked up the high chair—with Shannon strapped in it—and moved it around the corner of the kitchen into the hallway, where Shannon couldn't see her mother. Those five minutes seemed like an eternity to the child who didn't like to be separated from her mother. When her mom at last appeared, Shannon said quickly, "All done, Mama, all done."

To this day, 12-year-old Shannon remembers that life event and laughs. "I guess I figured out, 'Hey, that didn't work very well.' I was a smart kid, so I never tried it again. That was the first and last time my mom ever had to put me in a time-out. I knew she meant business and that she wouldn't back down."

> *Purposive behavior serves a person; it meets a need.*

Today Shannon and her mother have a very close relationship built on respect, and they have already weathered two of the early and intense hormone-group years.

Contrast that with Jarrod, who is 15 and treats his mom like she's the slave dog of the family. "Where are my gym shorts?" he belts out a minute before he heads out the door to school, and Mama goes scurrying to find them. And where did that behavior start? When Jarrod was three. Mama, trying to please him, had let him get away with his tantrums, then gave him whatever he wanted.

Those two examples show clearly what I call "purposive behavior."

How many of you have used the word *purposive* today? I'm looking for hands here. . . . I see none.

Okay, so how about this week? Uh, there's a hand.

How about this month? A couple more.

This year? A few more.

Purposive isn't one of those words you hear a lot, but it's important for you as a parent to understand what *purposive behavior* is. Purposive behavior serves a person; it meets a need. We all engage in it.

What is the purposive behavior of a child throwing a temper tantrum in a toy store? A good guess would be that Mom or Dad has given him a small dosage of vitamin N and said no to the "I want, I need" three-year-old. The three-year-old's way of saying, "You'll do exactly what I tell you to do," is throwing a temper tantrum grand enough that folks six aisles over hear it and peek around the corner to see what's up.

So what does that parent do to shortcut the embarrassment of this child's behavior? "Okay, okay, I'll get you the toy this time. But this is the *last time* I'm going to buy you a toy."

That little girl has just been rewarded for her behavior. She's gotten her strokes. No wonder she's smiling hugely as she goes through the checkout line holding that toy. Imprinted on that child's mind is the thought, *Hey, this works. I wonder what else I can get by using that method.*

So guess what she's going to try again the next time? Her tantrum has served a purpose. She knows now if she pouts, cries, throws a fit, or sometimes even settles for stony silence (that's passive control), she'll get what she wants.

Every person develops a "life theme"—a mantra or a way of thinking that informs the way he or she responds to events. In fact, if you know a person's life theme, you can, with great regularity, predict how they will behave in a certain situation.

> *Every person develops a "life theme"—a mantra or a way of thinking that informs the way he or she responds to events.*

Strong-willed children learn their life theme early: "I only count in life when I dominate or control." And they're very good at demanding and bullying. They tend to be very goal-directed, without thought or consideration for those who remain between them and the goal.

Other common life themes are: "I only count in life when I'm noticed." Or, "I only count in life when other people serve me." Or, "I only count in life when I win."

But not all life themes are negatives. Here are some positives: "I only count in life when I help others and please God." And "I only count in life when I put others and their needs before my own."

Don't be suckered in. You're smarter than that.

The point is, by the time your kid's a teenager, he's got a pretty well-developed life theme. Does he see himself in a positive light or a negative one? Is he good at blaming others, or does he step up to the plate and accept responsibility?

So let me ask you now: what is the purposive nature of your son or daughter's behavior?

The answer might lead you to the stark realization that you are being manipulated, set up, suckered, or used. And God didn't put you on this earth for any of those reasons. Kids' intentions are not always good ones. There are times when you as parent will need to reach in your back pocket, throw the yellow flag, and say, "That's a foul. That's a violation. That's a penalty." And there are consequences to such fouls.

So now back to Shannon and Jarrod.

Why did Shannon throw a stubborn fit over eating her food at lunch? Because she wanted to see who was top dog in the home and if there was any wiggle room. Such testing is the result of human nature. But when she found out her testing didn't work, did she try it again? No, because her behavior didn't work. Now, of course, there is a big difference between a 3-year-old and a 15-year-old. If the 15-year-old has been allowed to exhibit that behavior for 12 years, it'll be more ingrained and will take more work on the parent's part to get rid of it.

Why does Jarrod think he can treat his mom like a slave dog? Because during all his growing-up years, sweet Mama has put him at the helm of life, driving his own boat. *His* needs and *his* wants have always superseded hers or anyone else's. As far as Jarrod is concerned, he's the top rooster in the henhouse, so why shouldn't he sit on the highest fence, crow a little, and boss everybody else around? He's learned how to do that, and guess who's taught him? His beloved mama, who allowed herself to be run and harassed by a kid shorter than a yardstick, who has now grown up to wield that yardstick like a club over her.

There's a reason your teenager is acting a certain way. Every behavior he exhibits has a purpose. If it didn't work, he wouldn't be using it. Don't be suckered in. You're smarter than that.

Three Types of Parents

I grew up in Buffalo, New York, which is still to this day a blue-collar town. Back in 1950, it was one of the largest cities in America and known for its steel mills and its grain. I have vivid memories of huge General Mills silos along the waterfront. Recently I drove through that area and could still smell the aroma of the cereal the company was making.

Part and parcel to growing up in western New York State in the 1950s was that you were openly threatened as a kid if you misbehaved. The main threat was, "I'm going to send you to Father Baker's." Father Baker was a priest, a remarkable man who had established a home for wayward orphan children before his death in the early 1900s.

One day my seven-year-old cousin talked back to his mother. She put some clothes in a cardboard box, handed it to him, and told him to go sit on the curb. "Father Baker is coming to pick you up," she said. Then she walked back into the house and shut the door.

My uncle, a milkman, came home from work several hours later and saw his son sitting on the curb, crying. "You sassed your mother, didn't you?" my uncle asked.

"Yes," my cousin said through his tears. "And I'm waiting for Father Baker to come pick me up."

My uncle, being trained in sensitivity, said to his young son, "Well, you can't miss him. He drives a big black truck." Then he walked into the house and shut the door.

How times have changed! Contrast that authoritarian scenario with many of today's permissive parents: "Henry, would you please turn down the TV so I can concentrate on your homework?" Or, "Have you chosen to go to bed yet?"

Extremes are never good for anybody—and that includes teenagers.

If you want to have a new teenager by Friday, the rules must change—with no warning. And it all starts with you identifying the kind of parent you are now and how you've chosen to relate to your child in the past.

Whatever You Want, Dear

All Maureen wanted was for her home to be happy. She'd grown up in an unhappy home with her siblings constantly fighting, and her parents divorced when she was 13. So when Maureen had her own children, her life mantra became "Can't we all just get along?" and "Don't worry, be happy." Problem is, Maureen was wearing herself out by being the exhausted martyr of the family, trying to do everything for her children.

"Whatever you want, dear" parents are those for whom anything goes. There are few guidelines and boundaries in the home, and no one feels safe because the rules of the chess game are always changing. The permissive parent might say, "No, we're not going through the Starbucks drive-through for coffee this morning," but then, after begging and pleading from the passengers, what happens? That SUV steers itself right to Starbucks and orders grande white chocolate mochas! Hmm, funny how cars do that sometimes without their owners' help.

"Whatever you want, dear" parents want their kids to be happy. But as I say often, "An unhappy teenager is a healthy teenager." When was the last time in your life that you were happy 24-7? Life throws curveballs, and the faster your son or daughter gets used to them, the better. Cushioning your kid from life's bumps and snowplowing her road in life won't gain either of you anything. It'll only show your kid, "Hey, Mom will do anything for me. I'll throw her a bone, then sit back and watch her go after it!" That is certainly not a relationship based on respect. In fact, it makes your position as the parent laughable to your teenager. Your perceived value takes a plunge.

It Worked for Me

I always thought I was a great mom. My days were nonstop busy doing stuff for my kids. It took my dad getting sick, and me spending weekends taking care of him in another state, to realize I was raising two spoiled brats (15 and 17) who wanted everything their way—and I was letting them get away with it!

I came home to laundry piled high and demands of "where's this" and "where's that." It wasn't until I got overwhelmed that I realized I was doing a lot of things for them that they should be doing for themselves. It really got me when my son said, "Mom, you said you'd help with my science report, and you weren't even here." What he meant was, "Mom, I'd counted on you doing my science report so I could sit on my rear end and play video games all weekend."

So I decided to practice the word "no"—your tip. I said it to everything for the next three days. At first my kids were shocked, then angry, then confused. My son got an F on his science report and ended up in two after-school sessions because of it. He walked home the eight blocks because I'd told him he'd have to find his own way home. I didn't even pick up my cell phone when he called to try to get me to change my mind. My daughter wore a shirt she hated to school, since it was the only shirt that was clean. After that, she did a load of laundry herself.

My kids are strong-willed, and I know the battles are far from over. But I also know that I'm the one who allowed them to become selfish, since I'm the one who put up with their behavior (my husband works overseas for part of each month). No more. I'm finally standing up for myself, and that feels good!

Karissa, Michigan

Permissive parents also work hard to be their teenager's friend. Let me be blunt. Do you really think your teenager wants you acting hip, wearing the latest styles, texting her continually, yakking about the cutest boy, and hanging around with all her friends at lunch? Your teenager has the potential for lots of friends, but she has only one mom and only one dad. Your role is unique. Don't try to be something you're not.

When I was a dean of students at the University of Arizona, I ran the parent orientation for the parents of freshman students. I was dumb enough to give out my home telephone number, and as a result, I frequently got calls from parents who were concerned about their kids.

"Dr. Leman," the parent would say, "I'm so concerned about Mikey. I just got a frightful call from him. He's depressed, he hates school, and he has no friends. Would you talk with him?"

So I called Mikey into my office.

"Michael, how are things going at school?" I'd ask.

"Good," he'd say.

"Like the dorm?"

"Love it."

"Made some friends?"

"Oh, yeah, some great friends."

What was Mikey doing? Using his powerful personality to yank his parents' chain. By sounding miserable, he was controlling his parents' responses. And his "I want my son to always be happy" permissive parents were falling for it hook, line, and sinker.

Being a good parent doesn't mean acquiescing to the demands of your youngsters, or falling for their "woe is me" lines and trying to make things all better for them. If you have been a permissive parent in the past, now is the time to make a change. Let your no be no, not "Well, maybe, if you're good, I'll take you to the video arcade." If you say you're not going to do something, don't do it. Don't give in, no matter how much your kids plead with you.

Remember the purposive nature of your kid's behavior: he will do what he's doing because it's worked before. If you no longer give in, his pestering behavior won't work anymore, will it? If you want a new teenager by Friday, you cannot back down. Changing your mind only fosters more pestering and obnoxious behavior. But sticking to the plan will guarantee results.

> *What was Mikey doing? Using his powerful personality to yank his parents' chain.*

If you've always been a permissive parent, just saying no once likely won't do the trick. Your kid is smart. She's thinking, *Okay, so Mom has this new parenting book. That's good for a couple days until it wears off. So I just have to hang in there, and things will get back to normal.* But, parent, things should *never* get back to normal in your house if you want a new and a better normal. When your no remains no, your smart kid will get the picture in a couple days.

Giving in to your kids is a piece of cake, but it will never serve you or your teenager well in the long run. Allowing your teenager to mouth off only fosters rebellion, because your teenager thinks that you're such a pushover he can manipulate you any way he wants. And believe me, he'll try. That's why you, permissive parent, need to toughen up.

Just say no. I know you can do it.

My Way or the Highway

Mitch ran his home like it was a military boot camp, even though he'd never been in the army. He expected his kids to bend to his wishes and rarely allowed them to have opinions of their own. As soon as he got home from his job as supervisor of a plant, he began barking out orders of what needed to get done around the house. If his three kids didn't hop to their jobs immediately, the consequences were stiff. Grounding was a typical punishment; at least one of the two teenagers was grounded every weekend.

What was Mitch saying by his behavior? "I'm better than you are, bigger than you are, and older than you are, and I have all the power." Fathers in particular can fall into this parenting style. (Mothers tend to fall into the permissive parenting style, especially if they are trying to balance out the father in the home or they feel guilty because there is no father in the home.)

Authoritarian parents like Mitch believe that kids should be quiet and that their opinions don't matter until they're grown up. Such parents have a need to be in control, to exert their authority. There is usually a division between the authoritarian parent and the rest of the family (usually Mom included), since one gives all the orders and the others have no say in what happens in the home.

But authoritarian methods—"Do what I say because you have to and I won't have it any other way"—will only be met by outright rebellion. And it's a chilling thought for any parent to reflect on how a 14- or 16-year-old could outwardly rebel if she wanted to. If you dump your wishes on your daughter with the "it's my way or the highway" treatment, don't be surprised if she takes off as soon as she can legally . . . or even before.

Mitch's wake-up call came when his 15-year-old daughter, Justine, ran away from home with a young man she thought loved her. Three months later she was located by police—her arms riddled with needle marks and her body bruised by her 18-year-old boyfriend's brutal treatment. All Justine had done was trade one authoritarian figure for another.

Today Mitch is a changed man who is working hard to be the father his kids deserve. But he can never turn back the clock on what happened to his daughter, and he will live with that grief and guilt for the rest of his life.

"It's my way or the highway" parents often come from strict, traditional roots themselves, where they were not allowed to have a say in their own homes when they were growing up. Other times they are damaged individuals who need to control others in order to feel good about themselves. And yet others are individuals of faith who misinterpret the Bible's wording about submission—seeing submission as applicable only to women and children, with men having no responsibilities other than lording it over their families. Often-

> *Mitch ran his home like it was a military boot camp.*

times authoritarian parents struggle with anger issues. Their families tend to walk a tightrope, hoping not to upset Dad.

If your teenager is angry, take a look around. Where did he learn that behavior from? Is there an authoritarian parent in the home? If so, that parent needs to get a grip on his own anger before he can hope to change his kid's anger.

Think of it this way. Going potty is natural. Going potty at the mall in front of people will land you in jail. Similarly, it's the misuse of the natural emotion of anger that's the problem. Some parents and some kids will clobber each other over the head with anger like some people clobber baby seals. If that's what's happening in your home, it has to stop—now.

Home ought to be a place where each member of the family receives encouragement and is held accountable, where issues are discussed and resolved at the dinner table or in a family council, and where everyone's opinion is respected.

> *The point of being a parent is not to control your children; rather, it's to encourage and partner with them.*

If you have been an authoritarian parent, you don't have just a little paint job to do in the family living room; you need to do some foundational work, and it all starts with you. You must completely change the way you think and act toward your teenagers. Instead of barking out orders, say simply, "I bet your mom would really appreciate it if we could do the dishes tonight. If you wash, I'll dry." Then watch your daughter's mouth fall open. She'll probably be running for the thermometer to see if you have a temperature. That's because authoritarian parents are great at getting others to do the work at home . . . and taking it easy themselves.

When your kids are young, you may be able to get away with the authoritarian parenting style. After all, you're bigger and stronger; you can make them behave. But now that your kids are moving physically into adulthood, the same "I'm gonna make you" methods won't work. Your six-foot-two son may, in fact, be bigger than you.

Once your son is 18 and out of the house, he'll do what he wants to do. He'll no longer be subject to your strict supervision.

Authoritarian parents don't know how to react when their teenager begins to get his own ideas and opinions—when their kid wants to live differently. So the parents respond by trying to shut down the kid. By trying to suppress him and get him under control.

But the point of being a parent is not to control your children; rather, it's to encourage and partner with them, seeing the long view and the big picture. The older your teenagers are, the more they will have their own ideas and opinions. If you take them seriously, rather than assuming your ideas are always best and the only ones, you will begin to grow a relationship that will extend beyond the hormone-group years.

Either extreme—permissive or authoritarian—is dangerous. Balance pays off big-time. Your role as a parent is to train your teenager to be a contributing, positive member of society. If respect hasn't been a major ingredient in your home life, now is the time to start incorporating it.

If you are a "whatever you want, dear" parent, start by respecting yourself enough to stand up for yourself. Say no . . . and stick to it. Consistency is the name of the game for you. Be a parent, not your child's friend. Respect your child enough to not let her be a spoiled brat who thinks she can get everything she wants when she wants it.

If you are an authoritarian parent, realize that you are not better than your child. You are both equal in the sight of God Almighty. You simply play different roles in the family. You will need to work hard to think before you speak. *Is what I'm about to say encouraging and nurturing to my child? And when I have to speak hard things, am I speaking the truth in love?* You will also need to see your teenager's thoughts and ideas as important—and as important as your own. Respect is a two-way street.

> *Respect is a two-way street.*

Because the patterns of permissiveness and authoritarianism are ingrained for many years, you'll need to work hard to combat them. But keep this in mind too: as you move, so will your kid. And the amount that you move affects how far your teenager will move. Change starts with you and your own willingness to turn things around. Yes, you've lived longer and you're bigger, but this book is all about relationships. You're only going to go as far as your relationship with your teenager allows you to.

Equal but Different Roles

We've just talked about the extremes of parenting—the *permissive* parent and the *authoritarian* parent. But the best kind of parenting strategy is a balanced one, in which parents are in healthy authority over their kids. *Authoritative* parents believe that they and their teenagers are created equal. All are members of the family—win together, lose together. No one member of the family is more important than any other. Authoritative parents also know that they are responsible to set the temperature valve in the home. That means establishing guidelines and boundaries so that everyone in the home is safe emotionally and physically.

> **Be a SMART Parent**
>
> **S**elf-control is a great attribute. For your kids to get it, you must have it.
>
> **M**inimize negative expectations. Focus on positive ones.
>
> **A**ttitude, attitude, attitude. It's the ace in the hole when playing the game of life with your teenager.
>
> **R**ecognize your teenager is not you.
>
> **T**alk only after you've listened, thought, and prayed about something.

The authoritative parent looks back and asks the question, "What kind of environment did I come from? How will that environment affect the way I respond in my own home now?" Taking a look back on your life is grist for the mill in reacting to this new alien creature in your home.

How were you treated by your parents when you were growing up? Parents who came from authoritarian homes often had no say at home themselves; thus, when they become parents, they revel in the role of getting to be the one who controls all the action of the family game. But in doing so, they often become the only player while the rest of the family sits on the sidelines, not really entering the game because of the fear of or frustration with the consequences.

Those who came from permissive homes often are ones who were caught in the middle between warring parents and siblings. They want their home to be completely different from their growing-up years. But giving in to everything backfires and creates a stressful environment similar to what they grew up in, due to the lack of boundaries.

The authoritative parent says, "I'm the parent, you're the child. Those are our roles. Sometimes I'll have to play the parent card, and when I have to, there's no doubt I will. But I always want to know what you think and why you feel a certain way, and to keep an open, honest, respectful dialogue between us. I can be wrong, and you can be wrong. And when one of us acts inappropriately, we need to ask for and receive forgiveness."

No one member of the family is more important than any other.

The authoritative parent keeps the emotions in the home on an even keel as much as possible. Sure, there will be times when the temperature is elevated. But the authoritative parent doesn't allow it to remain high for long. Street-smart parents address the situation head-on, giving all parties the opportunity to tell their side, as long as they do so respectfully. Then a wise decision is reached that will benefit the entire family.

Authoritative parents don't rescue their kids from consequences either. They let the chips fall where they may. If your teenager makes a dumb move, then she should suffer the consequences of it. Certain actions will always result in consequences. That's life in the real world of adulthood, so it should be life in the hormone group as well.

Some years ago, my daughter Holly got pulled over by a motorcycle cop. As soon as she was parked on the side of the road, he approached the car. The first thing she spotted was a gold Christian fish pin on his lapel. "Oh, wow," she said, "you're a Christian. I'm a Christian too."

The cop looked at her. "Well, yes, young lady, I am. And since you are too, you'll surely realize why it's important for me to give you this ticket."

Authoritative parents allow their teenagers to experience the consequences of their actions; they don't snowplow their roads in life. But they also lather on the encouragement: "I believe in you, and I believe you'll do the right thing." They provide wisdom, balance, and a place of safety to discuss any and all topics. They expect the best, so they most often get the best.

If you try to accomplish the principles in this book and you remain a "whatever you want, dear" or a "my way or the highway" parent, nothing I say in this book will work. You won't have a new teenager by Friday. That's because your teenager is smart and will know you're merely blowing smoke. But if you admit the areas in which you need to change personally, and you set out to attack those areas head-on, you will gain your son or daughter's attention and respect.

Getting Your Game On

The hormone-group storm has hit. You have to have a plan. All of a sudden your cooperative, quiet kid has become a tiger you have to grab by the tail. He's mouthy or he flat out disobeys you. When this happens for the first time, you, like most parents, are probably in shock. You feel you're in crisis mode.

Well, let me tell you, you're not. You've just begun the battle of being a good, balanced parent of a teenager. However, as we proceed through this book, you'll find out the game plan really isn't complex. In fact, it's rather simple.

But the results depend on having a game plan that's simple, reasonable, and within reach. As the old saying goes, "KISS" (keep it simple, stupid). If that mantra works for start-up businesses that become multimillion-dollar companies, it'll work for your family.

It's Time for a Change

If you want to have a new teenager by Friday, what do you need to adjust in your own actions and home life? How will you deal with the daughter who challenges your authority, seems unmotivated to do anything, and is going in a direction 180 degrees opposite of where you'd like her to?

If she asks for the car keys, do you hand them to her and say, "Okay, go have fun. Oh, and if you would be so kind, maybe, uh, could you call me . . . if you don't mind . . . to let me know you're okay since I know you're going to miss curfew?" Permissive parent, stop right there! You're pampering her, making excuses for her, and foisting negative rather than positive expectations on her.

Most parents are driven by frustration.

Or are you going to be a dictator who insists, "You better be home by 10:00 or else. If you're home even at 10:01, you'll be grounded for life!" And are you also going to be there her freshman year of college, when she has car keys in hand, no rules to abide by, and no parent hanging over her? Just what will she do then?

Or are you going to be a balanced parent who is in healthy authority over her teenager, who simply says, "I'm glad you're going to have time with your friends. I'll see you when you get home," because you fully trust that your daughter will honor your family guidelines to be home at a reasonable hour?

Yes, being a balanced parent is risky. It's far easier to overparent, coddle, or try to control the results. But when you do so, you're not rearing a teenager who will think for herself. You're creating a clone of you who will be controlled as long as she's in your sight. But look out when she's not!

Watch Your Own 'Tude

When you parent teenagers, it's important that you don't sport a 'tude. If you do, certainly that dude or dudette in your family will sport a 'tude. And in the teenage years, there are plenty of 'tudes going around already.

Most parents are driven by frustration. They go around putting out one fire and then are plunged right into the middle of another. And guess who is keeping them hopping and enjoying every minute of it? That powerful teenager!

No matter what happens, you are going to be the chilled-out parent who will teach your kids by example how to handle the heat. In the midst of battle, you will remain calm, listen to all sides, be fair and respectful to everyone, and come to a just resolution of the problem. Part of a right resolution means that you hold your teenager responsible for her decisions, and doing so shows her respect. You're saying, by your actions, "You made a choice. When it's a good choice, you will reap the benefits. When it's a poor choice, there will be consequences, and they will be yours alone to shoulder. That way the next time you're faced with a similar situation, you can choose what you're going to do. I happen to think that you're a smart kid, and that you're going to choose wisely next time."

> *Most parents have reared their kids to feel like the center of the universe.*

Be Predictable . . . but Not Always

If you always deal with discipline issues the same way (for example, "Go to your room!") and it's not working, then you need a new game plan.

Most parents today have used—I say with tongue in cheek—the feared time-out. If you think that means anything to your teenagers, think again. When you're telling them to go to their room, you're not punishing them. You're giving them a nice little retreat for the evening! After all, in their room they have their cell phone, computer, stereo, flat-screen TV, and any other technological gadgets to keep them happy and occupied. They certainly aren't going to feel any discipline from that.

42

Most parents have reared their kids to feel like the center of the universe. So it shouldn't be surprising to anybody that selfish, hedonistic little suckers grow up to be selfish, hedonistic big suckers.

A parent is the conductor of the family orchestra. This is especially true of a mom, who is the point person of the family. In order for the family to work, the violas, violins, cellos, and basses all have to come together, starting out on the correct pitch. That pitch is the family guidelines and boundaries, starting with mutual respect. Each instrument is different and plays a different role, but it's only together that they can make beautiful harmony—a concert that sounds like a concert, or a concerto that sounds like a concerto.

> *The best way to teach self-control is by staying in control yourself and revealing the consequences of being out of control.*

Instead of thinking of *disciplining* your kid in their hormone-group years, think more of *discipling*. When you discipline, your attitude is, "Oh no. I can't believe my kid just did that. What am I gonna do? What punishment can I come up with that will be big enough so he won't do that again?" When you disciple, your attitude is, "How can I help prepare my teenager to live on his own? What's important for him to know?"

Being *predictable* in your discipling means your teenager can predict that there will be some action taken when she goes astray. She will know that her parent will assume a role of authority. But the *unpredictable* part comes because she won't always be able to guess what that action is going to be . . . and it will come at an unexpected time.

Let's say your daughter speaks to you extremely disrespectfully on a Saturday morning. Let it pass; don't make a big deal out of it. Your blood pressure doesn't need the hike anyway. But on Saturday night, she'll be looking frantically for the car keys. Guess where they'll be? In your pocket. When your daughter misses her outing, that will be a teachable moment.

Again, you're the calm one. You didn't yell back when she yelled at you; you simply waited for the right timing. Nine hours later, when you've had plenty of time to think through the appropriate discipling, you act. When your daughter asks why, you say matter-of-factly, "Because I don't appreciate what you said to me this morning. It was disrespectful." The best way to teach self-control is by staying in control yourself and revealing the consequences of being out of control.

> *Parenting in the hormone-group years is all about gaining the cooperation of your teenager.*

So, smart parent, if you have self-control, your teenager might catch it from you. And because you caught your teenager off guard by the discipling coming hours later—when missing that event would mean a great deal to her—you exercised the unpredictability card to the best of your ability. When your teenager is all about pushing your buttons, it's not a bad thing to let her be off-kilter every once in a while.

Let Your No Be No

This one is especially for you moms, who tend to be pushovers more than dads are. After all, many of you pushed that baby out through a narrow birth canal, so you have a lot invested in that kid. But just because you went through physical torture during labor doesn't mean you should go through it with the kid for a lifetime.

Let your no be no. Don't be cajoled or whined at or screamed at to say yes when you've already said no. Your teenager needs to know you mean business. It's only when the two of you are on the same plane of respect that you can truly have a relationship that will benefit both of you.

I love Louis Pasteur's quote: "Let me tell you the secret that has led me to my goal. My strength lies solely in my tenacity."[2]

Parent, be tenacious.

Up Your Perceived Value

Parent, you hold all the cards in this game called life. You're the one who has the means to make things happen for your son or daughter—including driving the car (I will mention that a lot in this book, but that's because such freedom is very important to the emerging teenager), going to college, having clothes (hopefully clean) to wear, etc. You hold the keys to all those things. Otherwise, your kid would be going off to school naked as a jaybird. So who's kidding whom? Now's the time to step up and be a parent.

The late John Wooden, probably the best college basketball coach of all time, was a wise man of faith, revered by all in the industry. He coached at UCLA, and interestingly, he never told his team to go out and win the game. He always told them to play the game the way it needs to be played.

> **What to Do on Monday**
>
> 1. Decide: total reconstruction, partial replacement, or a little paint job?
> 2. Identify your parenting style:
>   • Whatever you want, dear
>   • It's my way or the highway
>   • Equal but different roles
> 3. Develop a game plan.

Those are wise words for parents too. There is no "winning" in the game of parenting. If either you or your 13-year-old "wins" a fight, both of you actually lose. Parenting in the hormone-group years is all about gaining the cooperation of your teenager.

You do so by listening to him, respecting him, encouraging him, standing up for him—and yes, also standing up *to* him and holding him accountable. When you do so, and your teenager knows you care about him and what happens to him, your perceived value will rise, and you'll be amazed at the deepening of your relationship.

Every child needs three vitamins:

- vitamin E: encouragement
- vitamin N: no
- vitamin C: cooperation

Street-smart parents learn how to give each of these vitamins in the right dosage to produce a healthy, balanced teenager.

★ **THE WINNING PLAY** ★

*Your teenager will change
to the degree that you change.*

Tuesday

Talking to the "Whatever" Generation

Getting beyond the crossed arms, the grunt, the staring out the car window, and the "whatever" comments to reach your child's heart.

Imagine your 16-year-old son is sitting at the dinner table one night, and he blurts out, "When I'm 21, I'm going to drive a Corvette."

What would most dads, in their feeding frenzy after a long day at work, say? "Well, then, you better get your tail going in school. You're going to need good grades to get a decent job so you can buy that Corvette."

And what might Mom say? "Uh, excuse me, honey, what's a Corvette? An aunt of mine had something called . . . a Corvair. Or was that my grandmother?" (Yeah, and my cousin had something called a Shove-it—a Chevette—when he first started to drive too.)

Is it any wonder that boy sits there the rest of dinner with crossed arms and gives the remaining conversation an occasional

What to Say When They Complain about Dinner

TEENAGER: "Mom, chicken again? I *hate* chicken."

TRADITIONAL SHOCKED AND DISAPPOINTED MOM: "But last week you *loved* chicken. You ate four pieces at dinner. You're always saying how you love Aunt Harriet's chicken. It's your favorite."

HAVE A NEW TEENAGER BY FRIDAY MOM: "Honey, what would you like to have for dinner sometime in the next week or two? What dinner would be, to you, just the best?"

TEENAGER (startled): "Uh, I dunno. I'd like . . . I'd like, uh . . . prime rib."

MOM: "Okay, let me write that down. Prime rib. What else would you like with it?"

TEENAGER (still startled at the turn of events): "Uh, mashed potatoes."

MOM: "Plain or garlic mashed potatoes?"

TEENAGER: "Garlic."

MOM: "Okay, I wrote that down too. Anything else? Something special for dessert?"

Why would or should a parent respond in such a way? Because your teenager needs to know that *somebody* in the house cares enough to listen to what he says, even if what he says can sometimes be stupid and can change rapidly from week to week or hour to hour. The important thing is to leave your teenager with a distinct, lasting impression that he matters greatly in your family. Wouldn't you want to be treated the same way?

grunt, letting it play out without him? He's thinking, *Whatever! Dinner*, to him, has become a "just endure it; it'll be over soon" type of event.

But what if, instead, the street-smart dad said in response to his son's comment, "Wow, a Corvette. That would be so cool. What kind of a Corvette? The standard one with the automatic transmission or the ZR1 with the six-speed manual trans? And what color? Any special features?"

Now that's *engaging* your teenager—evening the playing field and revealing that his dreams, his ideas, his thoughts, and his life are valuable to you, as is an interesting topic of conversation that the entire family can share in.

You're Screaming So Loudly I Can't Hear What You're Saying

When a teenager says something ridiculous, most parents react. "Where on earth did you get that from?" they say. "I'm telling you, talk about stupid. Did you get that from the internet or something?"

Whenever you talk with your teenager, you're either opening the door for future communication or you're shutting him down. If you're Mr. or Mrs. Know-It-All and you have the final answer to everything, then what possible motivation could your 15-year-old have for bringing any subject up for discussion at the dinner table? He's not dumb. If everything he brings up gets shut down, he's thinking, *I ain't sayin' nothin'. I'll just give this family dinner thing a lick and a holler, and within 20 minutes I can be back texting my buddies.*

Teenagers who don't feel engaged with family life—who don't think their opinion is important because their ideas, dreams, etc., aren't treated as important and aren't even listened to—will get mum fast.

In all my years as a psychologist, the number one thing I've heard teenagers say

> *The number one thing I've heard teenagers say is, "My parents don't understand me."*

is, "My parents don't understand me." When I ask why they think that, they'll say, "They don't listen to me at all. They don't respect anything I say. I'm not important in their lives."

It doesn't take a rocket scientist to explain why we have a generation of kids who've decided not to talk to their parents . . . even if their parents are talking at them.

Did you catch that little word *at*? Most of the hormone group I've talked to feel their parents spend 99 percent of their time talking *at* them instead of talking *to* them. They boss them around, tell them what to do and what to say, and even tell them how they should feel or not feel. Parents spend only 1 percent of the time talking *to* their kids about what they're interested in and connecting with their hearts.

Simply stated, if somebody was telling you what to do, when to do it, and how to do it, and then telling you how you should feel about it, how would *you* respond? Especially if you weren't sure if that person was on your side or not? If, in fact, you were pretty sure that person was aligned against you and didn't want you to have any fun in life? Ah, now you've got the picture. Nobody likes to be bossed around. And the first place you see a teenager's attitude—before it comes flying out of her mouth—is in her body language.

Body language is mute, but it can still scream loudly. What is your teenager saying—or not saying—by her posture, her eyes, her gritted teeth? If you want to know what your daughter is thinking and she's not talking, check out her body language. It will say, "I'm discouraged," "I'm angry," "I'm hurt," "I don't feel important," or "I'm overwhelmed." Because she's part of the hormone group, that body language can change from day to day, hour to hour, or even, as one dad told me, "minute to minute, especially with my just-turned 12-year-old!" Body language can also say, "Please don't interrupt me. I've had a rough day at school, and I'm thinking through what, if anything, I can do about it. It feels out of my control right now, and that makes me really nervous."

Sometimes your child, like you, needs privacy and a time to work things out on her own. Trying to talk your teenager into talking will never work. It will simply firm up her already clamped lips.

It Worked for Me

> I took your advice. I shut up. I stopped pushing my 14-year-old to talk. The first three times I only said, "Hi, honey," when he got in the car after school. The silence all the way home was deafening. Kinda freaky for a natural talker like me. But the fourth time he looked at me a little puzzled and asked, "Hey, Mom, how was your day?" So I told him briefly, then shut up. And then he started talking. Thanks for helping me figure out how to get to my son's heart . . . even if my tongue is raw from biting it to stop from talking.
>
> *Maria, Tennessee*

Every day your child is assaulted with the pressures of not feeling good enough, pretty enough, athletic enough, etc., to be part of a peer group. What does she get from you? Realistic encouragement, kind truth, and empathy? Or criticism, put-downs, and "you ought to know better than that"?

Ouch. The truth does hurt, doesn't it?

The bad news is, you're not perfect. The good news? There isn't a parent or teenager on this planet who is perfect either. So that evens the playing field to get on to the business of parenting and forming a lifetime relationship with your son or daughter.

Instead of shutting down your kid when he says something off the wall, why not say, "Hey, tell me more about that." Or, "Wow, I'd never have thought of that. And you did. That's amazing." Or, "Mmm, you seem upset . . . or discouraged, maybe." Or, "Wow, something great must have happened today by the look on your face." These statements lend themselves to open communication, and you'll certainly get more than a grunt. You might even have an intriguing conversation the whole 10-minute car ride home. Even better, you'll learn something about your kid's life—and his heart.

Jumping over the High Bar

Parents the world over have expectations for their kids. Some want their kids to be straight-A students, or top athletes, or star musicians. My mom had great expectations—to see me at least graduate from high school (and believe me, that was a big expectation of the underachiever Kevin Leman back then). It's good to have positive expectations for your teenagers—to believe that they can succeed and to encourage them to try.

> *My mom had great expectations—to see me at least graduate from high school.*

But expectations go awry when parents hold the bar of life so far up that no kid on the planet can hurdle over it without landing face-first in the sand or mud. These high-bar parents say things like:

- "Oh, you cleaned your room. Uh, yeah, I could tell. But next time . . ."
- "What's with the B on this report card [when all the rest are A's]?"
- "You could be a part of the popular group if you tried hard enough."
- "Well, you should have done better. When I was your age . . ."
- "If you practiced more, you might be able to get a scholarship to the conservatory."

What are these parents saying? "I've erected this high bar for you, and I'm expecting you to jump over it. And when you do, I'll move it a bit higher, like they do in steeple-chase horse championships. Then, when you fail, I'm going to be very disappointed, and I'll make that clear to you."

Where did you get that idea from? Chances are good that you yourself had a mom or dad who insisted that *you* jump over the high bar. And you hated or feared failing just as much as your son or daughter does. Even though you swore you'd never do to your kid what your parent did to you, you find yourself doing the same thing. That's because the life tape you learned as a kid—"I don't count unless Mom and Dad are happy with me"—is still running through your head now that you're an adult. Worse, it's coming out of your mouth, now directed toward your own child. Old patterns die hard, don't they?

Life Training

One of the trends today is for people to have "personal trainers." They're the people who give you a kick in the seat of the pants (figuratively) when you need to make a change in your life and don't have the courage, stamina, or determination to do it yourself. You might have a physical fitness trainer who helps you get your middle section in order so you don't have to suck it in every time you zip up your pants. He helps you lift weights, work out, build up muscles. Or you might have a life trainer who is bringing some order to the chaos of your days and helping you figure out your personal values and priorities.

> *With even a little change on your part and in your attitude, you will see a huge change in your teenager's attitude.*

In this book, you'll become your own personal trainer. Each of us has something we want to eradicate from our lives. It usually develops as a result of events in the past that have influenced us. Or we have a void—something missing. Because you didn't have certain things while you were growing up, you're determined that your kid will have those advantages.

We're all creatures of habit. The tapes from past happenings run through our heads, telling us how to behave, what to say, how to interact in relationships.

But we don't have to be slaves to those tapes. When you have a genuine desire to be different, to behave differently, *you can do so.*

If you don't, your current ways of relating will take a great toll on your relationship. But with even a little change on your part and in your attitude, you will see a huge change in your teenager's attitude. She will go from moody and mouthy to "What can I do to help, Mom?" Just watch and see.

If your teenager seems defeated, or won't even attempt to do new things or something she used to do, or tends to tune you out, take a careful look at yourself. If you're raising the high bar on your kid, you're priming her to fail. She's smart enough to know it, so she'll figure that she might as well not even try. Or she'll try so hard that she'll exhaust herself attempting to make you happy because, whether you believe it or not, your teenager wants to please you. When she can't live up to your expectations, she feels like a failure. Just as you did with your parents.

So how about lowering the bar a little (or a lot)? You'll be doing yourself—and your son or daughter—a big favor. In America today there are millions of kids, in what would be considered "good homes," who aren't living up to their potential out of fear that if they did, they'd always have to achieve more and more, and the pressure would be too great. So instead they hunker down, burrow under, and cocoon themselves from family and friends. But it doesn't have to be that way.

Should You Call Them a "Teen" or a "Teenager"?

Parents speak out.

- "You can call them anything you want. But that doesn't really matter since they don't come anyway. I ought to know. I have three of them in my house."

- "My dad said we weren't allowed to become teenagers. We had to be 'young adults.'"

- "*Teen* sounds like a nasal disease. *Teenager* sounds like a person."

None of us jumps over the high bar of life every time; we all miss every once in a while (or a lot) and end up crumpled in the sand. So why do some of you continue to raise the bar higher on your children to make it nigh on impossible to meet your expectations?

Have a New Teenager by Friday is all about behaving differently—by Friday. But it has to start with you.

It Worked for Me

I felt like I'd been belly-punched when I heard you talk on the radio about critical, perfectionistic parents who raise the high bar on their kids. I'm a construction worker who's had to work really hard for a living, and I want life to be different for my son. I know I've been too hard on him. He's a great kid, and he deserves a better father. I'm not an apologizing kind of guy, but I did it. He didn't say anything. Just stood there. I don't know what'll happen next for the two of us—my son and I haven't had a good relationship lately—but I know I did the right thing. Pray for me when you think of it.

Josh, Illinois

Signs of a "Shoulding" Parent

Do you have a teenager who:

- starts projects and doesn't finish?
- always plans to hit a home run but has difficulty even getting to the plate?
- can be hot—spot-on—until something goes wrong, and then falls apart?
- runs in streaks—all hot, then all cold?

- always needs a kick-start?
- is down in the dumps even before he gets out of the starting gate on a project?

If so, you might want to take a good look in the mirror to find the solution. Teenagers take their cues from their parents. Do you "should" on yourself?

- "I really should get to the laundry today. It's been sitting there for three days."
- "I shouldn't have done that. Now I'm going to have to . . ."
- "I should help out. After all, I have a day off this week."
- "The next time he asks, I should . . ."

If you spend your day saying and thinking what you should do, you're missing out on life. Even worse, you're probably falling into the trap of treating your kid the same way:

- "You've got to be kidding! You call that good?"
- "I wouldn't call that clean."
- "You should have gotten an A."
- "Why isn't your homework done? It should be by now."
- "I should think you'd care about that."
- "You should have worked harder."

All humans hate criticism—and even more so, teenagers, who are sensitive to every comment made about them. Little comments grow to be big comments in their mind. And with the hormone group, even little comments you make can translate as snarky— whether you mean them to be or not.

Since most kids would do anything to avoid criticism, they simply shut up. *If I don't say anything, Mom or Dad won't know anything about my life and won't criticize me.*

Avoid "shoulding" at all times and at all costs. It effectively halts teenager-parent communication right in its tracks.

During these years, you need to find new ways to communicate your unconditional love and acceptance—and some truth-telling when it's needed as well. But never, *ever* use the word *should* with your kids. It'll shut the communication down every time.

My Mom's Smart Words

My mom was a very smart woman. She knew just the words that this baby of the family needed. "Listen and think before you open your mouth, son," she said. "And say you're sorry—and mean it."

Wise words indeed.

How many times in the past week would you have been better off if you'd listened—and thought—before you opened your mouth with your son or daughter?

It might have been the attitude and the smart mouth that set you off. Or it might have been because you had to ask your son five times to clean his pet tortoise's cage. Never mind that most of the hormone group don't hop off the couch and whip off their iPod earbuds just to hear what you, their precious parent, have to say. Nor do they stop in the middle of texting on their iPhone to say, "Sure! I'll get that chore done right now." For that to happen, the world would have to stop spinning on its axis. Most often you get the glazed eyes and/or the slight head nod since they're living in a different world—watching a reality show, texting a buddy, or thinking through a problem at school—so they don't even have the chore on their radar. That's why reminding your teenager to do chores will never accomplish anything except frustrating you.

You can work all you want toward the goal of being a perfect parent, but you'll never make it. That's because we human beings aren't perfect. But that doesn't mean we can't be good parents.

Part of being a good parent is being smart enough to know when you should shut up and listen, and when your teenager's ears are ready to hear what you have to say.

> *There will be times when you'll open your mouth ... and wish you hadn't.*

You're going to make mistakes. There will be times when you'll open your mouth ... and wish you hadn't. What flies out isn't going to be pretty, edifying, or even passable.

That's when you do the right thing. You go to your son or daughter and say, "I'm sorry. I spoke in haste, and I shouldn't have said that. Will you forgive me?"

Your kids are watching what you *do*, not merely what you say. They need to hear those words from you, Mom or Dad. Being humble and admitting when you've done wrong puts you on an even playing field with your kids and shows that you respect them as human beings.

It's hard to step off that know-it-all pedestal, but when you do, you build a lifetime relationship.

Sailing, Sailing . . .

"But you always . . . !" "You never . . . !"

If you realize that the hormone group will *always* talk in extremes and will *never* want to back down, you can stay serene on a wave-tossed sea in the worst of windstorms. Life at sea with a teenager is tumultuous, no doubt about it. Moods will change minute to minute, hour to hour, day to day. If you allow them to carry you along, your family ship will be tossed from side to side. But if you stay *calmly* at the helm, take deep breaths, and smile, this too shall pass.

Although your teenager may let fly a "whatever," she doesn't really mean that. She actually cares very deeply about what's going on, but the "whatever" says, "I have no idea how to deal with this right now! Help!" Your daughter especially needs you when the storms of life come (and they will)—when her heart is broken by her first boyfriend; when she fails an algebra test; when her best friend decides she doesn't want to be friends anymore; when she's teased because she speared toilet paper on her shoe and carried it around all day at school, and nobody told her about it until the end of the day. . . .

> **How to Get Your Teenager Talking**
>
> • Shut up.
> • Don't ask, "How was your day?"
> • Say calmly in response to a shocking statement, "Hmm. Tell me more about that."
> • Eliminate the word *why*.

When your teenager snips at you, be the parent. Don't react. Let the moment go. Cut the kid some slack (especially if it's right after school—a heavy processing time for teenagers who are trying to make sense of their day at school, their thoughts, and their warring emotions). Remember that *grace* and *mercy* are both beautiful words that make the world go round. Sometimes you need it; sometimes your son or daughter will need it.

But that doesn't mean you let the kid get away with disrespect either.

It's all about love and positive expectations. The love you show your teenager and the expectations you place on him are very important. That's because your kid cares what you think, will internalize your beliefs (for ill or for good), and will act in accordance with those beliefs. Contrast "Dad thinks I'm a loser, so I might as well act like one" with "Mom believes in me. I'd never want to let her down."

You wouldn't believe the number of times adults have told me that they were never encouraged in their home—never told they were loved or how special they were.

If you treat kids the way you expect them to behave, a miracle occurs. They really try to live up to that!

That's why teachable moments are so important. Kids are very good at tuning out yelling; after a while they just hear "blah, blah,

blah," and the words all run together. So if you're disappointed with her behavior when she's mouthy, you need to get quiet and stay quiet. "Run silent and run deep," as the old saying goes. Then wait until your daughter realizes, *Hey, there's something going on with Mom.* And she'll ask, "What's up? How come you're so quiet? How come you won't let me go anywhere or do anything?"

> *If you treat kids the way you expect them to behave, a miracle occurs. They really try to live up to that!*

Ah, that's your teachable moment to tell her straight out, "I don't appreciate the way you acted toward me two hours ago."

When you tell it like it is, *calmly* and with love, you are treating your daughter with respect. You're setting the bar at an acceptable level of behavior, not at the high jump area. Now you have your daughter's attention, and you are molding her heart and mind. You're also changing it from something negative ("I can get away with anything because my mom lets me") to something positive ("Wow, I can see that life is going to change around here if I treat my mom that way. I better start treating her with respect").

And you've accomplished all this *calmly* (note that I've used this word three times in this section, and there's a reason for that)—without putting yourself in the path of your teenager's wind.

Sometimes the wind will blow at hurricane decibels. But you, parent, are smarter than to let yourself get sucked in. Just sit back, have a cup of coffee, and wait for the winds to die down.

Best of all, you don't have to say a word.

Capturing Your Teenager's Heart

Recently my daughter Lauren showed me a math paper. "Shazam!" I said. "When did they start using letters?"

Lauren just grinned. She works really hard in math, and she was thrilled to get a B on her paper. We did a happy dance as a family and posted that paper right on the fridge, front and center. I was proud of Lauren; she had worked hard.

Lauren comes from a long line of Lemans who struggle with math. If I was smart enough to put my scores in mathematical terms, I'd do that for you, but let's just say I barely made it through consumer math. ("So-and-so went to the store with a dollar. Candy bars were on sale for 50 cents apiece. How many candy bars could he buy?") My final grade in elementary-level algebra in high school was a 22, and my SAT in math was in the 0 percentile. I went through college without taking a math class. I took statistics classes instead, and even took advanced statistical analysis all the way to the PhD level. I'll never forget the experience of explaining to my professors the analysis of covariance. But if you slapped a million bucks on the table now and said, "I'll give this to you if you define covariance," I'd walk away a sad man. I couldn't. Math still isn't my forte, but I do it when I have to.

> ### 5 Tips to Keep Your Sails out of Your Teenager's Wind
>
> - Don't take things personally.
> - Stay calm.
> - Listen, but don't fight your teenager's battles.
> - Offer helpful suggestions only when asked.
> - Don't tell your teenager what to do.

I have five kids, and every single one struggles in math. But Lauren has worked the hardest of us all, and it shows. When that B came home, I knew it was the product of tremendous work and focus on her part, so I couldn't help but say, "Good job!"

But so many parents would have responded differently. "A B? I know you can do better than that." Well, folks, a B is above average, and for a teenager who struggles with math, I'd say that's an incredible grade, and something to be celebrated. So that's exactly what we did: had a party and whooped it up!

But more than that, I care about Lauren's heart. She cares about people. She's compassionate and helpful toward those who are hurting. She's a giver, not a taker.

Now, which person would you rather have walking around in the world? A straight-A student who is all about himself, is competitive, and doesn't care about people, or an average student who clearly loves others and puts them first? If you're a businessperson, which one would you want to hire for your company? Which one would you want for a neighbor? Hands down, it would be someone like Lauren every time.

> *In all my practice of psychology, I've never run into the perfect human being.*

Our world gets caught up with the outside of things—what people look like—to the exclusion of their hearts or their minds. There are actresses I won't name (out of sheer kindness) who are very pretty women but don't have a lot upstairs, and have even less in their lives that would be considered faintly moral.

Funny thing—in all my practice of psychology, I've never run into the perfect human being. Your teenagers won't be perfect either. But if you tend to their heart and encourage real character strengths, your words will carry them through situations when you're not around. If you believe in them, accept them, and highlight the goodness in them, you give them the courage and the power to handle difficult situations.

An article in *USA Today* says it all: "Young People Prefer Praise to Sex, Money." The study was based on the responses of 282 students. Writer Sharon Jayson reports:

> Sex, booze or money just can't compare with the jolt young people get from a boost to their self-esteem, says a new study of college students that found the desire for praise trumped other desires or needs.[1]

Although I'd differ in the use of terminology and use the word *encouragement* instead of *praise*—since, in my definition, *encouragement* focuses on who the person is and *praise* focuses on what a person does—clearly your words make a difference. They have everything to do with how your kid thinks and feels about herself, as well as her confidence in facing life's storms.

> **What to Do on Tuesday**
>
> 1. Lower the high bar.
> 2. Don't "should" on your kid.
> 3. Keep your sails out of your teenager's wind.

So let me ask you bluntly: when you communicate with your teenager, do you talk *at* her, or *to* her? Do hairstyles and clothing take the front seat of your discussions, or does your relationship?

You need to be your kid's champion in these wind-tossed years. After all, you may be the one person who believes in your "whatever" kid right now . . . even if you do want to kill her sometimes.

My mom, who is now in heaven, had to believe in her little wayward boy Kevin for a lot of years before anyone else thought he was worth anything. But I have to hand it to her. She never put me down; she never criticized. She did, on occasion, set me straight, and rightfully so. However, in all she said and did, she always paid attention to my heart. As a result, she captured it forever.

You too can capture the heart of your "whatever" teenager—for a lifetime.

★ THE WINNING PLAY ★

Capture your teenager's heart.

Wednesday

Belonging Matters More than You Think

How to keep your teenager in your world while traveling through his or her world.

"All I wanted was someplace to belong," former gang leader LaWonna told me. "And I knew I'd go to any length to get it."

That's how this now 29-year-old became the tough female head of an inner-city gang . . . at the age of 16. Growing up in the Cabrini Green area of Chicago, LaWonna had only a dim memory of someone she used to call "Daddy." He left when she was four, and the remaining family of three was plunged almost immediately into poverty. With no high school degree or workable skills, LaWonna's mother did laundry, ironed, and took just about every job she could to help feed her family. She was rarely home, and LaWonna was left to take care of her younger brother. When she was in first grade, she was making them both dinners and lunches. "I loved my mama, but she just wasn't around. She got home at 11 at night, and we kids would already be asleep."

Longing for love and attention, LaWonna fell into a local gang when she was 11 and finally found a home. Not only that, the gang provided protection for her eight-year-old brother too. "They became family to us," LaWonna said. But LaWonna came head-to-head with the hard edge of gangs when, in a rival turf war, her brother was killed. "That's the day I died too, and became someone I didn't want to be."

> *Kids who feel strongly about their home turf—who feel respected and listened to there—are less likely to look for acceptance in their peer groups.*

To this day, LaWonna lives under an assumed name in a different state, in order to escape the gang warfare after she decided to get out. She says, "I was a hurting kid who wanted a daddy to be around and a mama to love me. Without that, I had to belong somewhere. But I had no idea the terrible price I'd pay for getting what I wanted."

The world's a rough place, and it won't do your kid any favors—whether it's your local high school, a small town, a private school, or an urban setting.

Every teenager needs a place to belong, and the best place for your son or daughter to belong is your home. Like LaWonna, teenagers who belong at home don't feel as great a need to belong elsewhere—like in a gang, in the "popular" group at school, with the "partiers," or with the "druggies." A research study confirmed that the closer adolescents are to their parents, the less likely it is that they will use drugs. The more independent the adolescents are from their parents, the greater the likelihood that they will use drugs.[1]

Teenagers who feel unloved are also more likely to feel depressed, and trivial events can lead to desperate solutions such as suicide attempts. Research shows that boys are about four times as likely as girls to actually *commit* suicide, while girls are twice as likely to *attempt* suicide.[2] According to the surgeon general's report: "Depressed children are sad, they lose interest in activities that used to please them, and they criticize themselves and feel that others criticize them. They feel unloved, pessimistic, or even hopeless about the future; they think that life is not worth living."[3]

Clearly, those who feel loved, who are connected to their families, make better life choices because they aren't as influenced by peers or by the life happenings that seem to swirl out of their control.

The best advantage you can give your teenager is to make her home turf the place she wants to hang out the most. The place she wants to bring her friends to. If you supply that kind of a home, you increase the probability that your kid will want to be home, which means you'll know where she is and who she's hanging out with. Even better, her identification with your family group will give muscle behind her words when she's away from you and approached to do something harmful or illegal. "No thanks," she can say firmly. "I'm an Anderson, and we don't drink. And no, I don't do Spice either. So don't ask me again."

Kids who feel strongly about their home turf—who feel respected and listened to there—are less likely to look for acceptance in their peer groups. But how do you go about providing that type of environment?

It Worked for Me

My husband and I were in the middle of revamping our basement when we heard you talk on *Fox & Friends* about making our home the place where kids want to be. Our kids are just turning 11 and 13, so we decided that, instead of making the basement into a larger office for my husband, who works at home, we'd turn it into a rec room so our teenagers can have a place to hang out with their friends. Your tip came with perfect timing, and we can already see the results. We've become "the hangout," and we like it that way!

Sarah (and Richard), New Hampshire

Establishing Your Turf

You can gain respect, even admiration, from your teenager. Truly. And here's how.

Your 13-year-old son is being bullied at school. He has a squeaky voice, he hasn't matured yet physically (he's the runt of the litter), and he ends up on the serving platter three days a week in the gym locker room. Then, last week, the football quarterback stole his clothes from his locker and left him naked, with not even a towel for cover. What do you do? If you want that kid to know he's got a safe place on your turf, you become his partner—his advocate.

First, pay a trip to his homeroom teacher at school. Do this so neither your son nor anyone else knows. It's very important—for your son's sake and for the mission to be accomplished—that your son's peers don't see you talking to the teacher. So make an after-school or before-school appointment, and bring the Starbucks and the lemon cake to sweeten the deal. A 10-minute meeting with a teacher can do a great deal if you address the issue straightforwardly, giving only the needed details to present the issue, and treat all parties involved respectfully.

If that doesn't get an appropriate response, the next step is your principal's office. The same rules apply, and double the Starbucks and lemon cake. But you always start with the teacher first and win her cooperation.

And how do you handle it with your teenager? "That's a really ugly situation you're in. And you're right—it's not fair. It's not right. But I sure am proud of you for the way you handled it. You didn't try to get back at the other kids; you didn't mouth off."

Then you talk with him about how weak bullies really are. "Anybody who has to pick on somebody who looks smaller or weaker is pretty insecure. They don't think much of themselves, do they, if they have to cut somebody else down to feel good?" Be your teenager's partner—empathize with him and his tough situation. But also help to provide some perspective for a long-term view. Then quietly keep tabs on what's happening with the teacher and school administrator. No bully should be allowed to continue wreaking havoc on your son.

Then just wait. This summer, between June and August, that 13-year-old son of yours will do a magical change act. He'll grow up right before your eyes—adding three inches in height, a deep voice, and hair in the appropriate locations. Those bullies might be staring up at your son come the first day of school . . . or at their 10-year high school reunion.

> *This summer, between June and August, that 13-year-old son of yours will do a magical change act.*

You will survive. Your kid will survive. And through this situation, you have gotten your son solidly on your turf by empathizing with the unfair situation and by showing that you're on his side and you care about what happens to him.

This is true in things both great and small. In the teenage world, the appearance of a simple pimple on your daughter's face is like having a rubber dart stuck to the middle of her forehead. She'll feel like the whole world is looking at her. Again, become her partner. Go to your local pharmacy with her and let her pick out products to try. Keep trying them until you find one that works.

When a friend dumps her, you become the shoulder to cry on. When he doesn't make the team, be the one to help him drown his sorrows in an extra-large pizza of his favorite variety. These little things you do go a long way toward establishing your turf.

When you listen and partner with your teenager, you'll gain his respect . . . even his admiration. And you'll give him the determination and courage to stand up for himself.

The Sibling Dog and Pony Show

You're sipping your morning coffee, and two of your precious darlings start the dog and pony show at the breakfast table.

"How *could* you?" one hisses.

"How could I *what*?" the other says.

"Wear my favorite jeans and bring them back with a big stain!"

"Well, you wore . . ."

And the battle kicks in before you can even get them out the door for school.

Where two or more are gathered, there will be division. Especially with families in the hormone-laden years, where comfortability can quickly breed irritability.

> *Where two or more are gathered, there will be division.*

An important thing to keep in mind is that every branch of the family tree will go off in a different direction. One of your sons might be musical and artistic; the other might be gifted in athletics. Your older daughter may get straight A's without cracking a book, while your younger daughter struggles to pass a couple of her classes. No two in your litter will be the same, and understanding their personalities and what they are up against in their peer circles, as well as understanding their roles in your home, can help you support them more effectively.

Firstborns tend to be the leaders, the perfectionists, the analytical and critical thinkers who get heaped high with chores because you know they'll get them done.

Middleborns tend to be the peacemakers—the "hey, let's not make waves and slide under the radar" people who are easygoing and major on outside-the-home friendships (because that's where they're noticed).

Babies of the family tend to be the charming entertainers, who are very good at getting off scot-free on their jobs.

Trying to make things "equal" (as many parents do) merely breeds contempt and competition.

I have five kids. I love all of them. I don't love one of them more than another, but I won't treat them all the same. Why? Because they're not the same. Just like the state of Arizona won't treat a 12-year-old the same way they'd treat a 16-year-old who's driving. One can freely and happily go for a ride in the passenger side; the other has to get a permit, prove himself, and then take a test to get a license.

Nobody wants to live in a war zone, where shells are landing willy-nilly and exploding.

Gangs have turf wars to gain "respect" (or so they call it), but turf wars in the family should be halted in their tracks, whether between parent and teenager or between siblings. Nobody wants to live in a war zone, where shells are landing willy-nilly and exploding. That kind of excitement you don't need in a home. Homes should be a place of peace and respect, even if a few skirmishes occur now and again. They should be handled respectfully, in an even-keeled manner, with the goal to come up with a balanced solution that is workable for all.

So how can you handle those skirmishes before they become full-blown battles on the home front?

There's something important you need to realize. Why are those siblings warring in front of you? Because they're hoping to draw you in. They want you to take sides so they can say, "See, I *told* you Mom likes me better than you." Fighting is all about competition. It's actually an act of cooperation! So let your kids fight . . . but keep it fair.

Next time the kids start their dog and pony show, and one says, "How come *she* got to do that? You never let *me* do that," try a little humor.

"Well, it's because we love her so much better."

That's how we Lemans handle it, and it's guaranteed to get the dramatic "Oh, Daaaad!" But then we're a family who uses humor a lot, so it works for us.

If humor's not your thing, try straight-forward reasoning.

"Well, do you really want me to treat you like your little sister?"

"Yeah, I do," your son says. "She gets all the good stuff."

"Okay," you say calmly, "starting tonight, for the next week, your bedtime is now 8:30 p.m. Your allowance is now $10 a week, and—"

"Uh, I don't mean that!" your son says quickly.

"Then what did you mean?" you say.

> **Ground Rules for Fighting Fair**
>
> 1. Speech must be respectful of the other person. No vulgar language is acceptable.
> 2. One person talks at a time until he's done, then the other can talk. No interruptions allowed.
> 3. Abuse of any kind—physical, verbal, or emotional—is off-limits.
> 4. The two warring parties talk it out in a room by themselves, out of anyone else's hearing.
> 5. They don't come out until it's resolved with mutual satisfaction.

You've just caught your teenager red-handed . . . or red-faced, in this case. The truth is, he can't stand it that his little sister got something he didn't get. But when you put it in the proper perspective (an adjustment of bedtime and money speak volumes to a teenager's freedom), it's amazing the turnaround in attitude that can happen.

And you didn't even have to raise your voice or your lecturing finger, now did you?

A Winning Strategy

"But, Dr. Leman," you're saying, "there's no way I can stop my kids from fighting."

No, that's right, you can't stop them from fighting. But you can stop them from fighting within your hearing. Funny how that takes all the fun out of it.

You may think that you don't have much influence over your child's life, now that he's a teenager, he has his own group of friends, and he's driving. But, parent, you still count. You're still in the game, and the clock is still running. Without you, your child wouldn't even have the underwear he's wearing. (See what I mean about you counting more than you think you do? And the world thanks you too.)

Let the bulls take each other by the horns . . . and stay out of it.

You have enough to do. The best place for your child to learn about relationships—and fighting fair—is in your home. So let the bulls take each other by the horns, so to speak, and stay out of it. That's the best way to short-circuit the battle.

Too many parents spend a significant amount of their time at home refereeing sibling squabbles. But don't become Judge Judy and ferret out the almighty punishment upon the deserving party. Parents who choose to do it that way will be ready for the loony bin by eight o'clock in the evening.

Instead try this: when your kids start fighting, usher the two of them to a room somewhere—preferably the least desirable place in the house, like your cramped office, where they have to be face-to-face. Outside is even better. Then give them instructions: "You guys need to solve this, and I'm going to give you 20 minutes to come up with a solution together. I'll be back to check on you."

I guarantee your kids will be out of that room in a couple of minutes with, "Everything's cool, Mom."

73

But what is the solution? You're doubtful the warring parties came to an agreement that easily. So you ask very matter-of-factly, "How, specifically, did you solve the problem?"

If one of your kids is wily and strong-willed and the other is much more laid-back, I can tell you that with great regularity the powerful kid will be the one who decides what the solution is.

However, the street-smart parent will defer to the more manatee-like type personality—the one who floats along in the water of life—and ask, "Is that really how you want this to be?" You give that child the opportunity to speak up.

"Well, not exactly," she says.

"Then," you say firmly, "you guys need to talk longer until I get a fair, balanced solution to this problem. It sounds pretty one-sided to me."

Now your teenagers will play their guilt card on you. They'll accuse you of treating them like little kids.

"Well," you say, unruffled, "you're acting like little kids, so I guess that fits."

No teenager wants to be called a little kid. Your message will get across. They'll be less likely to fight in your hearing the next time.

And if they do, put the ball right back in their court again. Walk away. Let them resolve it. Don't own problems that aren't yours.

It Worked for Me

I know from your *Birth Order Book* that I'm a middle-born, a pleaser. So when my four kids—6, 7, 14, 16—fight, I just want everybody to be happy. I didn't realize until I heard you talk at a women's luncheon how much I was letting my kids control me. As I drove home, I vowed that it was going to stop. The next time they got into it, I actually put the two fighters in the bathroom (hey, you said the smallest room in the house) and made them work it out. I did that twice in less than 24 hours with the older ones, and only needed to do it once with my younger two. It really works!

Saundra, Utah

A Note about Children with Special Needs

If you're the parent of a teenager who has special needs—who is physically, mentally, or emotionally challenged—what do you need to be aware of with sibling battles? One of the things I learned early on in my psychology practice was that siblings often are jealous of the extra attention that special needs kids get in the family. A lot of additional things come their way too, because of their disabilities. Although their siblings know of the challenges and see them firsthand, it's easy to think in the midst of mood swings, *Wow, he gets all the good stuff. No fair.*

> *Siblings often are jealous of the extra attention that special needs kids get in the family.*

Mickey is the middle child in a family. She's the peacemaker, the one who steps into the middle between her two warring brothers. Her older brother is a definite firstborn, with an opinionated, there's-only-one-way-to-do-things personality. Her younger brother, Frankie, has Down syndrome and other physical challenges as well. The family's schedule revolves a lot around Frankie's needs since he's in extra programs instead of a regular school. Mickey sometimes feels lost in the shuffle and gets a little jealous. She's not able to drive the family car and get away, like her 16-year-old brother, so she ends up playing babysitter for Frankie a lot. Yes, she loves her brother, but she once told a family friend, "Everybody always talks to and about Frankie. Frankie this and Frankie that. Don't I matter too?"

But interestingly, kids who experience initial jealousy over a special needs kid in their family often end up as very protective of that same brother or sister as they grow older.

I've also seen firsthand how families with special needs teenagers are especially blessed. They're often a very tightly knit group who has waged war together over health issues, emotional issues, schooling, and other life discussions, and come out stronger.

Life is precious. We come in different shapes and sizes and strengths and deficiencies. But special needs kids give far more to their families than they take.

Just ask Mickey, who recently defended her beloved little brother with a diatribe far better than an attorney could have, when someone called him stupid. Bet the other kid won't try that again with a special needs kid . . . ever.

A Home—or a Hotel?

Have you ever seen someone standing on a street corner in a city, holding a sign that says, "Will Work for Food"? Well, your teenager needs to work for food. Here's what I mean.

There are a lot of "givens" for teenagers in today's world. As such, they tend to view a reward as their right for anything they're involved in. But if your teenager is truly going to be part of your family, he too needs to "work for food"—to be part of the home, which includes things like cleaning up his room, taking out the garbage, being kind to his little sister, running errands, etc.

Home isn't a place where one person kicks back, relaxes, and sleeps in while everybody else works. It's not a hotel with room service that takes care of dirty sheets, serves meals with a cover, and then doesn't mind if the plates are shoved out into the hallway for pickup.

Home is a place where every member of the family is equal to every other member of the family—where each person is respected, and each person pulls their weight.

However, let me be clear: just because all are equal doesn't mean you, as parents, shouldn't be in authority.

Two of the hottest words in our culture—words that spark an immediate response—are *submission* and *authority*. Some people have a knee-jerk reaction because they see those words as negative. However, if you think about it, if you're

> *If you don't give your teenagers responsibility, how will they learn to be responsible?*

subject to someone's authority, you are submissive. That doesn't mean being less than or inferior to, though. Submission speaks of order. Without someone in charge, the home would be in constant chaos.

We've all seen the golden child who is treated like a prince in his own home—and he acts like it elsewhere. He's the miserable, spoiled brat that the teachers discuss in the lunchroom. He's not gaining friends in his classroom either. So did the parents really do the kid any favors by establishing him as the center of their universe? I think not.

Some kids today also think nothing of hurting their parents—hitting them, kicking them, etc. Worse than that, the parents take the abuse. In fact, it happens all the time. Allowing your kids to strike you is not only wrong, it's unhealthy for them—not to mention unhealthy for you. God did not put you on this earth to be anyone's punching bag. If this is your situation, it has to stop. You must stand up for yourself. If your son or daughter has become too violent or too powerful, then get outside help to handle the situation. Never, ever tolerate abuse of any kind in your household.

When you as the authority figure rear your kids to respect authority, you are training them to be authority figures whom others can respect someday. How else will the baton of responsibility be passed?

But if you don't give your teenagers responsibility, how will they learn to be responsible?

That's why it's so critical to make sure that your 11- to 19-year-old has a piece of the action—that he is able to give back to the family. An 11- or 12-year-old is more than capable of paying the family bills online once the account is set up or sorting out receipts and charity donation slips for taxes. A 16-year-old can call the local garage and schedule the car for an oil change, drive it there, and do homework while he waits. A 17-year-old can figure out meals for a week and do the shopping.

> **Family Mantras to Live By**
>
> • Each person is like a snowflake—no two are the same.
>
> • Row your own canoe.
>
> • Respect each other's differences.
>
> • All for one and one for all.

When your teenagers contribute to the family, they will become more a part of that family. In order to feel connected, they need to give back to the home.

Think back to the agrarian roots that America came from. Teenagers in that society had a definite purpose. Even our school year of nine-plus months, with two and a half months off in the summer, was built on the concept that youngsters had to be available to help harvest the crops.

Now for those of the younger generation for whom *work* is an alien term, *work* is when you get up in the morning, get dressed, go someplace, barely have time for lunch, and come home tired at the end of the day just in time to sleep . . . and get up and do it all over again.

So many kids today don't do any work; they don't give back to anybody. No wonder we're raising "Generation Me." Even toddlers and preschoolers are telling their parents, "You're not the boss of me"—and getting away with it!

The reality is, we're not the "boss" of our kids; we're their parents. And with that position comes built-in authority. Again, it's not the authoritarian, helicopter-hovering, know-it-all parent who hands out edicts right and left. Nor is it the "hey, honey, anything goes, and can I wipe your nose while I'm at it?" parent. Authoritative parents are loving, balanced, and mindful of the welfare of everyone in the family.

> *No one member of the family is more important than the whole family.*

I've said it before in this book, but I'll say it again: no one member of the family is more important than the whole family. That means no prima donnas are allowed. There are no free rides. Everybody contributes.

So why is it that we're allowing kids shorter than a yardstick to call the shots? To develop a demeanor and attitude early in life where they put themselves in diametric opposition to wherever the parent is?

As the commercials say, "Don't try this at home." Really, don't. It's not good for anyone.

However, let me give you something you can try at home. If you have access to an ankle-biter between ages two and four, extend your arms toward that child and simply say, "Come here." My best guess (in 99 cases out of 100) is that the child will go south . . . as far away from you as he or she can get.

> **What to Do on Wednesday**
>
> 1. Partner with your child.
> 2. Don't own problems that aren't yours.
> 3. Run a home, not a hotel.

But if you want that child to come toward you, all you have to do is simply say, "Come here" softly, then start to walk backwards . . . slowly. Watch the miracle that happens before your eyes. That little toddler will come toward you.

That's the position of a parent of a teenager today.

Open your arms in welcome, and walk backwards. As you do so, you're saying, by your action, your attitude, and your character, "Teenager, follow me."

Your son or daughter will follow someone. Who do you want that someone to be?

He or she will belong someplace. Where do you want that place to be?

Belonging to you can change your teenager's world. The family who works together and plays together stays together.

★ **THE WINNING PLAY** ★

It's all about the relationship.

Thursday

"You're Grounded!" (I Hope So)

Are your teenagers grounded for what they do . . . or grounded
in who they are? How to raise a street-smart kid.

I know a kid who is always grounded. He's grounded if he forgets to take out the trash. He's grounded if he doesn't clean up
his room on schedule. Just last week, he was grounded because
he brought home one B—amid all his A's—on his report card. (I
know some of you are saying, "What? You've got to be kidding.
If my kid brought home one B, I'd be jumping around the living
room for joy!") No matter what your policy on grades, grounding
a kid for getting one B is a little overkill in the parental grounding
department, I'd say.

But when you think about it, don't you want your teenager to
be "grounded"? Not in the way that teenage boy always is, but in
the sense that your teenager is solid in what he thinks and believes,
and confident in making the right choices and doing the right
thing, whether you're looking over his shoulder or not.

Only those who are given responsibility can become responsible. So what kind of choices are you giving your teenager? Soon he'll be out on his own. What kind of life do you want him to live?

Every day you are putting items in your teenager's bags—packing them for life both now and beyond your little nest. But just what are you putting in those bags? Are they the things that really count? Clothing and hairstyles will change like the wind (or the entrée of the next fashion magazine), but things like a good work ethic, integrity, respect, responsibility, character others can count on, someone who can be trusted, someone who tells the truth, etc., are the important traits that will ground your teenager for a lifetime.

Heading into the Teenage Morass

No teenager would want to admit this, but it's true. Unless there has been a significant amount of abuse and turmoil during their early years in your home, most teenagers head into the hormone-group years with a naïveté that can be charming, frustrating, or downright frightening to parents. Your precious darling, whom you've nurtured in your home (okay, so you've coddled a little too) and whom Grandma treats as the center of the universe, is now going to rub shoulders with kids in middle school and high school who:

- use the F-bomb every other word
- grew up in a home environment foreign to what your kid grew up in
- don't believe lying is wrong
- are all about getting what they want, when they want it, and by any means they want
- are about looking good to their peers and don't care about anyone's welfare but their own

What? You don't think those kids are out there? If your background and home environment are rather sheltered, take a walk sometime down the middle school or high school hallways when the students are changing classes. Or hang out on the grounds after school and simply listen and watch. I guarantee that your eyes and ears will be opened to a new and startling world.

As your kid moves into the hormone group, it's critical he feels solidly a part of your home and your home turf, because the values you've taught him will be tested in more ways than one during these years. Your daughter will see other kids doing things that she knows are wrong but will be tempted to go along with it just to fit in. Your son will feel that push to compete—to be cooler than cool in his new environment.

Establishing Healthy Boundaries

Now that your son or daughter is a teenager, you can't stand by his or her side constantly to weather life's storms. But you can help by making sure you establish healthy, respectful boundaries in key areas.

Curfews

One of the questions I get asked the most by parents of just-turned teenagers is, "What time should my teenager be home at night?"

But it isn't the time that's important. If you've given your children age-appropriate choices early in life so they can learn to make responsible choices, you won't have to worry about the time.

When my teenage kids went out with friends, they would ask me, "Dad, what time should I be home?"

I would shrug. "At a responsible hour."

Why would I say that? Because as my kids have grown up, I've given them age-appropriate choices and the opportunity to be

83

responsible, and they have been. So I didn't need to say, "Well, make sure you're home by 11 p.m.—or else." In fact, they were usually home well before I would even think to start looking for them!

That's because, along the way, we've built blocks of trust and respect for each other. We've been able to talk *with* each other instead of *at* each other. My kids knew they belonged to the Lemans, and that we Lemans have certain family values we hold to firmly.

Driving the Family Car

When three of our kids were driving, Sande and I decided that, instead of us coming up with guidelines for the use of the family car, we'd let our kids—Holly, Krissy, and Kevin II—come up with the rules themselves. Why would I do that? Here's what I told them.

"Okay, guys, I'm going to show you how much it's going to cost me for each of you to drive. It's a lot of money." I showed them my State Farm bill. "But I didn't take you down to the DMV to get your license because I thought you were goofballs. You have a good head on your shoulders, and I like the way you think. But since I'm the guy accountable to State Farm for what you do behind the wheel of our family car, I'd like you to take some time and jot down rules that you think should govern your use of the family car. Then we'll look at them and post them on the fridge."

If you let your kids come up with the rules, you might be surprised. Here are three of the rules our kids came up with on their own:

- Never bring the car home with the tank on empty.
- Be home by 10:00 p.m. Never later.
- Have no more than two friends in the car with you.

If you let your kids make the rules—like no texting while driving—they will be less likely to rebel and break them (after all, they

84

came up with them in the first place). So let your teenager have ownership of establishing the boundaries.

Personal Responsibility

I've stated throughout this book that it's important to make sure the ball lands in your teenager's court. It's not your ball, so you shouldn't be carrying it. What your kid does from this point forward is her responsibility—*not yours.* There is no passing the buck about whose fault anything is. The old adage is true: "Those who point a finger at someone else are pointing three fingers at themselves." Your teenager's actions, behavior, and character are all her own. She needs to experience both the benefits and the backlash from them without any interference from you, because that's the way the real world works.

However, with that blunt statement, let me also say that today's parent has to be street-smart. Too many parents don't notice—or don't want to notice—that there is an elephant on the sofa. For example, if your teenager always has a lot of money but no job, perhaps you'd be smart to investigate just where his money is coming from.

No matter what beliefs and values your teenager is testing, you must communicate in a way that is respectful to him or her, but also no-nonsense and straightforward. "Drinking is not acceptable in this house." "Your girlfriend is not allowed in your bedroom with the door closed. No exceptions." You must care enough to confront when necessary. Otherwise, let that little bit of reality do the talking.

It Worked for Me

I can't count the times in the last two years that my son has said, "But why didn't you tell me?" Like it was my fault when he wasn't somewhere he was supposed to be. Then I heard you talk about putting the ball in the court where it belongs. I realized my son wasn't the problem; *I* was. I was letting him get away with it! Talk about stupid.

No more, I vowed. The next time he missed a football practice, he came storming into the kitchen and let me have it. "Mom, how come you didn't tell me?"

"It's not my football practice. It's yours," was all I said.

My son opened his mouth, then shut it. He must have stood there for a couple minutes, looking confused. But now he checks the school schedule for himself and tells *me* in the morning when he has activities. What you say really works!

Joleen, Kansas

Sexual Exploration

The other evening one of Lauren's friends came over while I was watching a TV show. As we engaged in a short conversation, I happened to catch something on the TV screen and said, "Well, that's a little over the top for prime-time TV." A guy was getting it on with a girl right there on the show—and right at dinnertime, for kids all over the nation to see.

> **What a Teenage Boy Needs to Know**
>
> - Girls don't like to be grabbed.
> - Keep it in your pants.
> - Treat your date with respect and kindness.

Lauren's friend jumped in. "Dr. Leman, I haven't forgotten what you told us when you visited our class in seventh grade."

"Oh," I said, "what was that?"

"You told us to keep it in our pants."

I laughed. "That's really good advice. That little puppy will get you in more trouble than you can ever imagine."

Teaching your kids about sex and sexuality isn't just giving them "the talk" when they are eight or nine, then wiping your hands clean and saying, "Whew! I'm so glad we got through that." (All this done, of course, as you talked to the kid through her closed door.)

86

Instead, talking about sex and sexuality is a continual thing. You comment on things like that on TV, revealing where the world's view doesn't align with your value and belief system. You treat persons of both genders with respect. You answer questions about what real, committed love is and the emotional and physical results of sex outside of marriage. You also talk about topics that might make you uncomfortable, such as homosexuality, oral sex, etc., when your kids want to know the facts.

If your teenager is getting into the dating scene, then Mom, you need to talk with your son. Dad, you need to talk with your daughter. These cross-gender conversations are extremely important. Who better than a male to tell what's on a male's mind? Who better than a female to say what she likes or doesn't like about how a male treats her?

Although I've discussed this entire subject in depth in *A Chicken's Guide to Talking Turkey with Your Kids about Sex*, here are a few guidelines for your discussion:

> **What a Teenage Girl Needs to Know**
>
> • You don't "owe" your date anything—that includes kisses, a hand up your shirt or down your pants, or any kind of sexual behavior.
>
> • A boy who says he loves you but can't wait for sex isn't "in love" with you, he's "in need."
>
> • The way you dress will affect what boys think of you, because they are stimulated by looking. You might like that tight shirt because it shows off your figure, but it's likely saying something else to your date: *Tonight might just be the night.* . . .

- Focus on biology—how the male and female bodies work.
- Explain what sex is. Yes, one aspect of it is the entering of the penis into the vagina, but I also define sex as: "Any activity in which body parts normally clothed by a bathing suit are touched, massaged, played with, kissed, or sucked." That's why, in today's world, it's not enough to emphasize abstinence. Many people can abstain from the "sexual act" of the penis into the vagina, yet still be carrying out all sorts of

sexual behavior, including oral sex. What we must emphasize is *purity*—of both body and thought.

- Emphasize that sex is sacred—it's meant for one man, one woman, in a committed marriage relationship, for a lifetime. Relationships should always be based on respect for each other, not "need."

- Stick to the straightforward facts: "In order for a man or woman to have sexual intercourse, his penis will get inserted into her vagina."

- Tell them why it is important to wait. Present the statistics, along with the statement that "it'll never happen to me" isn't true about STDs or pregnancies. And using a condom doesn't make sex completely safe either.

- Explain why it's important to not kick off a process that you can't stop once the train of hormones is running. Once you give of yourself in sex, you can never have a "first time" again.

- If your teenager is dating, you set the parameters. "As you're going into this dating time of your life, we need to talk through a few guidelines. If you're having a girl over, where do you think the best place would be for you to have privacy?"

"Oh, my room," your son will say.

"No, that's not an alternative. But I know something that would be. If you bring your date over, I'll greet her and talk with her, then get busy for a while somewhere else in the house so you can have privacy in the family room. If you want to rent a movie and hang out, Dad and I will find something to do in the back room."

Yes, you all share the same family room, but you want your teenager to know that the family room is to be used for his social engagements as well. Having your son's dates on your home turf gives you a premium box seat to see how he handles life on his dates . . . and also the kind of girls he's dating.

Because teenagers are all about "the moment," it's difficult for them to think ahead 5 years, 10 years, or even to next weekend. But put it this way: If you were at your high school reunion 10 years from now and you saw the guy or girl you went on a date with, could you smile and greet that person? Introduce him or her to your wife or husband? Or would you be embarrassed? Ah, now that puts things in a different light, doesn't it?

It Worked for Me

My daughter is 14, but she looks 18. Every male at the mall checks her out, and she says she hates being noticed. I could never get across to her, though, that wearing hip-hugger jeans and a tight camisole isn't just a fashion statement; it's a "hey, take a *really good* look at me" statement. A friend who'd heard you speak gave me a tip to try, and my husband was game. He took Rachel out for dinner and explained to her how guys think.

Rachel didn't say anything to me about how the night went, but I noticed a change the next day. She was still wearing the same jeans and cami, but this time she had another longer shirt over the top of it that hid her otherwise "right out there" curves. She got it. And you were right: all I had to do was provide the opportunity for her to hear from her dad what guys think. It's sure a lot easier and less stressful than harping on what she's wearing all the time.

Susan, Washington

Value and Belief Systems

Do you really want your teenagers to match your beliefs and value system? Strange as it may seem to your ears, I hope not. You've spent years teaching, preaching, and living out (or not)

Let Reality Do the Talking

Situation #1: Your son forgot to return the car keys for you to get to your dentist appointment on time.
Answer: Next time he wants the car, it's simply not available.

Situation #2: Your daughter spent all of her allowance, and it's only day 10 of the month.
Answer: "Oh, that is a problem, isn't it?" you say. "Hmm, well, it looks like you'll have to get creative since you won't get your next allowance check until the end of the month."

Situation #3: Your son borrows your husband's golf clubs, and the seven iron isn't there when he comes back.
Answer: "I know your dad loves you and he loves me. But I'm not quite sure where that seven iron fits in the big picture. It's pretty high. So you'd better find a way to either find it real quick or make some financial plans to replace it, because I know your dad, and he won't be a happy camper."

Situation #4: Your daughter bad-mouths dinner.
Answer: You say nothing. You simply remove the food from her plate without any comment, but the kitchen is closed for the night. Later, when she wants to go out, you say no. When she asks why, you say, "I didn't appreciate your comments at dinner. It took me two and a half hours to make that food, which I removed from your plate so you wouldn't have to look at such trash. If you can't respect and appreciate my efforts, I don't feel like driving you anywhere."

your beliefs and values in front of your children. Often your actions spoke much louder than your words. Ouch. That thought hurts sometimes, doesn't it? But we're all imperfect people, and we often act inconsistently with our values when under pressure. Now, as your kids enter the hormone-group years, they'll begin to think for themselves about those values and morals you've tried to live out. They'll have to decide whether they're going to accept or reject them.

It's like pouring water over tea leaves into a teacup. This is the time for them to take the values they've absorbed thus far and test them in the real world. The result can be either a beautiful, golden-colored water, or a muddy, steeped-too-long mess. Yes, you can help and guide (you are, after all, still the authority in the home), but your teenager is now a thinking, functioning, almost adult. Soon she'll be out on her own. So if she's going to test those value systems, the best time for her to do so is now, while she still has you as a ready resource for questions.

If you are a person of faith, a great chapter in the Bible that would help you kick off a discussion about life values that really matter is Colossians chapter 3. It's a wonderful "family plan" that could revolutionize the relationships in your house.

Family, School, and Then Other Things

Teenagers in general tend to be busy socially. They can, in fact, have so many things going on that they begin to disconnect with their families because they end up spending less and less time at home. That's why making sure your kids are solidly entrenched on your home turf is so important to their well-being in their teenage years. What happens in the family—family activities, outings, dinners, chores, vacations—needs to stay the top priority even in this time of great social growth. The next priority has to be schoolwork—giving it the time and attention it needs to bring in grades that reflect the personal talents of the student. Anything besides that—jobs, friends—are the "extras" of life that come when the first two roles are fulfilled.

But take a look at most teenagers' schedules and you'll see this order of priorities:

1. Friends
2. School and school activities
3. Family (when it can be squeezed in between items 1 and 2 above)

It's no wonder families today are feeling more disconnected than ever, and teenagers don't feel like anyone at home cares about them. They're hardly home to find out!

The Activity Trap

My sweet wife, Mrs. Uppington, loves the Christmas holiday. In fact, she loves it so much that she decorates the house festively from top to bottom. Our Christmas tree is usually 10 feet tall. It's adorned by 3,000 lights (and that's a conservative number), and of course these lights all have to be connected and plugged in. I, being the nonelectrical genius in the home, decided one Christmas that we'd connect all of the strings of lights into one big receptor, rather than having to plug them in separately.

> *Activities are not good for your kids!*

All of a sudden there was a big *poof*! Sparks flew my way. I jerked my head back toward the tree and found that 17 pine needles smashed in the back of your neck doesn't feel very good. The shock taught me something, though. You can't overload an electrical circuit without some kind of backlash.

If your teenager is overwhelmed, you don't have to look further than the calendar you put before her on a weekly basis. Many kids are very competent, skilled in a lot of areas, achievers, hard workers, and straight-A students, but look at everything they do. If your kid is doing four hours of homework a night, involved in a school play, taking piano lessons, and playing on an athletic team, no wonder she's overwhelmed. I'd be overwhelmed too if I had to do all that.

Now, me? I was sort of underwhelmed as a student. I used to cut school on Mondays and Fridays with great regularity; I liked the three-day-a-week plan. I only gave school a lick and a holler, and that was it.

But some teenagers are like Energizer Bunnies who keep going and going and going . . . until eventually their batteries wear out and they collapse.

Anyone who has read a single Leman book knows where I stand on this: activities are not good for your kids! By that, of course, I mean an excess of activities. Some kids are overwhelmed in life because they're not cutting it in school and they feel the pressure to succeed where they're failing. Other kids are overwhelmed because they excel at so many things they're involved in—it's hard to pick just one thing.

On all days you will be a parent. But on some days you also need to be a shrink. So turn into Dr. Phil for a moment and do an analysis with me of what's happening with your kid and in your home.

Is your kid running full speed, like the Energizer Bunny? If so, why? Is she thinking:

- "I only count in life when I achieve."
- "I only count in life when I get straight A's."
- "I only count in life when I'm involved in everything people ask me to be involved in."
- "I only count when I say yes, and I won't count if I say no."
- "I only count when I don't disappoint other people."

I've known straight-A kids in high school who have been diligent bookworms, have graduated from their class as valedictorians, and have failed in life miserably.

Every kid needs downtime—times when he or she can create, dream, and just *be*, without always having something to *do*. Your son or daughter needs relief from the constant stress of busyness. All kids need to be kids. Does your teenager have any time in his or her schedule like that?

You, the parent, the authority of the family, have the ability to say no to your teenager. "No, you can't do everything. You'll have to make some choices here."

93

And then you, parent and shrink, need to add the muscle of determination to encourage those decisions . . . and to stand behind them and support your kids wherever necessary to accomplish that purpose.

It Worked for Me

We're finally off the treadmill, and it feels good! With four kids in our family, Monday through Saturday was an insane experience since each kid was in multiple activities. It helped a little when our two older ones became teenagers, but then they just got more involved, and we saw less of them. There were some weeks I felt I never got out of our SUV except for when I was sleeping.

But no more. I love your policy of one activity per semester, and we adopted it as a family at the beginning of this school year. Thankfully, two of our kids love soccer, and they're close enough in age that they're on the same team. The two older ones are involved with after-school activities the same three days. So now we all get home at 6:00 on three nights a week and can have a real dinner (the Crock-Pot is my friend), and the other two nights a week we're all home right after school, and we stay home. Our lives are still busy (busier than I'd like them to be), but it's way better.

Angie, New Mexico

Developing Kids with Character

A couple months ago, Sande, Lauren, and I were going to have a family outing. But since she's the last little bird in our nest—with her siblings already out on their own—we told her she could invite someone else to go along.

---

9 Great Ways to Grow Compassion as a Family

Take a simple inventory of your family's time and talents. Then brainstorm how you can serve others—as individuals and as a family. Here are a few ideas for starters.

1. Provide free music lessons (guitar, piano, etc.) for a kid in the neighborhood who would love to learn an instrument but can't afford it otherwise.

2. Help a family who is in need. Our daughter Hannah is involved with a group called Children's Hopechest in Colorado Springs, Colorado (www.hopechest.org), a thriving international ministry to orphans that connects them to the life-transforming power of community-based relationships with Christians in the United States and Canada.

3. Offer to babysit a single mom's children so she can have one evening a week to herself.

4. Spend a Saturday morning helping an elderly person with yard work, bill paying, or grocery shopping.

5. Shovel your neighbor's driveway.

6. Wash cars—and don't accept donations.

7. Pet-sit your neighbors' dog while they're away on vacation.

8. Bring an elderly neighbor's mail to her door each day in the winter, when it's dangerous for her to cross the snowy sidewalk.

9. Invite the new kid at school over after school and let him help make the snack. Make sure all the members of your family meet him and welcome him.

I was surprised at the companion she chose. He was a kid I didn't care for personally, for many reasons. After the activity was over, I asked Lauren, "Why did you invite that kid? You know I don't like him, and I'm surprised that you do."

"Oh, Dad," she said. "I didn't invite him because I liked him. I invited him because nobody in our class likes him."

If you want kids who aren't always thinking about themselves or what they can get, but who are thoughtful and considerate of others, you need to model that kind of compassion in your own home. When you see others' needs, try to meet them by working together as a family. By doing so, you model generosity of time, finances, and other resources.

We Lemans view our home as the neighborhood rescue mission—a place where anybody can come and get some love, attention, and a listening ear. Is your home a place of safety? Where your own kids—and others' kids—like to hang out? Do you care about those other teenagers who flock into your house?

So many parents want to treat their kids like a pheasant with orange sauce under glass—pretty to look at but isolated from the rest of the world. Isolating your kid under the glass dome is the easy way out. But it's not healthy for you or for your teenager. Why not invite over a kid who doesn't have the same advantages your family does? Or a kid nobody else likes? I was humbled by the knowledge that my daughter, to whom I'd role-modeled compassion and a generous heart over the years by the family activities we chose to be involved in, was more compassionate than her father. And you know where I got the idea to do family activities together to assist others? From my own parents. They loved me and I never doubted that, but they were also concerned about other people—even those we didn't know.

As you interact with others who are unlovable, unlikeable, or less fortunate than you, perhaps you and your teenager can make a difference. Do you want your kid to be a giver or a taker? If you want her to be a taker, then raise her like your neighbors' children (the ones who drive you crazy and their parents crazy with all their demands and irresponsibility). If you want her to be a giver, concerned about others, then provide opportunities for her to help others.

I heard recently of a youth group who was doing a car wash. Nothing new there. But the way in which they were doing it was completely different. They didn't charge people, and they didn't take donations. They just smiled, washed cars, and told people,

"Have a fabulous evening!" Another family has permission from a local mall to show up every Friday evening to play music for two hours. (This eight-member family is their own band.) The mall's manager is so thrilled with the crowds they draw—and this free service—that he sometimes treats the family to pizza afterwards. It's the family's favorite day of the week—and they've made shoppers smile too!

> **What to Do on Thursday**
>
> 1. Decide what you want to pack in your teenager's bags for life.
> 2. Establish healthy, respectful boundaries.
> 3. Model giving as an antidote to selfish behavior.

Now, that's pretty far removed from the American dream of getting paid and paid highly, isn't it? But it's a great way to teach kids that they don't always get the carrot at the end of the stick for all they do in life. When you do something to help others without expecting anything in return, it feels good. And that's a wonderful boost to your teenager's self-worth—and the right kind of focus for them. (See "9 Great Ways to Grow Compassion as a Family" on page 95 for some other ideas.)

So let me ask you: what are you packing in your teenager's bags for life outside your home? The concept that she's the center of the universe and others better kowtow to her demands—or else? Or are you rearing a kid who understands the need for, helps establish, and sticks by the family's boundaries; accepts responsibility when her choices aren't wise; and is growing a compassionate heart?

Parent, it all starts with you, for as your teenager sees you do, she'll do too.

See the power you have?

★ THE WINNING PLAY ★

Let reality do the work so you don't have to.

Friday

Ka-ching, Ka-ching, Dividends on the Way

No more pull-ups. No more sippy cups. How to take advantage of these free 'n' easy years.

In late 2010 the company of GM reorganized and made an IPO (initial public offering). They sold stock in their company and set the price at $33 dollars a share.

At least 11 years ago, you made a significant investment in life. You bought the initial stock offering on your little guy (made of snails and puppy dog tails) or girl (made of sugar and spice), and you've helped build the stock options on that guy or girl a little at a time with your love, acceptance, guidance, humility—even your forbearance.

Over the years, your stock has been growing; you've been able to watch it inching up. There are no dividends yet, no public payoff, but with such an investment and all the time you've spent, how can you go wrong?

Yes, your little stock has made a lot of choices on his own. But *you* were the one who was there when he went a little too far and you had to bring him back on course.

The teenage years are where your stock will finally start to pay dividends after you've watched it grow over the years. All the foundations you've built for your child, the things you've put in her bags—accountability, respect, responsibility, etc.—will start to show publicly and privately as she becomes "her own person" as a teenager.

> *Far too soon, your teenager will turn the page of a new chapter in life.*

Yes, there will be times when you'll wonder if you'll survive the storms—or if your kid will just blow away from you like a tent in a desert sandstorm. But in such times, look back on the skirmishes and battles you've already won. No, the teenage years aren't ones where you can go sit in the easy chair and put up your feet. You'll have new challenges around the corner, so it's best to stay light and easy on your feet.

But far too soon, your teenager will turn the page of a new chapter in life. Every teenager's next move will be unique. Some kids will enter the service, others the job world, others college or university, others vocational training.

If you want your child to succeed, to develop who she is to the best of her abilities, and to be a healthy, balanced, contributing member of society, then her best bet for a partner in life is you. So what do you want to do while your child is a teenager? Think through what you want to accomplish together in these all-too-short years remaining. What last-minute instructions will you give her for the game called life—without Mom and Dad—as she flies out of your nest and makes her own way in the world?

Training the Big Three

We live in a world of instant information. When a news event happens on the other side of the world, we know about it within minutes. But news isn't always what it's cracked up to be. For years, people considered Bernie Madoff, American stockbroker and investment advisor, a genius. In the world's eyes, he had it made. His firm was one of the top market-maker businesses on Wall Street. But on June 29, 2009, he was sentenced to 150 years in prison—the maximum allowed—for defrauding thousands of investors of billions of dollars. He even described his business to his sons as "one big lie."[1]

And he's not the only one who's not doing things on the up-and-up. Pastors of megachurches cry their eyes out apologetically on national TV, asking for forgiveness for what they've done. Sports figures like Tiger Woods, who seem invincible and appear to have life thoroughly grasped by the throat, come down hard when their private lives are exposed to the eyes of the world.

People can make stupid decisions that ruin great careers, amazing opportunities, and sterling reputations. Richard Nixon could have gone down as one of the greatest statesmen who ever occupied the White House, and he would have been remembered particularly for the tremendous strides he made with China. But what are people going to remember Nixon for? The fact he did the wrong thing. If Tricky Dicky, as he was called, would have gone before the American people and said, "You're not going to believe what I did. Talk about being dumb as mud. I erased those tapes. In retrospect, that was a terrible thing to do. I was wrong, and I apologize," he wouldn't have left office until his term was up.

Then there's Bill Clinton, who probably could have gone down in history as one of the greatest presidents of the United States. He was, after all, a brilliant guy—the only US president who was a Rhodes scholar. But he lacked common sense and the ability to do the right thing. What did he say over and over? "I did not have sexual relations with that woman."

It Worked for Me

I always hated my kids watching the news because everything presented on it was so negative. But recently I changed my perspective when I heard you talk about the importance of talking through real-life news with your teenagers. When a city councilman was caught with a prostitute, I discussed it with my sons, ages 16 and 17.

"Boy, that guy was sure dumb," one of my sons said.

"Yeah," my other son said, "and it seems like his wife is a really nice lady. Why would he want to throw that all out the window for a night with a hooker?"

My sons got it. But even better, the point stuck with them. When my 17-year-old started dating a couple months later, his girlfriend started pressuring him for sex. My son said he told her the story about the councilman, and that he wouldn't throw his virginity out the door for her either.

His girlfriend broke up with him, and I was secretly glad. But my son's response made me so proud of him. "Mom, her breaking up with me told me that I wasn't really what was important to her. Sex was. I'm so glad I didn't fall for it." He looked at me and grinned. "Guess that councilman taught me something after all."

That was one of my proudest mom moments yet.

Janey, Texas

A wise person once said:

Have two goals: wisdom—that is, knowing and doing right—and common sense. . . .

Learn to be wise . . . and develop good judgment and common sense! I cannot overemphasize this point. Cling to wisdom—she will protect you. Love her—she will guard you. . . .

Don't get into needless fights. Don't envy violent men. Don't copy their ways. . . .

The man who knows right from wrong and has good judgment and common sense is happier than the man who is immensely rich! For such wisdom is far more valuable than precious jewels.[2]

You may be a person of faith; you may not. If you are, you might have recognized those words as coming from Proverbs, a book of wisdom in the Bible. But whether you believe in the Bible or not, this is wise advice for all. If your teenagers learn to have wisdom, good judgment, and discernment, they will know and do right instead of wrong.

It's interesting. There isn't a lot in the Bible that speaks specifically of rearing children. The best reference says, "Children, obey your parents; this is the right thing to do because God has placed them in authority over you." And if your teenagers do so, there's a promise for them: "Yours will be a long life, full of blessing." But it doesn't stop with just telling kids to obey and behave. It has a note to parents that hits home: "Don't keep on scolding and nagging your children, making them angry and resentful."[3] Instead, it says to give your children suggestions and godly advice! These are wise words indeed for the hormone-group years.

> *Your teenager needs to head into life outside your nest with what I call the "big three": wisdom, good judgment, and discernment.*

In today's world, more than ever, your teenager needs to head into life outside your nest with what I call the "big three": wisdom, good judgment, and discernment. There are plenty of traps awaiting them if they don't have these three solidly in their pocket. Many shysters are ready to sucker them otherwise. One well-meaning, kind woman I know got suckered into sending six thousand dollars to a "police officer" who said her grandson was in jail and needed bail money. There are all sorts of folks who will prey on the weak. Bernie Madoff bilked people out of money—including his own family—for years before he got caught. Smart adults couldn't even see through the scheme! All power to his kids for turning him in to the authorities.

Your teenager needs to know that if something is too good to be true, it probably is. He must carefully investigate before moving ahead.

How can you increase your teenager's street-smarts? When you see articles about people like Bernie Madoff, bring them up in the car or at the dinner table. "Hey, did you hear about . . ." and fill your family in on the news item. Discussing real-life situations clues your kid in to the fact that there are both people who prey and people who are suckers out there, and that he doesn't want to be either of those. Encourage your kids to talk about news they find on the internet or hear about. It makes for lively dinner conversation and ups your kids' street-smarts so they will be less likely to fall for the spiels of those who would lead them down the wrong path.

Teenagers may think they're streetwise and smart, but the majority of them are fairly naive (something they certainly wouldn't want to admit to their peers). That's why so many of them make easy targets for scam artists. And in the teenage world, with the push to do what everybody else is doing, if one falls . . . a multitude will fall.

Don't let your kids be suckers. Talk about real life. Train your teenagers in wisdom, good judgment, and discernment by practicing them every day yourself, and talk through situations with your teenagers so.they can develop the "big three" for themselves.

Saving for a Rainy Day

With the scary state of today's economy, you can give your teenagers a tremendous gift: the gift of managing money wisely and investing for the future. Why not jump-start your teenager's finances by encouraging him to put money in a savings account (even telling him you'll match the amount he puts in each time, if you're able financially to do that)? Show him how his money will grow with just a little effort on his part.

And why not throw in some lessons on how the stock market works by giving your teenager the opportunity to invest in a stock or a bond? Giving your teenager a stock certificate for her birthday can kick off the process. But don't stop there. Turn the gift into a lesson in how the stock market ebbs and flows by checking the value of the stock from time to time with your kid. If your 12-year-old spends a lot of time on the computer playing games or surfing the web, she's a prime candidate to research more about the stock market, since she's comfortable with the internet. She might even want to invest in one of the companies she buys video games from.

> *Don't let your kids be suckers.*

Here are some tips from the article "How to Give Children the Gift of Investing":

- Buy some stocks or bonds to teach your child how to diversify his investments.
- Start a custodial investment account in the child's name for as little as $100.
- Open up a Roth IRA if a teenager has earned taxable income this year. Match some or all of his or her contributions.
- Start a 529 college savings plan. Encourage relatives and friends who are undecided on a gift for college to contribute to the account.[4]

Use these tips and advice from any other financially smart people you know to help you teach your teenager to use money, save it, and invest it wisely.

School and Job Shopping

You've reached the years where your teenager is, most likely, going to start thinking about the overwhelming question, "What am I going to do with my life after high school?"

If your son or daughter is in the top 10 percent of his or her class and is getting early acceptance to a number of colleges and universities, with scholarships to boot, you're already hearing in the background the *ka-ching* of your hard work as a parent up to this point.

For myself, the above question didn't come until close to high school graduation, followed by the shocking thought, *Holy crow, what am I gonna do? Everybody else I know is heading off to college.*

Yes, I was a slow learner. Your kid might be like me (hopefully not). It took a long time before my mother heard the *ka-ching* of her hard work.

As your kid is heading to that next chapter in life, your street-smarts have to kick in more than ever. If you have a "smart kid," does that mean she should go to the top-notch university that many hold in high esteem, which costs nearly 50 grand a year? Or would this daughter, whose one life goal is to work with kids, be better served by going to a community college for a couple years (and be able to save money by living at home) and then transfer to a local state university?

I'd like to give you a bit of perspective from my time as a dean of students at the University of Arizona, when I was in charge of all the dorms and more than 6,000 students living in them. Inevitably, if you asked the freshmen to tell you their major, you'd hear

---

The Gift of a Lifetime

For a little reminder that so much of life is about your perspective, here are just a few of the moments my parents lived through with their son:

- I picked imported-from-Norway ornaments (my grandmother's family heirlooms) off our Christmas tree with my pellet gun . . . and then blamed the cat.
- I hit golf balls toward the New York State thruway.
- I graduated at the bottom of my class in high school.
- I got thrown out of Cub Scouts . . . and college.
- I ate Milkbone dog biscuits.
- I was sent home from fourth grade for sticking my finger out my fly and wiggling it at girls.
- I was cut from the JV basketball team . . . and ran home in the middle of winter with just my shorts on.
- I dropped pumpkins off viaducts onto the expressway behind cars.

Yet my dear mother believed in me. She'd always say, "You were such a good boy." Later in life, when I reminded her of what I'd done as a kid, she said, "Oh, yes, I do remember that time. But you were such a good boy."

When you believe in your kids (whether they deserve it or not), you give them a gift for a lifetime. My mother sure did. It took a lot of years, but her positive expectations turned this ol' boy around. It can turn your kid around too.

"premed" and "prelaw" over and over again, like a stuck record. However, if you took a look at some of those kids' high school records, that career was highly doubtful.

With parents, the phrase "hope springs eternal" is almost laughable sometimes. A hopeful parent can take a solid D high school student and try to turn him into a med student at a top-dollar university. But is that really likely to happen?

Parent, when thinking through your teenager's future with him or her, it's street-smart to consider his or her personality, talents, level of personal motivation, and life goals. Unless your daughter is very responsible, directed, a great student, passionately motivated to be a helper of people, and getting high grades in science, why would you pay to send her through four years of university, then another two for nurse training? If your son wants to work with children and loves the daycare where he's working after school, the last thing you'd want to do is spend 48 grand a year and end up with loans in excess of $100,000 for him to get a BA in elementary education.

> *With parents, the phrase "hope springs eternal" is almost laughable sometimes.*

If your son is a B student, then a community college would probably fit him better than a high-pressure university. On the other hand, if your kid gets straight A's, wants to be a pharmacist, and has the push and the brains to do so, you don't want him working at the local Walmart either. Help him to accomplish his dreams of getting schooling at a top university.

Should your child go to a private school or a private university? If you have the 50 grand a year it takes for your kid to explore a liberal arts education at a prestigious school, and you're okay with that, then fine. But if, like most of us, you're looking for the next dollar, that move wouldn't make a lot of sense. You need to be prudent. What is best for the student, and what is best for your family? You know your teenager better than anyone else.

Some kids are better off staying at home and commuting to a local university, with just the book and class fees to pay for since the housing is covered. There are also a plethora of small colleges and universities throughout the United States that are perfect for kids who are average or above average and who want to get to know a lot of other people in a small environment. Some teenagers would flourish in a big school environment, with the big football games and all the extracurricular activities. Others would feel lost in such a place. Some kids can work part-time and attend a community college part-time to get their feet wet in both worlds.

There are some students who aren't ready for college. But they may have high technical skills and are a perfect fit for technical training. (Those people are worth their weight in gold to me, since the technical stuff is definitely not my natural gift.) Others need to mature, develop responsibility, and decide what they're interested in doing in life. Such teenagers shouldn't be pushed into a college environment to "find themselves." Taking a few years to work in different jobs may help them fall into something they like.

For example, Adam was a solid C student in high school. He didn't really have any particular interests. His dad wanted him to go to the same university he had attended, but it was a high-end one, and Adam didn't have the grades it would take to get himself in—or keep him there. When they consulted with me, I told them it seemed best to let Adam explore some job options. So Adam started with a summer job, cleaning the floors at a local industrial shop. While he was there, he became intrigued with how the machines worked and asked if he could stay during his lunch hour one time to watch how they were programmed. Because of Adam's insightful questions, the foreman there gave him the opportunity to stay after work once to help set up a new machine that had just arrived from China. Adam's interest grew. Soon the foreman was pulling him from his clean-up duties to set up other machines. Fast-forward a year—Adam was working full-time. Now, 10 years later, he's the supervisor of that shop!

It certainly isn't the career path that Adam's wealthy parents would have chosen for him initially. But they are proud of him. Adam is now known in that industry for his insight, integrity, and creativity. His skills have helped to launch his small company into being one of the forerunners in that industry.

Adam's sister trained at a small college that focuses on equestrian riding, and is now working with special needs kids who are trained to ride horses as part of their physical therapy. His brother is in advertising and just now taking some college business classes.

It just goes to show, if you have three kids in your family, one will turn right, one will head straight down the middle, and the other will turn left. Encourage each of your teenagers to go his or her own path, in a street-smart way.

> *Encourage each of your teenagers to go his or her own path.*

These after-high-school decisions must be made carefully, for they will affect your son or daughter for a lifetime. So get in the car or take an airplane ride and visit the schools with your child.

Just now, as I'm working on this chapter of the book, my wife, Sande, and I are traveling with Lauren, now a high school senior, to check out UCLA and Otis College of Art and Design—both in the Los Angeles area. Lauren loves to draw and to write, so we wanted to focus on schools that had good programs in both of those areas. But it's only by visiting the schools that Lauren herself will figure out which one best suits her personality and interests.

Yes, your teenager has to make the ultimate choice for his future, but you can encourage him to look wisely at the choices, help to gather information, and talk through realistic expectations. A kid who struggled to get homework done probably isn't a candidate for a BA, an MA, and a PhD. (Of course, there are exceptions—myself, for one. But I had to work some years in between those accomplishments and get serious about studying first.)

The basic principle is: before you put yourself or your teenager in debt for a long time, make sure you're getting the bang for your buck that you deserve for your investment.

It doesn't matter what your neighbor Mike, your co-worker Sally, or your aunt Matilda thinks. What matters is what's best for your teenager and her future, with some due respect paid to your pocketbook as well. Nobody wants to exit four years of college being 100 grand in debt. Yet that hangs over hundreds of thousands of young adults in America. Don't make that your teenager's story unless it's absolutely necessary. Help her make wise choices, then do what you can to help send her on her way in life without a financial burden.

It Worked for Me

I'm a girlie girl, so it's been hard for me to relate to my three sons, all a year apart. (Yeah, God has a real sense of humor, doesn't he?) The testosterone level is pretty high in our house, now that they're all teenagers. Recently it hit me, when you talked about moms and sons at a women's retreat, how much I've been trying to make my boys like me. In other words, I've been working to *take away* their masculinity. That day I realized how unfair I've been.

Now I go out of my way to encourage them when they do "manly" things—like help me carry in the groceries, open a door for me, etc. Thanks for helping me see the light so that my boys become men who will be protectors of women—the kind of man my husband is—instead of the "sensitive boys" I was trying to raise.

Nancie, Indiana

A Special Note for Moms of Boys

About four hours before a game at a major university, the players have chapel. I've had the pleasure of speaking at many of them, but recently I sat in when Andy Lopez spoke. He's the head baseball coach at the University of Arizona and has won the NCAA baseball championship at Pepperdine University. He talked about the fact that football is a violent game—the players, especially at the Division 1 level, are big and fast.

Andy is one of those amazing guys who grew up in a rough neighborhood yet pulled himself up by the bootstraps and has done well in life. But his life turned around when he became a Christian. Still, he was worried about one thing. As he told his sister, who had become a Christian before him, "I don't want to be soft."

Andy shared with the football players that day in chapel that he began looking at the guys in the Bible—Jeremiah and Isaiah, for example. Those guys weren't soft; they were tough. They did what they needed to do—and it wasn't always easy.

Dr. Louann Brizendine, founder of the first clinic to study gender differences in brain, behavior, and hormones, recently released a book called *The Male Brain: A Breakthrough Understanding of How Men and Boys Think*. Impeccably researched and at the cutting edge of scientific knowledge, it's a book every wife and mom (or anyone who has a man in her life) needs to read. It's an intriguing study that follows the male brain through every phase of life from infancy to adulthood, and it will help you understand the male creatures in your home. Here are three of Dr. Brizendine's revelations:

- The male brain is a lean, mean, problem-solving machine. Faced with a personal problem, a man will use his analytical brain structures to find a solution.
- The male brain thrives under competition, instinctively plays rough, and is obsessed with rank and hierarchy.
- The male brain has an area for sexual pursuit 2.5 times larger than the female brain, consuming him with sexual fantasies about female body parts.[5]

Moms, I know you love that sweetheart boy of yours. But wouldn't you admit that your guy needs to grow up to be tough? To be a "lean, mean, problem-solving machine"? To learn how to effectively deal with his natural desire for position and sexual achievement? Yes, as your son gets weirder than weird in the teenage years, you still want to nurture that tender heart. But someday your son will be a dad and a husband. What do you want him to be like?

Think about it for a minute. If you're married, what attracted you to your husband? His softness of heart toward you, for one. But weren't you also attracted to his manly strength? His competitive spirit to fight for your interest? Most women want a combination of tough and tender. Anything you can do to encourage that wonderful combination in your son's teenage years will benefit not only you, your son, and your family, but the family he'll have someday as well.

Shoulder-to-Shoulder Parenting

About a month ago, I got a phone call from two parents who were in the midst of a "discussion" (a nice way of saying they'd nearly come to blows over this issue and finally had to call in some third-party help—enter, Dr. Leman). Their 19-year-old son had already wrecked two cars (not new but late-model used cars). Of course, it was never his fault—one time he was texting, and the other time he was finger-wrestling his buddy in the passenger seat, and he just didn't see that other car coming. Worse, those two cars had been purchased for him by his parents—or, more specifically, by his mom. The father had been resistant from the get-go, claiming that the son ought to buy his own car.

After this second wreck, Mom was adamant about getting the kid another car.

"What is wrong with you?" Dad asked.

Mom was defensive. "Well, how can he get to work if he doesn't have a car?"

The kid had a basic, barely-over-minimum-wage job. Clearly he didn't have the funds to pay the insurance—he was even stretching it on the gas—yet Mom wanted to provide him with a *third car*, when the son hadn't shown any level of responsibility? I agreed with the dad: "What is wrong with you?"

Clearly Mom was in charge of this family, to the kid's detriment. He was on easy street, thinking, *So, if I wreck a car, Mom will just get me a better one. What's the big deal?* Also, Mom was buying into the mantra, "I have to be my son's *friend*."

And here's what was worse. When I talked with Mom, she was full of venom about Dad. "He doesn't do this; he doesn't do that. . . ."

Yet I know that dad. He is very responsible, he's hard-working, he's well-liked by his peers, and he has integrity. But he's one of those people who thinks you ought to have discipline in your life and work hard for what you purchase.

The mom, on the other hand, is a perfect example of a discouraged, defeated perfectionist. Upon talking with her further, I discovered that she grew up with a critical-eyed father. She could never please him, no matter what she did. She headed into her marriage thinking that she'd never be able to please her husband either. So instead she decided, without realizing it, that she'd just manipulate him and push him around to get what she wanted (becoming, in fact, very much like her father).

And her son? Well, the mom never had a sibling, so she wanted a "buddy." If her son was happy, then her world went around just fine, thank you very much. No wonder that son was one lazy critter who didn't do squat around the house, was completely self-absorbed, and was in line to get a third car only a year old.

Worst of all, guess who was watching this fiasco unfurl? The son's younger brother and sister. Believe me, they've been learning some relational patterns that both parents are going to have to deal with when those two children become teenagers.

The mom's desire to be loved and appreciated was short-circuiting her son's learning about responsibility. A car is the last thing I'd get that kid. A lot of folks who don't have cars get to work. In fact, there are these things that look like big cars and seat over 50 people. You can find out when they're going to arrive, and then they even come on time to take you where you want to go. They're called *buses*. Or what about a used bicycle taken out of his allowance money? Now we're talking!

The son's job would be only a 15-minute bike ride from his house. But then, of course, the kid would actually have to exert some energy to get there. Instead, because of Mom, that kid had it made. He was taking advantage of the war for control going on between Mom and Dad. And everybody in the family was losing in the process.

It Worked for Me

My wife came home last weekend from a retreat where you spoke about how important it is for parents to stand united in front of their kids. Far too often we've let our kids play us against each other, and that's caused a lot of problems in our marriage. That day we made a decision to stand together, no matter what.

It took only an hour for our resolve to be tested. My daughter first tried me, then tried my wife. When we stood firm together on the decision, my daughter tried again to sway one of us. Finally she said loudly in disgust, "What is *wrong* with you two?"

We looked at each other and smiled. "Nothing is wrong," I said. "In fact, everything is all right."

Ray, Arizona

Parents, are you standing united, or are you letting your taller-than-you ankle-biter control your home and divide your marital relationship? This area is critical to your success as parents. That's why I'm going to give you another example of why standing shoulder-to-shoulder is a key to your success in parenting—and to your teenager's success in life.

I received a phone call from a troubled dad last week. He said:

> Dr. Leman, you gotta help me. I'm caught between the devil and the deep blue sea. My wife and daughter go after each other all the time. It's an everyday, constant thing. I'm sick of it, but I don't know what to do.
>
> My wife, Norma, grew up in a home where nobody could be trusted, and she did a lot of things as a teenager that she shouldn't have. So she can't see our daughter Julie as someone to be trusted either. Yesterday we had to shop for a new refrigerator, so I asked Julie to watch the two younger kids for a couple hours. She agreed and was fine with it.
>
> But then Norma found out and blew a gasket. "We can't leave three kids alone. There's going to be pandemonium!"
>
> Julie told her, "Mom, I can take care of the kids. Everything will be fine."
>
> "No," my wife insisted, "it's not okay."
>
> So they had another big blowup, with Julie saying that her mother didn't trust her (well, she's right, Norma doesn't trust her, but she doesn't trust anyone), and Norma yelling, "See, that's why I don't trust you. Your attitude stinks!"
>
> By the time it was over, Julie had gone to her room and slammed her door shut, and Norma slammed our bedroom door. I went in to talk to Norma and told her she was being too tough on Julie. I tried to make the case that Julie has always been responsible. But Norma said, "Don't you dare tell her that she's right!" and glared at me. I knew then our discussion was over.
>
> So I left the two mad women behind and took our younger two out for ice cream to get them out of all the fuss. Doc, I don't want to undercut my wife, but I can't live like this anymore.

Here's what I told him:

You sound like a smart guy, so you already know a lot of what I'm going to tell you. I'd bet you a million bucks that both your wife and daughter are firstborns. Added to that, they're both girls, so they'll always be knocking heads. Both will always want to be right. They're clearly in competition with each other. All your daughter was trying to say was, "Hey, Mom, I got your back," but your wife wasn't willing to accept that. Clearly your wife has some deep problems from her past that mean she isn't able to trust anyone. She needs to get some counseling for those issues before she rips your family life apart.

You don't have a kid problem; you've got a wife problem. She has to lighten up and understand that she has to stop competing with her daughter, or you'll all pay for it in the next couple of years.

And just how do you think a 17-year-old girl could get back at such a controlling mom? You don't have to let your mind wander long to figure that out. Talk about a control-freak mom. She knew exactly how her daughter should live, what sweater she should wear, where she could go and not go. There was no wiggle room for Julie to be an individual. Norma was like a modern-day Don Quixote, charging windmills at every step.

Thankfully, this dad had a great relationship with his daughter. It was also easier for him to relate to his daughter without competition since it was a cross-gender relationship, and he had a middleborn-pleaser personality. But I also encouraged this guy, who just wanted the pathway of life to be smooth, to take the situation to the next step. When his wife was calm, he got her behind closed doors and said, "Honey, you need to work on lightening up." He was honest with her about how her inability to trust their daughter—or anyone in the family—was wreaking havoc on all of them. After giving him the silent treatment for a couple days, Norma finally admitted that he was right and agreed to go see a counselor.

I was glad to hear it, because that situation had "family disaster" written all over it. There's a funny thing about families—they know each other's soft spots well. And in the light of battle, they're very good at locating them. They also know what buttons to push to escalate the battle.

As you're getting ready to launch your teenagers into an unsuspecting world, it's imperative that you stand shoulder-to-shoulder with your spouse—with no daylight between you. In front of your kids, you must stand united. If you do that, the results will be a slam dunk. You can undertake any kind of change and have a new teenager by Friday. In fact, you may not even have to wait until Friday.

> *The adolescent years are topsy-turvy enough without sending kids back and forth between Dad and Mom like a ping-pong ball.*

You may have had two "easy" kids who didn't need a lot of life shaping or attitude shaping from you. But this third one of yours? He's an entirely different matter. Now's not the time to pull back. You need to step up to the plate and be a parent. If one of you wimps out, you'll never accomplish the goal of having a new teenager by Friday.

The adolescent years are topsy-turvy enough without sending kids back and forth between Dad and Mom like a ping-pong ball. So saying, "Go ask your dad" or "Go ask your mom" is a cop-out. Your kids deserve better. Your spouse deserves better.

Kids thrive when they see their parents on the same page—when they know that there are family guidelines, a safe environment, and positive expectations of them. But if you and your spouse are on opposite sides of the page, all you're going to do is confuse your teenager. Frankly, if that's your position, you ought to close this book and go read a book on marriage (I suggest *Have a New Husband by Friday*) before you try to tackle any problems with your kids.

But if you really want to have a new teenager by Friday, then you need to pull together, affirming each other's decisions. You need to say clearly, in all your words and actions toward and about your spouse, "Honey, I've got your back." Where two stand united, teenagers don't have to think, *Hmm, I wonder if the rules are gonna change. Maybe if I ask Mom when Dad's not around . . .*

Don't let any daylight show between your shoulders, Mom and Dad. You're a team, and your teenager needs to know it.

A Little Rah-Rah Never Hurt Anybody

Every person needs a cheerleader in life—someone who believes in him. When your teenager does something well, celebrate it. Be his cheerleader. Believe me, there are enough people ragging on your kid for doing something or not doing something that your realistic encouragement will go a long way. Make sure he knows you're proud of *who he is*, not just what he does.

Words like, "Matt, I can't wait to see what you're going to do in life. Wow, I'm so proud of you. Look at all you've accomplished in your first 15 years of life. But who you are—to me and to your dad—

> *Every person needs a cheerleader in life—someone who believes in him.*

well, I'm amazed. I believe you're going to go far." Those are golden words to any teenager. Speak them to your teenager and he'll likely live up to them.

How you think about your teenager, talk to and about your teenager, and communicate with her will establish your relationship for a lifetime. And what you put into her bags will help to prepare her for the future.

But along the way, don't forget the fun. Do life with your teenager. Buy a bra for your AAA-cup daughter, whether she needs it or not. Make a fun, all-day excursion out of this milestone, and include lunch, ice cream, and plenty of chat and laugh time. To celebrate your 15-year-old son's first guitar lesson, do something crazy like play on the swings in the park. Go to the local A&W like you used to do with your dad (if you can still find one around), and get root beer floats to celebrate the B she got on her science test.

Go backpacking and camping as a family. Remember that night when your tent was nearly swept away in a surprise rainstorm? Or the time when your two teenage boys, attempting to cook a chicken over the fire, launched the bird into the lake, then retrieved the carcass to continue cooking it? Such experiences will be fodder for laugh fests when you gather together and your teenager is a forty-year-old father of two kids himself. Those are the moments. your son will remember and hold closely for a lifetime. The moments that will go in his "mental scrapbook"—whether you take pictures or not.

Make Sunday afternoon your board-game time. Use those hours to enjoy each other and talk about what's really important in life—even things you wish you'd done differently yourself. Or save money for a special trip, and don't let anything stop you. There's nothing like a long drive to get conversations flowing (but leave those iPods at home).

So go somewhere, anywhere, together. And oh, the fun you'll have along the way!

Just before my fourth child, Hannah, got married, she gave me the gift of a lifetime on Father's Day—a letter from a precious daughter to her dad about all the ways I've made a difference in her life. I'm not ashamed to admit I cried. And to this day, that letter is one of my prized possessions.

It's a letter that any parent would be thrilled to get. Sure, it's a pat on the back to me as a dad for what I did right. But that's not what makes me so misty-eyed. That letter shows me that my daughter Hannah, now out of the nest, will be flying high because she's well prepared for life.

To My Dad

Happy Father's Day!

This is always the hardest card to write because I can hardly put into words what you mean to me. I can't believe in just a few days you will be walking me down the aisle. I am so glad that you will be right beside me on the most important day in my life. I want to thank you for preparing me for this moment since I was a little girl. You have taught me how to love and shown me by your actions what a loving marriage looks like. I have never wanted to disappoint or let my dad down. I have always trusted every word of advice because I know that MY father knows best. And because of that I am so thankful that I have saved myself for my husband—and him for me. I know I was able to make that decision because of my relationship with you, and that is a blessing I am beyond thankful for. Thank you for being supportive of Josh and me. I know he is going to love and take care of me as you have for the rest of my life. I love you, and I will always be your little peanut.

Love, Hannah

As I've watched this nest-leaving process with four—soon to be five—of my own teenagers, I've become convinced that the hormone-group years really *are* the best years you'll have with your kids.

Just speak the truth in love and shoot it to your kids straight. Believe in your kids, but hold them accountable. Excuses only make the weak weaker. Don't snowplow their road in life; let reality do the talking.

What to Do on Friday

1. Emphasize wisdom, good judgment, and discernment.

2. Kick off savings accounts or investments with your teenager.

3. Enjoy the ride!

Lather on the encouragement, and when those proud-parent moments come, enjoy every minute!

These are the days you'll talk about and smile about for years down the road.

I guarantee it.

★ THE WINNING PLAY ★

Time flies. Don't waste these moments.

Ask Dr. Leman

A to Z Game Plans That Really Work

The 75 hottest topics parents have asked Dr. Leman about in his seminars across the country—and his time-tested advice that really works. Plus more "It Worked for Me" stories of parents who tried Dr. Leman's tips—and are now smiling all over.

See pages 309–10 for an index of A to Z topics.

Shh! It's a Secret!

A no-nonsense approach to having a great teenager . . .
and being a great parent.
Just look up the topic,
but don't tell your teenager what you're up to.
(Hint: There's a quick index at the back.)

If we had ten minutes together in person where no one else could overhear us, what's the one thing you'd most want to know about parenting a teenager?

Over nearly four decades, it has been my joy to help families succeed. I want to see *your* family succeed too. So in this section, allow me to be your personal psychologist. I'll just perch here on the arm of your chair while you look up the topics you're currently facing for some timely and time-tested advice.

Then think about your own situation. Ask yourself:

1. What is the purposive nature of the behavior?
2. How do I, as the parent, feel in this situation?
3. Is this a mountain or a molehill?

The answers to these questions will help you formulate an action plan for your own family. If the issue is a molehill, a can of Raid might help. If it's a mountain, the ante is upped significantly. You must handle the situation right, because it will affect your family dynamics, your well-being, and your teenager's well-being.

So pick the topic that's hottest in your family right now. The topics are organized A to Z to make them easy to find, or you can check the index at the back of the book. If you want a Parenting 101 crash course, just read straight through the section. I've included 75 of the topics that parents of teenagers ask me about most.

For additional help on specific topics, consult the resources on pages 313–15. You'll also find a lot of practical help at www .drleman.com. Have a specific parenting question I haven't answered? I'd love for you to join me on Facebook (www.facebook .com/DrKevinLeman). I'm always answering questions and having discussions about issues that will affect you and your teenager daily. That's because I care deeply about your ever-changing relationship with your teenager, and I want to see you both thrive.

Above all, remember the secret: do *not* let your teenager in on what you're up to. What you're doing must remain *your* secret. There are no warnings in this system—and no wimps allowed either. Backing down once you launch your action plan will only get you pushed back into the corner you started in.

You *can* be a great parent. And you *can* have a great teenager. So go ahead—plunge right in. The dividends await!

Acne

At first blush—no pun intended—acne doesn't seem like a huge thing to most parents. But for a lot of teenagers, acne is huge. It's weird enough growing up during these years—having your voice change, a gangly body that sometimes isn't as coordinated as you'd like it to be, and having raging hormones that make you feel like you're on a roller coaster. But then, on top of all those stresses, your face breaks out, and the helpful kids at school decide that Pizza Face would be a nice nickname for you.

The emotional scars of kids who grew up with severe acne in particular run deeper than the physical scars that remain from having it. Zits are not an issue for a parent to take lightly.

So let's say that your 12-year-old daughter is spending hours in front of the mirror, bemoaning that fact that she has zits. If you tell her, "Hey, every teenager has zits, so don't worry. I had them when I was a teenager too, and I got over them," that won't help. A teenager lives in the moment, and that moment *right now* is what's important to her and to her psychological well-being.

Parent, this is a time when you need to step up to the plate as a problem solver before your child starts saying she doesn't want to go to school because she has a big zit on her chin and everybody will see it.

Yes, acne will always be around in the teenage world. But the good news is that all kinds of great strides have been made in the area of dermatology—everything from specific medicines to topical washes, astringents, etc. So say to your kid, "Hey, I know you're concerned about your zits. So let's deal with this as best as we can. Come on, we'll take a little trip to Walgreens. I'm sure the skin consultant there can help us."

Let me tell you, a 12-year-old kid doesn't know a skin consultant from jack-diddly, but it sure sounds important, doesn't it? Follow it up with, "And I'm sure the consultant knows something that will help your acne tonight." Kids have short attention spans, so you'd be street-smart to play into that.

Then off you go. Locate that skin consultant or pharmacist and let *her* give your teenager instructions about how to wash her face—gently and with a certain type of cloth—how to use the astringents, etc. Let your kid decide on several things to bring home and try.

If those strategies don't work, take her to the dermatologist. To the peer group, a simple pimple *is* Mount Vesuvius. It's huge. And that's a lot for teenagers to handle emotionally, especially with all the other changes going on in their bodies and lives.

For parents who crave those psychological brownie points of being their child's friend, this is a practical way you can be a friend. Your actions will be interpreted by your teenager as, *Hey, my mom understands what I'm up against.* A kid who believes that won't isolate himself from someone trying to help. He won't head for his room after school, slam the door, and tune that parent out.

Most parents are only vaguely in touch with who their teenagers are and what the hormone-group life is all about. Kids who perceive value in their parents—as empathizers, problem solvers—are much more likely to keep the chain of communication open during these critical years.

So set aside a little time to get your kid some help for her zits. You'll be glad you did.

LIFESAVER

Partner with your kid.

Anger

I recently got a letter from a father who was at the end of his rope and out of ideas:

> My son has always been a tantrum thrower, but it's gotten worse. He's now 15, and last week he punched a hole in the wall of our kitchen when I wouldn't let him go out with his friends. My wife cries and retreats when Michael gets angry. I give him a piece of my mind right back. Michael's behavior is tearing apart our family. We need some advice, and we need it fast.
>
> Jason, New Jersey

Jason isn't the only one. As I talk with parents face-to-face across the country, anger pops up everywhere as a subject of concern among parents of teenagers. Anger is a very natural emotion, and all of us have experienced it. There are times when it is *good* to be angry—when injustice has been served.

But anger can also be used in a manipulative, powerful way by teenagers who have learned in their earlier growing-up years that it produces what they want from adults: results. Want that new iPod? Just start yelling about how your little brother gets everything and stomp off angrily to your room, and if Mama feels guilty enough, she might just order you a new iPod online that evening.

It goes back to the purposive behavior we talked about earlier in the book. *Anger produces results,* your teenager thinks, *so why not up the ante a little and get bigger and better results more quickly?* That's how anger escalates in a home.

But here's something to remember: anger is produced, manufactured, and distributed by the person who is angry. People often say, "Boy, he really made me angry!" In reality, you *choose* to be angry (or not) over something someone else says or does.

That's why teaching a child, even one at a young age, to handle anger in an appropriate way is so important. A powerful little ankle-biter who throws temper tantrums at ages 2 and 3 and gets away with it will become a powerful little buzzard at age 8 . . . and then an even more powerful and angry teenager at age 13. Being angry and manipulative might pay off nicely if your son or daughter ends up in a courtroom as an attorney, but for the most part it will spell all kinds of trouble in your home, at school, and in every environment where your kid is.

> Anger produces results, *your teenager thinks,* so why not up the ante a little and get bigger and better results more quickly?

When he gets angry, keep your sails out of his wind. If you do battle with your teenager, you will lose every time. He has nothing to lose. Nothing. When he starts spouting off at you in the mall or any other public place, people in the mall will be looking at him, thinking, *Wow, what a piece of work he is.* But guess what else they'll be thinking? *What kind of parent is THAT to produce a kid like that?* So who will be more embarrassed and most likely to give in to your angry teenager's demands? You!

But don't fall for it. All of us get angry; it's a natural part of growing up. Even Jesus got angry. But the things we say and do in anger need to be dealt with. Once angry words come out of your mouth, they can't be taken back. (And I'm talking both sides of the fence here, parents: what your teenager says to you, and what you say to your teenager.)

> *If you do battle with your teenager, you will lose every time.*

So how can you take the sizzle out of your teenager's anger? And yours too?

Remember when you were a kid and you blew up balloons for fun? One of your favorite things to do was to annoy your sister by that terrible screeching a balloon makes when you let air out a little at a time. For a person who has anger issues, talking about what's bothering him is like letting the air out of a balloon a bit at a time.

If you let small issues build up, you continue to blow air into that balloon until it gets bigger and bigger and harder and harder. Eventually, it gets so hard and tight that it explodes. But what if, instead, you let some air out of that balloon by talking with your teenager about what's bothering him? A limp balloon is more flexible; it won't pop.

Give your teenager the opportunity to talk about what angers him. Keep your mouth shut and just listen without judging or talking over your child. Remember that your son's perspective won't necessarily reflect reality ("you *always* do this," and "you *never* let me do that"). But his words do reflect his own reality—how he is thinking and feeling at the moment.

The next time your son blows a fuse, get him to a place where you can talk just with him without interruption. "Honey, I'm very unhappy about what happened in the kitchen with your sister and your dad. Your reaction and the words you chose to use were totally inappropriate, but I want to know from you what triggered that response. What made you feel like you had to say what you did? To act like you did?"

Then give your teenager the opportunity to talk through his feelings. Keep in mind that feelings aren't right or wrong; they're just feelings. But most parents think they have to counter with, "Well, you shouldn't feel that way!" Instead, take your son's feelings at face value.

"I'm sick to death of how you all treat me," your son spouts. "I hate taking out the garbage and always doing . . ."

Hear your teenager out before you open your mouth. Really listen to not only what he's saying but his feelings behind the words.

Then surprise your son. "I'm open to rearranging the chore chart. After all, you're 15. It's time for some changes. Why don't you draw up a new chart for our family this week and bring it to the dinner table on Friday? We'll all look at it together. Come to think of it, your little brother would make a great garbage man."

There's a great term in the business world: *empowerment.* All good leaders want to *empower* those under their leadership to do their jobs well, to feel a part of the group, to know that their contributions are listened to and appreciated. Talk to any first-grade teacher and ask the teacher how important it is to a first-grader to be a line leader or door monitor—the kid who gets to choose who lines up first. Kids love that kind of empowerment. And so does your teenager. You need to empower him so he doesn't feel powerless.

If you've ever been on the phone, going through menu after menu with automated computer voices responding, you know how frustrating it is not to have the opportunity to say what you really want to say.

Keep that in mind with your own teenager. Not allowing your kid an opportunity to say what's on his mind will lead to that popped-balloon syndrome or the frustration of never being heard.

Anger is the match to gasoline; it leads to explosive situations. If you don't deal with it in your home, you'll have bigger problems, such as the father who was dragged into court when his son punched a teacher at school. Or the mother who received a call that her daughter had killed somebody with her car because of road rage.

These are the critical years, and getting a grip on anger is extremely crucial for your teenager. It's why I've spent so much time on it in this section. It affects everything your teenager will do both now and in the future.

> *Anger is the match to gasoline.*

Take a look back at the anger situation in your home. At what point did it begin to escalate to where it is today? People who are now over the top with anger were able to get away with it before.

The time to stop the anger is now.

LIFESAVER

A soft response turns away anger.

Anorexia

Anorexia nervosa is a debilitating disorder. Those who are afflicted with it refuse to maintain a healthy body weight because they are obsessively fearful of gaining weight. A 98-pound girl can look in the mirror and see a 160-pound image. It is a serious mental illness and affects people of all ages, races, and socioeconomic and cultural backgrounds. Singing legend Karen Carpenter, for instance, died of anorexia.

But the disease really has nothing to do with food. That's a huge surprise for most people, since it seems that the whole life of an anorexic person centers around food. Instead, it has everything to do with a myopic view of life and a distorted self-image.

Please note that anorexia doesn't start in adults. It begins in the teenage years with the weight of expectations. One mom told me this story:

My daughter, Andrea, was a little chubby as a kid and got teased about it at school. Now she's 13, and over the past month she's eaten less and less at dinner. One night she just ate green beans and said she wasn't hungry and left the table. Then a friend of hers told me that she was really worried; Andrea never ate her lunch at school. She always threw it out.

How could I be so clueless? I just thought she was going through a not-so-hungry phase. But now she's losing weight—too much weight. And I don't know how to address the problem. When I try to talk to her, she says, "I'm fine, Mom. It's no big deal."

In all my years of professional counseling, I've never counseled an anorexic boy, and I've heard of only one other practitioner who ever dealt with one. The disease obviously is particular to young women. But how does it start?

The other day, as I was talking with my little granddaughter over dinner, I was shocked to find out that Adeline gets her hair cut at Great Waves—the same place my wife, Sande, does. (I'm still back in the $15 fix-me-up haircut scenario.)

"Well, Grampy can cut your hair," I told her. "You don't have to go to Great Waves."

Five-year-old Adeline eyed me like an NFL defensive end coming after the quarterback. "But, Grampy," she announced, "at Great Waves they shampoo and blow-dry my hair."

I gave up.

Great Waves it was.

Think for a moment about how society reinforces the perspective of "your looks are all-important" from when girls are a very young age. They are surrounded by the "thin is beautiful" mantra in living color. Every female is faced with ultra-high expectations for what she should look

From the perfect Barbie doll your daughter receives as a child to the models she sees in magazines, on TV, or in movies, there's one common theme—perfectionism.

like—her hair, her body, her makeup, her clothes. To be sexy and interesting to the male population, the misnomer goes, you have to be thin. From the perfect Barbie doll your daughter receives as a child to the models she sees in magazines, on TV, or in movies, there's one common theme—perfectionism. And perfectionism is slow suicide. Your daughter can never compete with those retouched images, nor should she ever try.

Yet so many girls are caught in just that trap. Girls like Andrea.

If you suspect that your daughter is anorexic, get her immediately first to your medical doctor and then to a specialist who deals with anorexia. This is a life-threatening disorder—one that is produced by the expectations and demands of our society and the resulting false views that girls develop of themselves. Anorexia demands your *immediate* attention.

If you think you can deal with this one yourself as your child's parent, you're wrong. I've seen parents try, only to have their beloved daughters sink further into the clutches of the disease until they were at death's door. (And keep in mind that I'm the guy who tells people the last place you want to end up is your local shrink's office.). In the case of anorexia, you need a professional's assistance to help your daughter recover.

LIFESAVER

*Some things demand immediate attention,
and this is one of them.*

Arguing

If you look on the bright side, arguing is great exercise for one's lungs!

On the downside, it can be annoying and wear you down as a parent. When people argue, they talk in "you always" or "you never" extremes that set up the competitive back-and-forth.

That's right. I used the words *set up*, and that's exactly what I mean. Most arguments with teenagers are setups. Your darling, simply stated, is manipulating you, and she's good at it.

What is your teenager really saying when she argues? "Hey, I don't like what happened, and I wanna fight because I feel like it."

But arguing is voluntary. It also can't be done with only one person in the room; it takes two to argue. So if you take your sails out of your daughter's wind—exiting gracefully to another room or keeping your mouth shut—the argument won't continue. That is, unless you as the parent fan the flames!

As 11-year-old Darlene told a friend, "I don't argue with my mom. It doesn't work."

Ah, now you've got it.

When kids start their arguing, you have a choice to make: will you be combative in return, or will you defuse the situation?

What if, instead of saying, "I'm sick of your arguing. Stop it right now, young lady!" you said, "Wow, that's an interesting perspective. Tell me more about that." Then check out your daughter's deer-in-the-headlights look, because that's exactly what you'll see. You've stopped her in her tracks; you've halted the argument. It's back to the purposive behavior again. If her behavior doesn't work for the results she wants—a knock-down, drag-out fight to take the edge off her bad day at school—then she won't continue using it.

> *Most arguments with teenagers are setups.*

With younger teenagers, you have more time for training. They'll soon learn, like Darlene, that arguing doesn't work, and you'll have fairly cooperative kids. But for kids who have an attitude, saying a simple, "Hmm, you could be right. Why didn't I think of that?" followed with the invitation, "Tell me more about that" will do wonders for your relationship.

If your son or daughter is angry and venting, you could say, "I bet there's a ton of reasons you're upset about that." Then sit back and listen. Let your kid vent a bit, as long as he or she isn't personally attacking you, but keep it on the subject at hand.

The other way to nip arguing in the bud is to remain silent and wait, and sooner or later your son or daughter will come around and ask what's going on.

"I'll tell you what's going on," you say. "Mom's unhappy." And then walk out of the room.

Chances are that kid will follow you and, looking confused, will ask, "Why?"

At that point you'll have the opportunity for a teachable moment. "Because I don't appreciate the way you spoke to me earlier. It was disrespectful and rude."

But here's the tough part, Mom. When your daughter turns those baby blues on you and says, "I'm sorry, Mom," accept that apology. But *never, under any circumstance*, back down.

When your teenager says, "So I can go to the movie now, right?" you respond, "We're going to take a pass on that tonight." In other words, don't let your kid think that a simple "I'm sorry, Mom" fixes everything and life can go back to normal. There still must be consequences for her action, and that means no movie tonight with her friends. If you stick to your guns now, she won't be as likely to try the same tactics again, because they didn't work.

So let your no be no and your yes be yes. If you waffle, you're only asking for argument because your daughter knows if she argues long enough, you'll change your mind.

Arguments stop when you don't argue back.

LIFESAVER

It takes two to tango.

Attitude

As you've read in the preceding pages, attitude is huge. And no, I'm not talking about your son's or daughter's attitude, I'm talking about yours. A good attitude will be your best ally when it comes to getting through these hormone-laden years with humor and balance.

Your teenager's attitude could be the worst in the world right now. It'll change from day to day, and even moment by moment. But you're the adult here. When you choose not to argue or engage in battle with your kid who is sporting a 'tude, your relationship will improve quickly—and the searing temperature in your home will lessen almost immediately.

Usually just saying the word *attitude* conveys negativity. But let me point out that there's also a positive to the word. When you see your teenager doing something positive, pounce on it. Say to him or her, "I'm so impressed. You showed great maturity and judgment when you did that, and I couldn't be more proud to be your mom." You give him the gift of your good attitude for a lifetime. For those of you still searching for a way to increase your child's self-esteem, you can edge your kid in the direction of positive, healthy self-worth by noticing and commenting on the things he does well in life.

Keep in mind that your 17-year-old can do anything he wants to do, but it is only out of respect for you—and your positive, uplifting, I-believe-in-you attitude—that he doesn't.

Your encouragement makes all the difference. So pass on your good attitude and your belief in your children. Slip 'em the commercial that says, "Hey, you done good. I'm really proud of you." Then sit back and watch their—and your—attitude improve by the day.

LIFESAVER

Slip 'em the commercial.

It Worked for Me

I grew up in a home where nobody thanked anybody for anything. We were always told when we did something wrong but never were praised for what we did right. It never hit me that I was doing the same thing with my four kids until I heard you talk about it on *Fox & Friends*. I now make it a point to slip each of my kids a commercial every day. I didn't know how much it meant to them until Kasey, my 14-year-old, came into the living room about 11 p.m. one night and said, "Uh, Dad, you didn't tell me what I did good today." I was stunned. And even more stunned when she showed me her journal, where she'd recorded every good thing I'd said over the past month since I started doing it. Slipping my kids a commercial is one habit I never want to break.

John, Texas

Authority Figures

If you've done things right as a parent up to when your kid hits the hormone years, responding respectfully to authority figures shouldn't be a problem for him or her. But for a teenager who hasn't been taught to respect authority (i.e., the demanding ankle-biter who got his or her way growing up—and there are a ton of kids like that out there), life can hit that kid in the face. When she ignores a police officer who has pulled her over for a traffic stop, she's in big trouble. When he disses a teacher, a basketball coach, or his girlfriend's father, he's going to pay for it big-time.

If you have a teenager who has a hard time with authority figures, tell him, "I know you don't like being told what to do. But people in authority make a living telling you what to do and how to do it. Now, I'm not you, and based on my experience in life, you don't have to like being told what to do. But you do have to live with it and show at least the minimal respect that should be given to a person in authority."

The kids who really get in trouble with authority figures are those who have strong-willed temperaments. The boy who, at 15, throws a tennis racket across the court when he doesn't score a point is the same powerful buzzard who, at 4, whined, complained, and threw a temper tantrum until his parents gave in to keep their sanity and some peace in the household. But what did the parents create? A monster who is now rebelling against all authority—including theirs.

> *The military doesn't take any guff, so why should you?*

If your 11- or 12-year-old is showing signs of being powerful and not mindful of authority, it's time to shape that behavior, and the sooner the better. If you have a 17-year-old who has no respect for authority, is already in trouble, and shows signs that he'll be in more trouble ahead, the consequences that come as a result of his rebellion will probably be a far better teacher in life than anything you could say or do at this point. If your son gets speeding tickets, he's going to pay some stiff fines and do some court time. Depending on how many tickets he gets, his license may be revoked. If your daughter isn't paying attention and gets in an accident, which doubles your insurance, a natural consequence would be, "Well, I guess you're going to have to hoof it; you no longer have access to a car."

Some kids learn the hard way late in life.

Interestingly, some of those strong-willed kids have sat in my office, telling me they're going to enlist in the military.

I want to choke with laughter. Do they really know what happens in the military?

But then I sober when I hear them say, "Well, if I go in the military, they'll help me shape up because they won't take any guff."

Ah, they've hit the nail on the head.

The military doesn't take any guff, so why should you?

All kids learn. Some learn the hard way.

Bad-Mouthing Others

As I was growing up, my parents taught me some life basics. One was, "Find at least one quality to like in someone, even if you don't like that person." As old as that advice is, it still holds true for the twenty-first century. When you bad-mouth someone—put that person down—you're looking down on someone that God Almighty himself created. That fact alone should garner a certain respect. Otherwise, by putting down others, you're saying, in essence, "Hey, God, you made some really bad creations here."

The reality is, no one of us is better than another. We sometimes delude ourselves into thinking that because we're of a certain ethnic group or faith, or we live in a specific country that's wealthy. But God Almighty sees us all as the same . . . imperfect people in much need of—guess what? Grace.

When your son bad-mouths somebody, what is he really doing? Trying, in an immature way, to feel better about himself. Putting someone else down means climbing a rung on the ladder of success.

If your daughter is facing bad-mouthing and gossip at school, explaining why others do that can take a bit of the edge off. "People bad-mouth others only when they don't feel very good about themselves. That person must not be very confident if they have to pick on you."

If your teenager is the one doing the bad-mouthing, set the record straight. "I heard from so-and-so's mother that you bad-mouthed her again today. Do you really feel so bad about yourself that you have to do that to somebody else to feel better?" Then shut your mouth and walk away. Let your few words do the talking . . . and let the well-deserved embarrassment and guilt trip begin.

> *People bad-mouth others only when they don't feel very good about themselves.*

Can you really stop bad-mouthing among teenagers? Probably not. But you can sure stop them from doing it within the confines of your home, which needs to be a stress-free zone.

Let's say your 13-year-old and 14-year-old get into a shouting match on a Tuesday morning. Now would be a good time to take them both by the arm, escort them to a different room in the house (the least comfortable one and small enough that they have to be eye to eye), and say, "You two need to solve this. I'll be back to check on you in 20 minutes." Then close the door, walk away, and go enjoy your breakfast in peace.

Even better, if you're blessed to live in a warm climate, like I am in Tucson, Arizona, escort your children out the door to discuss their fracas outside your home.

By the way, those two darlings of yours will try to be out of the room in two minutes, telling you everything is cool.

Tell them firmly, "No, I want you to think this through. I'm sick of the bad-mouthing going on between you two, and I want you to solve it. So get back in there, and I'll be back in 18 minutes."

If the 20-minute delay causes them to be late for school, all the better. Because now you have an opportunity to write a note to the school office that says:

My kids don't have a reason to be late. They chose to bad-mouth each other at the breakfast table. Feel free to do whatever you think should be done on your end. But from my end as their parent, I feel they have absolutely no reason to be late.

Thanks,

Mr./Mrs. Smith

Is it a pain in the keister to have to drive your teenagers to school because they missed the bus? Yeah, it is. But I have news for you. Just having kids is a major inconvenience and a disruption, and you chose to be a parent. This is part and parcel of your responsibility.

The point is to keep the ball in the right court. If your teenager is bad-mouthing, the ball belongs in their court. Don't own what isn't yours, and don't get in the middle.

If nothing else, they'll learn not to bad-mouth each other in the house in front of you.

And they most certainly won't do it at breakfast on school days. Touché!

LIFESAVER

Don't own what isn't yours.

Body Language

Body language conveys thousands of words. Everything from "You've got to be the dumbest parent on the entire planet" (the massive eye-roll and humph) to "I'm so bummed because my best friend blew me off today and won't hang with me anymore" (the slumped, dejected, staring-at-nothing-out-the-car-window look) to "I'm totally overwhelmed and want to fight" (the narrowed eyes, the crossed arms, the defiant pose), and so much more. Even "the grunt" comes across loud and clear, doesn't it?

When you get that grunt, here's the first thing I'd say: grunt back. Oftentimes it'll break the ice and get you both laughing (or you'll at least earn a lovely eye-roll). You need to be a street-smart parent who recognizes the changes in body language.

Now, before you start laughing, let me tell you I know what you're thinking. *Hey, Leman, the changes in body language around our house happen not only daily but hourly. How on earth am I supposed to keep track of all that?*

Change is part of the nature of the beast with the hormone group. But it's one of those important clues, parents, that you have to tune in to if you want to be street-smart.

When you see body language that portrays, "I feel really beaten down, burned out, or bummed out," an appropriate thing to say might be, "Honey, you seem really down today. Anything you want to share?"

> *Body language conveys thousands of words.*

If your teenager shakes her head no or shrugs and walks away, let her go. Don't come at her like a bloodhound, intent to sniff out the prey. Most parents try to pry things out of their kid. But you would do far better to keep your ears open and listen when she's ready to talk. Then you'll usually get an earful regarding what's going on in your teenager's life.

But let's say your kid is still mum the next day, and you see the same demeanor. Then say gently, "I took you at your word yesterday, but you still look bothered (or upset, or worried). I'd consider it a real privilege if you'd share what's troubling you."

Such observations show that you do notice and that you're paying attention to how she feels. A lot of teenagers these days don't feel like their parents pay any attention to them; they're left to fend for themselves. And those who don't have parental support have a tough go of it during these critical years. If you invite instead of push, your teenager will feel comfortable sharing . . . when she's ready.

When she does share her problem—about school, a health issue, a boy/girl relationship, a friend skirmish, or an issue with a teacher—don't leap to conclusions. Don't judge. This is your time to keep your mouth shut and listen. Sometimes just listening will help her solve her own problem.

Your teenager cares what you think more than anyone else in the world. That's why you taking time to listen and care about things in her world means more than you'd ever imagine.

Observe, then invite—don't demand.

Bossy

Kids are bossy. They love to tell each other what to do—siblings most of all.

Holly, our oldest, was always telling her 18-month-younger sister, Krissy, what to do. Lots of times I had to remind Holly to row her own canoe. "You're not in charge of your younger sister," I'd tell Holly. "That's our job as her parents."

Holly would infuriate Krissy when they played Marco Polo—you know, the swimming pool game where somebody says "Marco" and somebody else says "Polo," and you have to keep your eyes closed and find each other. The rules say you have to be in the pool. Well, Holly would stand outside the pool with one toe in it. Krissy, playing by the rules, would be swimming around and around, trying to find her. Finally she'd open her eyes and see her sister's smirk. When Krissy found out she was being duped, she'd get out of the pool, cross her arms, and say quietly and defiantly, "I'm not playing anymore."

Then Holly would call her "Quitsy" and would infuriate her more. There are times when I, as a parent, just had to say, "You two deserve each other."

144

Being 18 months apart and the same gender, they were staunch competitors, and both had their share of bossiness in their vocabulary (especially Holly).

When Holly was 14 and Krissy 12, I listened to them boss each other around for a while about who wore whose sweater and brought it home dirty and what they should have done differently. As the bossiness escalated, I pulled out an edict like Julius Caesar: "Thou shalt no longer wear each other's clothes." I did it for my own protection, not theirs. The bossiness and the bickering came to an abrupt halt. The silence was music to my ears.

Two girls who are close in age will boss each other around and do battle more; ditto with two boys who are close in age. If you have two teenagers of different genders, you'll likely hear less bossiness, though no home is immune.

If your kids are bossing each other around, ask them to do one thing: take it out of your hearing. It's amazing what those little words will accomplish. After all, the purposive nature of bossiness is to get your attention as a parent. When it doesn't work, the behavior stops . . . or at least it goes around the corner and you can read your emails in peace.

LIFESAVER

Row your own canoe.

Boyfriends/Girlfriends

Yes, your teenager should have friends, and the most important relationships in his or her life are those of the same sex, not the opposite sex. Watch groups of young men and young women 11 to 13 years old at a basketball event, and you'll quickly see the communication differences that exist between males and females.

The girls move quickly like a covey of quail, cooing simultaneously and many times holding hands. Girls talk about their BFFs ("best friends forever"). The boys? They're most likely to walk slowly, as cool as one could possibly look, and often in single file—either right ahead of, or right behind, their buddy. And they wouldn't be caught dead in a BFF hug or holding hands with their "best buddy." A high five or a wrestling session is more like it.

> *It's a proven fact that too much time spent together can make the glamour of an uneven match wear off.*

If you end up driving those kids to sporting events or social events, it's tempting to turn the radio or CD player on to block out the nonstop chatter. Instead, be street-smart: sit back, be quiet, listen . . . and learn. You'll hear some things that might shock you but will also give you insight into the kids you're driving around—the ones your son or daughter is hanging out with.

Some of them you'll like. Those are the kids who are most likely to have families with values similar to yours, who share your son's or daughter's interests, and who actually grew up with at least a minimum of manners (translate: they know how to say "thank you" when you drop them off at their house).

Some of them you won't like—and with good reason. But before you start pontificating your opinion, let me give you a secret tip. Suggest to your teenager, "Why don't you invite so-and-so to go with us [to the mall, the movies, dinner, etc.]?" In fact, make the suggestion a lot for a few weeks. Let the two spend as much time as possible together.

"Dr. Leman," you're saying, "are you crazy? I hate that kid. He's rebellious, he's disrespectful, he's thoughtless, and he has a crass mouth. I don't want him around my kid."

It's a proven fact that too much time spent together can make the glamour of an uneven match wear off. As Ben Franklin says, "Fish and company smell in three days." Enough said.

After a while, your kid will come to his own decision about that friend. The next time you mention, "Oh, do you want to give so-and-so a call and ask him to come with us?" you'll likely get a shrug and the response, "No, not this time, Mom." That's your first clue the relationship has started heading south.

When you hear those words, you can smile to yourself for a job well done behind the scenes. The best thing is that you didn't even have to make any pronouncements such as, "You will not see that guy! He's not good for you." You didn't have to glare at the other kid or make him feel unwanted (which would have been nasty on your part). You didn't have to say a word. After all, you're a street-smart parent, so you already knew that whatever you said would make your teenager determined to prove you wrong, and that would have put him solidly in his friend's court.

Furthermore, as a street-smart parent, you'd be wise to make your home the centerpiece of your teenager's life. Invite his friends over. Yes, that might mean springing for a lot of pizza. You better join Costco right now to get the bulk deals. And it might cost you a stain or two on your prize rug (better yet, why not simply move the rug to the guest room for a few years) and bucket-loads of brownies. But it's worth having those friends around because you can see firsthand who your kid is hanging out with, what he's talking about, and how the friends treat each other.

It's interesting—back in my growing-up days, we teenagers hung out with kids from around the neighborhood. Usually families didn't have a second car, so it wasn't often we got to hang out anywhere we couldn't walk to. That meant my parents knew my buddies' parents, because everyone lived in close proximity.

Times have changed today. Your teenager isn't hanging out just with the teenagers in her neighborhood—schools gather in kids from a much wider range. The smart parents get to know the parents of the kids their teenager is hanging out with.

Okay, I see that eye-roll. "Dr. Leman," you're saying, "I have enough trouble working 40-plus hours a week, trying to pay the bills, keeping my spouse happy, and getting the mountains of laundry done, and now you want me to do what? There isn't enough time in the week!"

Everybody has the same 24 hours in a day. What's important to you? Is knowing the other kids and their families, who are influencing your teenager, important or not? Make a simple call. It'll only take five minutes, and it'll win you massive dividends down the road. "Hi, I'm Jennifer. I've never had the pleasure of meeting you, but our two kids sure enjoy spending time together. I'd love it if you'd be open to meeting me at a Starbucks for a few minutes sometime to chat. . . . Over lunch on Thursday? Hey, that would be great."

> *The smart parents get to know the parents of the kids their teenager is hanging out with.*

That simple call and a half hour at Starbucks over your lunch hour can accomplish far more than you think. It opens a line of communication with your teenager's friends' parents. If the parents don't know each other, one teenager can get away with saying, "Hey, I'm over at the Wilsons'," and the other teenager can say, "Hey, I'm over at the Olsons'," and both sets of parents might fall for it. But a simple phone call to the parent you've met at Starbucks even one time will set the record straight about exactly where the kids are . . . or aren't. And they might not be anywhere you think.

As your teenager fine-tunes her interests, she'll start hanging out more and more with other kids who share those interests. For example, Kayla, who plays the violin, enjoys classical music, rides horses, likes wearing jeans, and writes her own fantasy stories isn't likely to hang out with the Hannah Montana wannabes who belt out the latest rock tune and dress in leopard-print everything.

The important thing is for you to enter your teenager's world. Note I said *enter*, not *intrude*. If your child likes to ride horses, don't just drop her off. Hang out at the horse barn and get to know the other parents. If your teenager likes concerts and you're the driver for the event, ask one of the parents of your teenager's friends to go along and sit in another section with you. Yes, you can endure a two-hour dose of Justin Bieber or Usher. (Nobody will see those earplugs you inserted before the concert anyway.) After all, your parents most likely endured a little of your music. And what you gain is a deeper relationship with another parent, as well as a window into your teenager's music and world.

> *There's nothing greater for your teenager than to see that their friends like you.*

You see, life with your kids is all about relationships. Give yourself a chance to get to know their friends—and their friends' families.

I have to chuckle. One solid-as-a-rock given in the Leman household is that anyone who enters through our door gets a gift before he or she leaves. Mrs. Uppington, my lovely wife, is the greatest gift giver of all time. Each Christmas, every single one of the kids who hang out at our house gets a little something from us Lemans in a beautifully wrapped package. I want to go on record as saying I have absolutely nothing to do with that (I just carry the shopping bags and hope my wife will be done soon so I can go home and catch the next ball game or TV Land rerun), but I'm glad my wife does. Our five children always had their friends over, and the kids who came over came back . . . again and again. They were truly the gift that kept giving.

But why did those kids come back? Because they liked us! The ultimate compliment was when one boy who was known for his few words said, "You're all right, Dr. Leman."

There's nothing greater for your teenager than to see that their friends like you. In your teenager's peer group, that makes you cooler than cool.

More importantly, it moves the peer group to your house, where you can (quietly) keep an eagle eye on everything that's going on.

You can't put a price tag on that . . . ever.

It's all about the relationship.

It Worked for Me

Maybe it's common sense, but I loved your idea of getting to know the parents of my daughter's friends. Since all four of us are working moms, we finally managed, after nearly a month of emailing each other, to set aside time when all of our girls were at the same school event. Then we four headed for coffee and salads at a restaurant.

Three hours later, we were still talking, and we were almost late picking the girls up from school. We moms really hit it off; we could understand why our kids had so much in common. Even better, now we moms often get together when our girls do, and we really enjoy it. It sure isn't the outcome I expected. But now I have three great new friends . . . who have three fabulous daughters. My daughter sure knows how to pick 'em.

Melanie, Ohio

Bulimia

You don't have to be a genius to figure out the signs of bulimia. Seeing boxes of laxatives in your teenager's room or in the bathroom is one clue. Hearing your child throwing up (and I'm not talking the occasional flu here) when she's fighting weight is another good indication of a teenager struggling with the illness.

What is bulimia?

> Bulimia is an eating disorder. Someone with bulimia might binge on food and then vomit (also called purge) in a cycle of binging and purging. Binge eating refers to quickly eating large amounts of food over short periods of time. Purging involves forced vomiting, laxative use, excessive exercise, or fasting in an attempt to lose weight that might be gained from eating food or binging.[1]

Just like anorexia nervosa, bulimia isn't something you see 40-year-olds struggling with, unless they started with the illness when they were teenagers. Again, this disorder is associated with young adolescent females. I believe that bulimia, just like anorexia nervosa, is socially induced by the search for perfectionism, due to all the images young women are bombarded with. A person with bulimia often feels a loss of control over their eating, as well as guilt over their behavior (which they usually realize is abnormal). What makes a bulimic different from an anorexic, though, is that someone with bulimia is often of normal or near-normal weight. By eating 12 donuts in a sitting and then purging the contents of her stomach through vomiting or laxatives, she gets the high of binging but maintains control of her weight at the same time. That's why a bulimic isn't always noticed as quickly as an anorexic. But the street-smart parent spots the signs of huge quantities of food secretly disappearing (especially junk food—I've never heard of a bulimic overeating lettuce) and goes straight to the source.

Bulimia isn't something you see 40-year-olds struggling with.

If you see signs that your teenager might be bulimic, a direct approach is best. "Honey, I saw a dozen Dunkin' Donuts in your room, and later I found the box in the garbage. I suspect that you ate all of those donuts and that you're struggling with bulimia. Could that possibly be true?"

Bulimia has great psychological, emotional, and social consequences for your teenager. When she gorges herself, she feels bad about her lack of control but can't seem to help herself. Then she feels guilty, and that guilt runs her life, which is never good. Someone with bulimia exhibits self-defeating behaviors, and this affects everything she is and does.

Parent, you need to step in. No, your child may not be wasting away literally like someone with anorexia, but bulimia is just as serious. Get professional help now. If you don't know where to start, talk to your physician. Your daughter needs you to stand firm—for her sake both now and down the road.

LIFESAVER

A direct approach is always best.

Car Key Wars

Keys come in four distinctive types: hearts, spades, clubs, and diamonds. What am I talking about? The car keys are like four aces. They are the conduit for freedom in a teenager's mind.

But with freedom also comes *responsibility*. For years, I've said that when it comes to discipling teenagers, hit 'em with the car. And not at 50 miles per hour, please. Driving a car, for most kids, is a big deal. There will be times when, because you haven't been listened to or respected, you'll have to take the teenage bull by the horns and show by your actions that driving the family car isn't a given. It's a privilege granted to those who listen, obey, and are trustworthy, helpful, kind, and considerate.

Most kids today feel a sense of license ("you owe me") when they get their license and have access to a car. They simply can't imagine that they could get a "no" from you regarding driving the family car.

But, parent, this is the balance beam you have to walk with your teenager every day. You are the parent, not their buddy. You have to know—and be able to say it and stick firm on it—when enough is enough and your teenager has crossed the line.

> *The car keys are like four aces. They are the conduit for freedom in a teenager's mind.*

No teenager will walk a perfectly straight line. (Neither will you.) There will be many days where they fall off the plank, and you'll need to watch them fall off and then help pick them up.

But when certain things that you expect of them as members of your family don't happen, don't be afraid to hit 'em where it hurts. For 99 percent of teenagers over the age of 16, that's their driving privileges.

Think about it this way. If your teenager can't be responsible to carry out her duties as a member of the family, then why on earth would you want to put her behind the wheel of a car, where the stakes are so much higher—both for herself and for others?

Shutting down your teenager's driving privileges—for three days, a week, whatever—allows her time to realize, *Mom and Dad mean business. They're in authority over me (as much as I don't like to admit that), and they hold all the aces. I just don't like it when they play them. Guess I'd better shape up, or I won't be driving until I'm in college.*

Some teenagers will dare you to stand up and be the parent you need to be. Some of you are already at that point. Your teenager has taken the car without your permission. What do you do? You report your car missing to the police. And you tell them that you believe your son has taken it without your permission.

Then you let the police handle it; that will certainly get your teenager's attention. And, by the way, if he has taken off with the car without your permission, he's demonstrating that you, parent, should take more prudent care of those car keys and put them in a place where he can't have access to them. That's being a street-smart parent.

The relationship between you and your teenager is worth only the amount of mutual respect you show each other.

Take the bull by the horns.

It Worked for Me

What you said about the "you owe me" generation hit home. And I was growing a good crop right in my own living room. I decided things had to change. When our oldest demanded the car keys, I said no. She pushed. She got mad. But I ignored her until finally she said, "Why, Dad?"

I was able to explain how her attitude of "you owe me" and her irresponsibility with doing things around the house hurt both her mother and me. I'd decided I wasn't going to hand over the car keys to somebody who couldn't be responsible. She was so shocked she shut her mouth and spent the rest of the night in her room. The next day she got up and ate breakfast with no complaints. She was quiet and respectful after school. Then she asked for the car keys again. When I said no, she looked thoughtful and went off to her room again. Since that night, a month ago, she hasn't pushed once for the car keys. She's been thoughtful of her siblings and done her school work, and the mouthy, "you owe me" bossiness has stopped.

Tomorrow is her 17th birthday. I'm thinking it would be a good night for all of us as a family to go out for dinner. And guess who'll get to drive? Thanks for the tip that gained us a daughter with a completely different attitude.

Sean, Kansas

Cell Phone

I was in the car with my daughter Lauren, who was 17, and she was texting like a woodpecker with ADHD.

"Who are you texting, honey?" I asked her.

"Zach," she said (her boyfriend).

"Why don't you just pick up the phone and talk with him?"

I got a cute eye-roll. "Dad, I don't have enough for a whole conversation."

Friends, this is the world we live in—like it or not for you non-techie people. In working on this book, I asked Lauren, now 18, what the minimum age should be for kids to get a cell phone. I wasn't surprised to hear her response: "Thirteen."

I've been quoted as saying that when a teenager drives a car (about 16 years old), they need a cell phone. Today's kids are mobile; they are sometimes in groups with adult supervision and sometimes in groups without it, where surprises can happen. I like the knowledge that I can get in contact with my daughter when I want to, and she with me.

The cell phone is not the monster some paint it to be. It can be a friend, helper, and lifesaver.

But there's a bigger point here: having a cell phone is a privilege. There's a cost involved. There are two schools of thought on this (and again, every argument can be taken to a fault). Some parents insist that their teenagers pay for part of everything they participate in. Frankly, unless your teenager has a stock fund that's doing better than mine, plus unlimited wealth tucked away, that scenario is frustrating and improbable. A better idea is telling your teenager, "As a member of this family, you have certain inherent benefits. We play together, pray together, and work together. When you lose, we all lose; when you win, we all win. We support and encourage each other. And because you are a part of our family, there are certain perks. One of them is having a cell phone on our family plan." You see, your relationship is all about respect.

> *The cell phone is not the monster some paint it to be. It can be a friend, helper, and lifesaver.*

What I've learned is that, with a teenager in the house, be sure you have unlimited texting on your cell phone plan (we chose a family plan, which saved us money), because if you don't, you won't quite believe the bills you're going to get . . . or the zeros behind the numbers.

I've now got a Droid, and I love that puppy. I get Facebook on there; I read the newspaper on it. There are so many things I can do on that phone.

I'd like to tell you that cell phones will get bigger and better, but in all probability, they'll get smaller and better. Yet one fact is certain: they're here to stay.

And their influence is spreading to younger and younger children every year. *USA Today* ran an article titled "Parents Worry about Toddlers' Tiny Fingers Itching for iPhones," which talks about three-year-old Charlotte Stapleton, who began mastering her mother's iPhone two years ago.

"She's always been drawn to it," says Ainsley Stapleton, 33, a CPA. . . . [She] says her daughter constantly begs for her high-tech playmate, but Mom has her limits. . . .

Call them iTots. *Wunderkind* of the 21st century. One-, 2-, and 3-year-olds who know their way around an iPhone or an iPad better than you do.[2]

There is concern on behalf of child psychology experts and parents that introducing children to such technology too early will lead to antisocial behavior and an inability to connect with peers. "Could today's tiny tots be following their Baby Boomer elders—tuning in, turning on, dropping out?" says Craig Wilson, the writer of the *USA Today* article. "Five percent of kids ages 6 to 9 own their own [cell phones]," he reports, "and the number is growing every month. It's just part of childhood now. For better or worse."[3]

With technology here to stay, we parents need to be smart—about our own use and our teenagers' use of cell phone technology. The key word is *balance*—in all things.

LIFESAVER

Privileges are just that—privileges.

Chip on Shoulder

There are all kinds of reasons a teenager might have a chip on his or her shoulder.

- He spends half the time at his dad's house and half the time at his mom's house.
- She's got three new stepsiblings she doesn't care for.
- His grades aren't very good.
- She doesn't seem to be fitting in well at school.
- He's got a bad case of acne.

- Not many kids call her on her phone.
- He got cut from the basketball team.

Trust me, when you see kids with a chip on their shoulder, there's a reason for it. Everyone develops a "life theme" early in life. There are teenagers whose life mantra is, "I'm a victim. Life is always unfair to me. It will always be unfair." They feel slighted for real and/or imagined wrongs.

If your teenager was abused, he can carry a big chip on his shoulder. There's an old song that says "You Always Hurt the One You Love," and the psychological results are wreaking havoc on families across the country. When your kid feels that life has been unfair, and he is hurt by life, he thinks (often subconsciously), *I have a right to strike out at other people.* And when he does strike out, does he do it toward strangers? Not usually. He doesn't have as much access to them. Instead, he strikes out at those he has the most access to—his family.

> *There are teenagers whose life mantra is, "I'm a victim. Life is always unfair to me. It will always be unfair."*

The reality is, some kids have been damaged by life. Rubbing this book on their head like it's a magic lamp won't give you an automatic fix. Maybe your kid isn't very lovable. But as the adult in the situation, you need to do your best to love the unlovable. There's an old song that says, "What the world needs now is love, sweet love." Love is a choice . . . and not always an easy one. So in the heat of battle, *you* be the first to say, "I'm sorry. I shouldn't have said that."

You won't get anywhere with a kid who has a chip on his shoulder by rubbing his nose in it and taking an authoritarian stance: "Hey, buddy, you better snap out of it."

Instead, say, "I'm concerned about you," "You seem bothered," or "You seem angry." These can be dialogue openers to begin restoring your relationship.

Sometimes just telling him, "Wow, if I were in your shoes, I'd be angry too," establishes equality. It puts you on even footing. You're not coming across as better than your teenager; you're identifying with him. Furthermore, add, "Based on what's happened to you in a few short years, I'm amazed that you've gotten as far as you have. Tell me, what can I do to help?"

Watch the floodgates of conversation open. Then stay quiet and just listen until his words have poured out and he's done.

LIFESAVER

Establish equality.

It Worked for Me

Ever since Dan and I joined our families three years ago, it's been like World War III around the house. Our kids just don't get along. Talk about loving the unlovable; we've had a lot of experience with that. But we were sick of the wars and the chip-on-the-shoulder attitudes.

After hearing you talk about what kids of divorce go through, we decided to call a family council. We told them that we understood they weren't happy with their new situation—or gaining siblings they didn't want—and they had a reason for being angry about it. But we all had a choice—either to stay angry at each other, or to try to work things out. Then we asked, "What can we do to help?"

Our kids were stunned into silence at first, then they started talking. The things they said were hard to hear— their disappointment in our previous marriages falling apart, that Dad or Mom wasn't part of their lives any-more. But for the first time we were talking instead of yelling. That night was a turning point for us. Now we have family councils once a week—to let the air out of the balloon, as you suggested, before it blows. Life isn't perfect, but it's working!

Eileen, New Mexico

Chores

I have a perfect solution to any fracas about chores: lighten the chores as the kid gets older.

"Dr. Leman, what did you say? Did I read that right?" you're asking.

You sure did.

Once your child is in her teenage years and is doing other activities outside the home that take more of her time, pass on to the younger kids some of the chores that she's routinely done around the house. This is a great way to even the stakes for your teenager since usually every time a job needs to be done around the house, parents holler for the oldest.

But in a family, no one member is more important than another. Everybody works to get the jobs done that need to be done. In today's hectic world, many moms and dads work outside the home. Others are single parents who don't have the luxury of a mate to plow the parental fields, which makes it even tougher and more incumbent on the kids to give back to the family. I don't know of a working-outside-the-home mom who isn't thinking on her way home: *Okay, so what are we going to have for dinner? Are there any meetings I have to go to tonight? Do the kids have any activities?* As she's driving in traffic, she goes through a long mental checklist.

All I'm saying is that everybody should carry their weight. It isn't always Mom and Dad's responsibility to make dinner, do the laundry, or pick up the house—especially if they're working outside the home. Children who are 8, 9, 10, and 11 years of age can certainly help prepare dinner, make sure the dog is let out and fed, bring the mail in, and pick up the living room.

This morning, my lovely wife, Mrs. Uppington, is sleeping in. I walked into the kitchen and saw dishes in the sink. I'm like a trained seal. I put away the clean dishes and put the dirty ones in the dishwasher so my tired wife could continue sleeping. I didn't wait for her to get up to do it.

Everybody in the family works; nobody skates by for free.

That's why it's not smart to pay your kids to do their chores around the house. After all, do you, Mom, get paid for making dinner? And do you, Dad, get paid for doing the laundry, folding it, and putting it away? Instead, each member of the family should receive an allowance because they are part of the family.

Everybody should carry their weight.

But what happens if your teenager doesn't do his given chores? Ah, that's when it gets interesting. If he doesn't do his chores, then a little something is missing out of his allowance—and that little something is paid either to you or to his sister for finishing his chores for him. It won't take long for your son to get the picture and get off the couch.

When I give seminars across the country, I always ask for those who grew up on farms to raise their hands. "Okay," I say, "those of you who grew up on farms are now free to leave my seminar, because you won't learn much." That's because, on the farm, everybody works; everybody gives back to the family. And that's a healthy thing because it makes a family stronger.

(LIFESAVER)

Everybody in the family contributes.

Clothing

Clothing tastes are individual, and most likely what your teenager wants to wear isn't something that you'd wear. So how do you know where to draw the line?

Let's say your well-developed 13-year-old daughter goes on a shopping trip with friends and brings home a shirt that will not only highlight her obvious endowment, but will make it more than visible to strangers from 50 feet away. That's when you as the parent reach in your back pocket for your yellow flag and pull it out. You firmly say, "We're not going there with that outfit."

When you put money in your teenager's hands, you'll be surprised at what a good shopper she'll become.

"But, Mom!" she'll say, and the argument will ensue. (But remember what you've already learned—that it takes two to argue, and you're too street-smart to do that, now aren't you?)

You simply say, "Honey, there are certain things you have dominion over and certain things you don't. When you're out of the house, working for a living, and paying your own way, you can wear anything you choose to. But for now, that shirt is going back to the store because it is not appropriate."

Now would also be a perfect time for Dad (or another male role model, if you're a single parent) to have a talk with his daughter about how men view women. A lot of things young women think are just stylish, young men may see as provocative. Not to sound like someone who has two feet in the grave, but modesty—whether in clothing or anything else—is a great quality that has somehow eluded our present population in general.

Modesty is the best policy in any generation.

So how do you decide what your teenager can spend on clothes? Here's my easy solution. Every family is different regarding their available clothing budget. The important thing is to set whatever budget you as a family feel is doable for each child's clothes. Then tell your teenager the amount on hand and let her make the decision of where she wants to shop. Say, "We have $300 total to spend on school clothes this year. What you want to spend it on is up to you, but when it's done, it's done."

When you put money in your teenager's hands, you'll be surprised at what a good shopper she'll become. The first time you do so, she might blow the wad all in one place. But when you stick to your guns and say, "There is no more," she'll learn very quickly that if she buys two items on sale, then she can buy more items. Our five teenagers loved to shop at recycled-clothes places; they found fun items they loved at a fraction of the cost.

Does that mean you just hand the money over to your teenager and leave her on her own? No, you go shopping with her. Now, I'm a guy who hates shopping, and we men would probably rather leave shopping to the females in our lives. So that means the task is usually left to you women. Bless you.

LIFESAVER

Modesty—in everything—is a great quality.

It Worked for Me

You just ended a huge fuss at our house with your tip to establish a budget and then put the money in our teenager's hands. Our daughter always wanted the latest fad jeans, the most expensive purse, etc. My husband has been without work for the past year and can only find odd jobs to bring in money. I work at a local child care and don't make a lot of money. I was tired of hearing Charlene whine about how her clothes weren't cool enough. So I figured out how much money we spend on her clothes during the year, then told her what the budget was and that we'd give her money every month, and she could figure out how to spend it.

She blew the first month's money on one clothing item. When we didn't come up with more money for other items, like we used to, she got the picture. The next month she and a friend started shopping sales and repeat places. Now the two of them text about how much they "saved," not how much an item cost. It sure took the pain out of clothes shopping for me!

Andrea, Michigan

Curfew/Staying Out Late

Whenever I talk to parents about this issue, they're startled to find out that, in the Leman family, none of our kids ever had curfews.

"Dr. Leman, I've read your books, and they're all action-oriented and have a tough-love approach. You mean to tell me you didn't have any curfews for your kids?"

That's right, we didn't. Here's why.

When your teenager is out with a friend and driving the family car, you've already expressed confidence in her responsibility and decision-making abilities. Otherwise why would you let her out the door with a car in which she could potentially damage or kill herself and others?

So you believe in your teenager. Now it's time to put the ball on the side of the court where it belongs. When your teenager asks, "What time should I be home?" answer, "At a reasonable hour."

"Dr. Leman," you're saying, "if I said that to my child, he'd be home at 4:30 in the morning!"

Then I'd say that would be the last time he'd be out with my car for a very, very long time.

What am I saying? Expect the best of your teenager. Positive expectations accomplish far more than negative pronouncements they're bound to rebel against (even if they're asking for them).

You might be surprised to find out, as Sande and I did, that your kids will be home a lot sooner than the curfew you'd have given them. In our family, I also let our children come up with the rules for using the family car. They were far stricter than ones even we as parents would have imposed on them.

> *When your teenager asks, "What time should I be home?" answer, "At a reasonable hour."*

Most teenagers, when you say, "Be home at a reasonable hour," will come back with, "Give me a time."

Repeat yourself. "Just be home at a reasonable hour."

Though kids want you to post the hour for them—for example, "Be home at 1:00 a.m. or I'll turn you into a frog"—the message you want to convey to your teenager is, "I trust you to do what's right."

This is a teachable moment you can't afford to miss.

LIFESAVER

Expect the best.

Cutting/Self-Injury

The Mayo Clinic defines cutting or self-injury this way:

> The act of deliberately harming your own body, such as cutting or burning yourself. It's not meant as a suicide attempt. Rather,

self-injury is an unhealthy way to cope with emotional pain, intense anger and frustration. While self-injury may bring a momentary sense of calm and a release of tension, it's usually followed by guilt and shame and the return of painful emotions. And with self-injury comes the possibility of inflicting serious and even fatal injuries.[4]

How can you tell if your teenager is struggling in this area? Watch for the telltale signs, says Mayo Clinic:

- scars, such as from burns or cuts
- fresh cuts, scratches, bruises, or other wounds
- broken bones
- keeping sharp objects on hand (razors, knives)
- spending a great deal of time alone
- relationship troubles
- wearing long sleeves or long pants, even in hot weather
- claiming to have frequent accidents or mishaps[5]

If a kid is dealing with past trauma or facing overwhelming issues in his everyday life, he may turn to cutting or other self-injury as a way to cope with his problems. It may briefly make him feel better—as if he's in control of life again—but the pain returns and the cycle continues.

Kids who cut often want to stop but don't know how. Until they get help to understand why they want to harm themselves, learn healthy ways to cope with stress, and find resources to help them, they can't stop by themselves. Kids who cut often get grouped into the suicide camp. But most kids who cut do it as a way to regain control of life, not as a way to die. They use it to deal with strong emotions, to hide emotional pain (they can focus on the physical pain), to control their bodies, or to punish themselves. Also, they usually do it secretly (unlike kids who cry for attention by trying to kill themselves).

Notice that most 40-year-olds don't try to cut themselves. It's a behavior fairly unique to teenagers. Why? Because teenagers experience high highs and low lows. Kids who cut tend to be somewhat depressed and withdrawn; they spend a lot of time alone in their room. They feel they have no control over anything in life. These kids desperately need someone to talk to, even if they're not good at relationships. Their anger at themselves is directed inward.

Parents often tend to write things off as a "stage": "Oh, it's just a stage he's going through." But cutting is not a stage. Like anorexia nervosa and bulimia, cutting and other self-injury is serious. It happens for a deep psychological or emotional reason.

Kids who cut do it as a way to regain control of life.

If there was an elephant sitting on your couch in the living room, would you walk right by it and pretend it doesn't exist? Or would you sit down on the couch next to that elephant and ask why it's there and what's going on?

If your kid is cutting, it's not a reflection upon you as a "failed" parent. But it is a wake-up call that something is going on in your kid's life and he or she needs help. Now is the time to get some professional assistance for your son or daughter.

LIFESAVER

Sticking your head in the sand doesn't accomplish anything.

Death

One of my earliest memories—I was five years old—was going to my aunt Micky's funeral. I remember that somebody told me Aunt Micky was just sleeping.

I thought, *I don't believe that. She doesn't look like she's sleeping to me. I think she's dead.*

I honestly remember thinking that.

I wasn't stupid, and neither is your teenager. When I was growing up, most adults tried to protect children from death. So the fact that my parents chose to take me to a funeral at age five was certainly unusual for whatever reason. (They probably didn't have the money for the babysitter, since finances were tight in our home.)

But in today's world, your teenager faces the issue of death far more than you can know. For example, my daughter Lauren is a high school senior, and some of her classmates have already lost parents. Terri, who goes to an inner-city junior high, has lost five of her classmates in the past three years to drug overdoses or gang killings. Jared's best buddy at a private prep school couldn't take life's stresses anymore and committed suicide. Jenna, an 11-year-old, just learned that her 14-year-old brother's third round of chemo failed, and he will die. Marie's grandmother is dying of breast cancer. The media is filled with dying and death—teenagers killing other students and teachers for real or imagined slights.

> *The first time your teenager loses a family member or friend, the reality of "the end" can be devastating.*

How do you deal with death? How do you talk to your teenager about it?

Death can be sudden. The first time your teenager loses a family member or friend, the reality of "the end" can be devastating. The process of death can also be prolonged due to a lengthy illness, so your child would face a long period of loss (for example, his grandparent has Alzheimer's and is slowly failing).

For teenagers who have seen a lot of "exciting" death drama in movies, the hard reality of death in person is far different and hits hard. They see Grandpa go from a fun-filled, vibrant person to a detached person who is declining. Or the friend they thought they'd have forever is now gone overnight due to a car accident.

All living things die. That's one reason I believe in pets for children (short-lived ones like fish are a great start), because the death of a pet is an important life lesson to prepare your kids for facing the realities of death in human relationships.

My advice when your teenager is facing death? Always be open. Share your tears. Don't hide them from each other. Give your daughter a chance to talk about her feelings. Make sure she has the opportunity to say to her parent, brother, or friend whatever she wants to say before the end comes. Death is final; we don't get a second shot at saying what's important. So now is the time. If the person has already died, have your teenager write a letter to that person expressing his feelings to help him process his grief.

After all, part of death is learning how to live—to figure out what you would do differently if you had that relationship with that person to live over again. Then you can move on to take the principles you've learned into new relationships.

LIFESAVER

Be real, be honest, embrace the emotion.

Depression

Amanda was a bubbly, happy type of girl, always loudly singing the latest movie tunes. She was known for her laughter, her creativity, and her love of performing her own musicals for her parents and friends. Then Amanda turned 11. Within a few months of getting her period, her hormones started going wild. She cried at school at least twice a day. She felt overwhelmed with life's stresses. She became quiet and withdrew from friends. She stared off into space. Each morning she'd beg her dad not to send her to school, because the school she used to love she now hated. She felt nobody liked her, even though she was surrounded with the same loving group of friends.

Amanda was depressed.

Depression is not just a "down in the dumps," temporary thing.

Depression is a "whole-body" illness, involving your body, mood, and thoughts. It affects the way you eat and sleep, the way you feel about yourself, and the way you think about things. A depressive disorder is not the same as a passing blue mood. It is not a sign of personal weakness or a condition that can be willed or wished away. People with a depressive illness cannot merely "pull themselves together" and get better.[6]

People who are depressed often feel sad for no reason at all. They don't enjoy doing the things they used to do. They're listless and apathetic about life. They have trouble focusing or concentrating. They think people don't like them. They withdraw from the groups they used to hang out with.

If you're seeing these types of changes in your teenager's behavior or demeanor and they've lasted for more than a few days, that's a sign that your son or daughter might be struggling with depression.

> *Depression doesn't just go away. It's a medical problem.*

Since emotions in the hormone group can be very up and down, many parents have the mentality, "Oh, she's just a little bummed right now. It'll go away." But depression doesn't just go away. It's a medical problem, and it needs to be addressed immediately by your physician. Also, be aware that mental illness tends to run in families. Is there someone in your family circle who struggles with depression?

170

When you see major and abrupt changes in the personality and behavior of your son or daughter—most teenagers who are depressed do a 180 in their behavior and personality—pay careful attention. The more quickly you get professional help, the better it will be for your kid and your entire family.

LIFESAVER

Change isn't always good.

Divorce

Divorce isn't easy on anyone . . . most particularly on the children involved. Teenagers feel like wishbones pulled in all directions—stretching to please both parents. They don't want to have to choose sides between the people they love.

Street-smart parents keep their teenagers out of the firing range between them. For parents who couldn't get along in their marriage and are at war with each other during their divorce, I know this is a lofty expectation. But again, who's the adult here? Your children didn't choose the divorce; you and your ex-spouse did. So keep the stresses between the two of you. Don't dump them on your children.

That means you don't bad-mouth your ex (as tempting as that is)—*ever*. Even if your ex is a slimeball, your bad words about him or her will come back to haunt you big-time. Give your teenager some credit that he can figure out who's telling the truth in the situation—whether now or down the road. You don't have to be the almighty trumpeter of the situation.

Let me be blunt. The traditional living arrangements in divorce agreements are brutal—making your teenager live one week at your house and one week at your ex's house. I ask again, did your kids choose your divorce? No, you and your ex did. So why is it that your kids are being flip-flopped from place to place like a pancake at IHOP? What if, instead, the parents switched houses? That would be far better for the kids, in my estimation. Interestingly, a lot of divorcing and divorced parents have seen the light and are doing exactly that. But that may not be workable in your specific situation—especially if it is a messy, angry divorce.

> *Did your kids choose your divorce? No, you and your ex did. So why is it that your kids are being flip-flopped from place to place like a pancake at IHOP?*

All I'm saying is that, although you're bound by legal agreements, anything you can do to make things easier on your son or daughter is preferable. And if there's any way to make visiting the other parent more voluntary on the part of your teenager, do it. Giving your son or daughter the freedom to decide how much time he or she is going to spend at the other home is a good thing for the kid.

Some of you are angry just reading these words, because they are the last thing you want to hear. You only get to see your daughter once a month on the weekend as it is. But forcing your teenager to spend time with you out of obligation doesn't do anything for developing a lifelong relationship.

There is enough stress in a teenager's life without adding the stress of divorce. Yet divorce is a reality in our society. However, that doesn't mean that you as the adult in the situation shouldn't do everything in your power to take as much stress out of the living situation as possible.

I recently got a heartbreaking phone call from a dad. His ex-wife, an alcoholic, dragged him through court, proclaiming lies about him. She painted him as darkly as possible to the court system so that she received complete custody of her daughter except for Saturdays. Problem is, this dad usually has to work weekends, so it's hard for him to find time to see his daughter. The guy was in tears as he told me about his situation.

"Doc," he said, "I love my daughter so much, but I'm losing her. And she's only 14 years old."

The mother had so poisoned her daughter against him that the daughter didn't want to see her dad anymore; she believed the lies her mother was telling her.

This is what I told that father:

> Here's the good news. I've gone through this hundreds of times with hundreds of different families, and I've seen lots of happy endings. But you won't like what I'm about to tell you at first. Stop trying to force your teenage daughter to see you. Back off; don't push. Go silent. Yes, I know it'll kill you in the meanwhile, but wait and be patient. Any 14-year-old kid who lives with a depressed, alcoholic mom isn't going to be happy with her life in such a setting for long. And when you remove yourself as a psychological punching bag for both of them—and, bluntly, that's all you are to them right now, even though you're only trying to be a good dad—you'll be amazed at what happens.
>
> God didn't put you on this earth to get chewed up and spit out. Even if the court says you have visitation every other week on Saturday from this time to that time, would you really be in contempt of court if you didn't go? You'd have to talk to your attorney about that, but I don't think so. You have an *option* to see your daughter, but you don't have to. So remove yourself from the conflict. If you back off far enough, at least you know that when your daughter calls you, she'll *want* to talk to you. Don't fall into the trap of being the Disney dad—trying to do anything to win your daughter's favor. Both sides of the relationship have to be working.

Divorce is nasty business, any way you look at it. But if you take the high road and don't bad-mouth your ex—ever—you'll be doing the absolute best you can for your teenager. I know of many kids who, once they were out of the nest and on their own, developed a wider perspective on what was happening at home and then went out of their way to spend time with their other parent.

Keep your teenager out of the firing range.

Doesn't Fit In with Peers

Jimmy was a mostly A student, a brilliant musician, and a book lover. He was an even-keeled kid that everybody seemed to like. But his parents were concerned about him spending so much time alone. "We want him to find a group to hang out with—you know, where he has friends and he can fit in . . . be like the other kids," they told me.

I'm going to ask you the same thing I asked those parents: "Do you really want your kid to be like every other kid in the peer group? How badly do you want him to fit in?"

If your kid is like every other teenager, she'll most likely lose her virginity in her teenage years; he'll smoke some Spice or dabble in marijuana; she'll cheat on a test to get a better grade; he'll lie to you about where he is on a Friday night.

That's because most teenagers are like lemmings. They don't make decisions by themselves; they fall into group-think. They can't stand up for what's right because they haven't been taught how to do so. So they go right along with the masses, whether right or wrong.

Never be concerned about your teenager not fitting in to a particular group (unless, of course, you see him or her getting depressed as a result). In regards to Jimmy, he was an only child, and loners tend to be only children. They tend to be introspective, very capable people who don't need a party going on at every second. They are great at entertaining themselves.

If your teenager isn't part of the popular group at school, well, good for her! Take a look back at your own high school class. A lot of the Mr. Hot Shots and Miss Populars in high school haven't exactly become the most successful, happy adults, have they? But what about the kids you wrote off and thought they'd never amount to anything? Surprise, surprise. One is a brain surgeon; one is an astrophysicist; one just won a Newbery medal for her innovative fiction; one is a specialist in restoring World War II airplanes.

> *Most teenagers are like lemmings. They don't make decisions by themselves; they fall into group-think.*

As I always say, "If a man owns a beautiful horse, he must remember that the beauty lies in the horse, and not in the man." So teach your teenagers about what's really important in life—what's on the inside of them . . . the part that will last past the high school groups that change weekly. Talk to your kids about who they are and the decisions they've made. Reinforce their good actions and behaviors with words that say, "I couldn't be more proud of how you handled that situation. I'm so happy to call you my daughter/son."

Your encouraging words make all the difference in your teenager's life perception. You might think a peer group is influential, but guess what, Mom and Dad? You're much more influential in your kid's life than those peers.

Even when she looks like she's not paying any attention to your words, she's hearing *everything you say*. So make sure you lather on the encouragement (not false praise).

Your kid is one of a kind. So let her be exactly who she is.

Nobody needs another clone around anyway.

LIFESAVER

Let your kid be who she is.

Door Slamming

Your kid slams the door. What do most parents do?

Take it personally. Get upset, mad, and strike back. "You come out here right now, young lady!" Or, "If you want me to take that door off, young man, I can certainly do it. Just try me."

But does the yelling or the fighting back solve anything? Or does threatening to ground them for life (the teenage version of the child's feared time-out)? The most you'll get out of your threats is perhaps an "I'm sorry, Mom" when she wants to go over to her best friend's house later. But then life goes on with no consequences. Well, obviously a problem exists, or your kid wouldn't be slamming doors.

Again, you're the adult here. The more you come up with creative, even humorous ways to look at the same old problem, the better off you'll be. Life in your house doesn't have to be slamming doors and a constant screaming match. But many parents throw their hands up in the air and say, "I give up." Don't make your problems bigger than life itself.

What if you said instead, "I want to answer that door slamming, but I'm not quite sure what it meant. Does it mean you're sick of me asking you to do what you know you need to do? Are you telling me that I should go to h-e-double-hockey-sticks? Are you saying you're so glad you only have 2 years, 3 months, 7 days, 21 hours, and 31 minutes left to serve in this prison before you're out on your own? Or are you sick of living in a 2400-square-foot home that has wireless, three square meals a day, and a flat-screen TV? At any rate, I'll be downstairs waiting for you."

That's what a calm, street-smart parent says. And you mean, "We're going to deal with this before life goes on. That means you're not going anywhere tonight. We're going to resolve this because our home and family relationships are the most important. Everything else comes second."

In such situations, you need to exert the parental authority that comes with the territory of being the parent. But be careful to establish equality with your kids. You're not better than they are, and they're not better than you; you play different roles.

> *Come up with creative, even humorous ways to look at the same old problem.*

But slamming doors is never acceptable and a nonnegotiable. So calmly nip it in the bud.

LIFESAVER

Keep your sails out of your child's wind.

It Worked for Me

A year ago, we got so sick of our son slamming doors that my husband finally removed his door. But it didn't solve the attitude behind it. He was just as surly as ever. Then we heard you on the radio talking about "C doesn't happen until A and B are taken care of," and we got it. The next time he stomped through the house, we let him go. We didn't yell back; we didn't go after him. But the next time he wanted to go somewhere, we said no. When he screamed at us, we didn't back down. (You're right—a united front really does work.) He stayed home that night. It took several rounds until he finally got it. Mom and Dad weren't wimps anymore; we weren't backing down. Now we've got a whole new kid who asks nicely for us to drive him somewhere.

Karlene, Illinois

Driving Privileges

When is your teenager ready to drive, and how should you go about preparing him or her? Check your state law, of course, for the specific ages required for learner permits and driver's licenses. Most states have driver's education in school, but if you send your kid to a private school, in all probability they don't have it. But there's something else you should consider first. Is your kid *ready* for the responsibility of driving? Is she responsible? Does she help out around the house? Is she respectful? Is she careful and considerate? Or is she spacey and mouthy and disrespectful of authority? Driving is not a right when you turn 15 or 16. It's a privilege granted to those who are responsible enough to be behind the wheel of the car. Would you really want to put someone on the road who isn't responsible? Someone who might end up hitting you or others because she isn't paying attention?

So before you agree to let your son or daughter get a learner's permit and/or a license, think it through carefully. Is your kid mature enough to accept the responsibility of driving? Does she understand the basic rules of driving (no texting, no talking on the cell phone while on the road, etc.)? If not, wait until your kid matures more . . . yes, even if her friends are all getting *their* licenses. When that happens, you might be amazed at the sudden spurt of respect and maturity you get at home from your daughter. It's like a magical charm for getting help around the house.

I taught four of my five kids to drive. I'll never forget the time that our oldest, Holly, was driving with me in the passenger seat and Sande in the back. As we approached the intersection, Holly was so intent on her driving that she didn't notice the red light. At Sande's gasp, Holly, startled, slammed on the brakes (and I mean *slammed*). She was so shocked her foot slipped off the brake, edging us a few feet into the intersection. This time I hissed, "Holly Kristine Leman!" (because in such times, the first name alone won't do). Startled again, she let her foot slip another time. Out we shot into the intersection a couple more feet.

Two seconds later, I was out of the car, throwing my hands in the air and doing a rain dance around our van that I'm sure the other commuters enjoyed. (If any of them were fathers teaching their kids how to drive, they were nodding in sympathy.) Yeah, I was at my prime. See, even psychologists blow it with their families sometimes.

> *Two seconds later, I was out of the car, throwing my hands in the air and doing a rain dance around our van that I'm sure the other commuters enjoyed.*

Do you see why, when we got to child number five, I decided enough was enough? And with Lauren, my age was also a factor. I said to Sande, "Hey, I've done this four times—covering my eyes and putting myself in the brace position and yelling 'Stop!' I'm not sure the ol' ticker could take another round."

So, to prove that with age you really do get smarter, we called Mr. D's driving school.

It was a great experience all around. I knew it was worthwhile because later, when Lauren was in the car with me and I was driving, she would tell me, "Uh, Dad, you're over the line." (Lauren has the amazing ability to tell it like it is and still be nice about it.) Mr. D's was a godsend. The lady who taught her was very nice, and Lauren loved her. They did hours around town and on the freeway, and Lauren even learned how to parallel park. It was the best 300-buck investment I've ever made.

LIFESAVER

Sometimes it pays to pay.

Drugs and Alcohol

When you think of heroin, what do you think of? Some down-and-out skid-row bum shooting himself up? Living life in a haze? Asking for money at street corners?

Well, think again. One of the biggest problems in fairly well-to-do high schools (like one nearby me in Tucson, where the kids come from affluent homes) is heroin use. It's the kid who dresses preppy or who dresses Goth—you can't always tell from how a kid looks or the clothes he wears—who can fall into the trap of using heroin. No one is immune. Heroin use is here to stay, and so is smoking pot, lining cocaine, using meth and other drugs, and drinking six-packs and even harder liquor.

The street-smart parent doesn't bury her head in the sand, moaning about how times have changed. Instead, she realizes that drugs and alcohol are indeed around and easily available, and that, most likely, her kids will be approached soon to try drugs or alcohol (if they haven't been already).

Drugs and alcohol carry big-time dangers and costs for your kid and others. If you don't believe me, call your State Farm agent. He'll not only explain the facts to you but also tell you how much it'll cost to add your 15-year-old onto your family car's policy. Put the car in your 18-year-old's name and see your premium skyrocket within seconds. And if your kid gets a DWI under age, in all probability he will lose his license. When someone gets a DWI, whether under age or as an adult, he or she goes through a court system, and to get legal representation, that person is looking at 10 grand for starters. The loss of life due to drugs and alcohol is huge.

Why, then, are they so socially acceptable?

Perhaps it's because we live in a society where a lot of parents smoke dope and use alcohol themselves. A friend told me she was at a kid's birthday party where two of the moms were gabbing around the corner of the garage as they smoked dope. A lot of parents believe it's okay to serve alcohol to minor-age children in the home, because they imbibe in alcohol themselves and have a full liquor cabinet on display. But parents, you are not living in France, where parents do give their children alcohol with dinner.

The loss of life due to drugs and alcohol is huge. Why, then, are they so socially acceptable?

Kids who are using drugs and alcohol usually have access to one thing—money.

Marian grew up in a home with two working, influential, wealthy parents. She came home at 11 years old to an empty house day after day and found the liquor cabinet for comfort. A shot or two of vodka and she wasn't feeling lonely anymore. To hide her growing addiction, she refilled the bottles a little with water. It wasn't until two years later when she came home from a party in the middle of the night, looking bruised, rumpled, and drunk, that her parents got concerned—after they had frantically phoned everywhere to find her. They had no idea she was even drinking or that she'd been drinking heavily for two years—right out of their own liquor cabinet.

Eight weeks later, her parents got another shock. Thirteen-year-old Marian was pregnant—she'd been raped at the party when she was drunk, and she didn't even remember who had raped her. The remorse these parents were feeling seven months later, as they watched their sobbing daughter sign the adoption papers for her new baby, couldn't be calculated.

So, parents, pay attention to the signs that your kid may be struggling. Do something *now*. Don't wait.

There's also something new on the market that you may or may not yet know about but need to be aware of: Spice. I was recently talking about it with a group of 50 parents in one room, and asked, "Who is aware of what Spice is?" Only one hand went up. That's why I include this information for you.

Spice, or K2, isn't actually a drug, but it acts like a drug. It can give you a pretty good buzz, and it's popular with young kids today for a couple of reasons: (1) it's very inexpensive, and (2) you can buy it in any smoke shop as incense. Some states are now scurrying to make this substance illegal, but it's still available as of the date of this writing. Even more, you can't detect it in a drug test.

> *Kids who are using drugs and alcohol usually have access to one thing—money.*

A lot of high schools are now drug-testing their kids. This is starting in the private school sector since it's easier to pull off there, but before long I believe drug testing will be part and parcel of your kid's education.

Temptations to use drugs and alcohol will always surround your teenager. You can't change that fact; you can't surround him in bubble wrap or be by his side every moment as the hovering Mama or Papa Bear. So what are you going to do to make your kid be different? What will you do in your home right now to ensure that your son or daughter isn't going to smoke that weed, snort that cocaine, or do anything illegal?

Whether your kid is able to stand against drugs and alcohol or not has everything to do with your support of, encouragement of, and belief in him. Our kids, when approached with drugs or alcohol, were taught to respond simply, "Hey, I'm a Leman, and we Lemans don't do that." Then they turned and walked away.

When a kid feels strong in who he is as a part of your family, knowing he has a secure, solid place in it, he can say no to the things that will falsely make him "feel good" or that would otherwise lure him to be part of a group that isn't healthy for him. He's already part of a group—you, his family—and he feels good about that.

If you've done things pretty well as a parent as your child has grown up, your kid will, in all probability, not end up using drugs and alcohol. But if you've overdone things—been too prescriptive, trying to bully your kid into being what you wanted him to be, or been too permissive, allowing him to do whatever he wanted with no consequences—he might rebel.

When our five kids were little, every time I came on an accident scene, I'd shake my head and say, "Drugs," loudly enough for them to overhear. Later, when our kids came upon accident scenes, they'd ask me, "Dad, do you think it was drugs?" Imprinting the consequences of drug and alcohol use on your kids as early as possible in life will indeed make an impression. Four of my kids are already out of the nest, and each of them has told me, "Dad, I've never taken a hit on weed (marijuana), even though I was asked, because I didn't need to do that to be cool."

Now, was I a never-ending watchdog? No, because you can't hover over your children every minute like God Almighty himself. It's just not possible. Instead, I treated my kids with respect. They knew that we Lemans were non-druggie people. They knew that drugs had consequences (they'd often tell their friends about them). They knew that no alcohol or drug use would be tolerated in our home.

Contrast that with the parents who think it's cool to rent a couple motel rooms so their kids can party there "safely" on prom night. Excuse me, but those parents make Jim Carrey in the movie *Dumb and Dumber* look like an astrophysicist.

If you're reading this book and saying, "Dr. Leman, a lot of this is just common sense," thank you for noticing. This book *is* all about common sense, and what many people lack today is common sense. Sadly, it's often the parents of teenagers who are over the top in their own attitudes, behavior, and character. And guess who the kids learn from? Go to an athletic contest of young kids sometime, and you'll be surprised at how outrageous some of the parents act. They make fools of themselves. But the kids on the field are fine (in fact, they're out there rolling their eyes in embarrassment because of their parents' behavior).

> *Parent, you hold the cards, and the cards you can play are aces.*

So before you start lecturing your kids about drugs and alcohol, take a good look in the mirror first. As you do, they'll do.

Now what do you do if your son or daughter is caught smoking weed or is under any other influence? Ask yourself this question first: "Would I let anyone on drugs drive my car?"

I certainly wouldn't.

Remember, parent, you hold the cards, and the cards you can play are aces. If your kid is off base, going in a different direction than you want him to, you need to stand up and throw the red flag, saying, "This isn't going to fly in our home." When your kid is 18 or 19 and out of the home, he'll do what he wants to do. Nothing you're going to do or say will change that kid. But when he's residing in your home, he's residing under your rules. And if he doesn't adhere to them, he loses his privileges as a member of the family (which goes for allowances, spending money, and driving the car). Remember that drugs aren't cheap. They cost a lot of money, and your kid can only mooch off his buddies for so long. So where is the money coming from? If it's coming from you, end the flow now.

If your child is using drugs, a confrontation is in order. "I know you're drinking/using drugs. You need help, and I as your parent am going to make sure you get the help you need. So here's how it's going to play out." Be firm. Don't do battle. Just state the facts.

One father told me recently that the hardest thing he ever had to do in his life was put his son in drug rehab a year ago, but he knew it was the right thing to do. His son screamed obscenities at him and said he hated him. But today, father and son have a good relationship; they play racquetball together twice a week and make a point of Friday movie nights together. Those movie nights have kept the son away from his old druggie crowd. Last week the teary-eyed father said, "Yesterday, Sean told me something I'll never forget. He said, 'Dad, you know I never really did hate you. I was just all messed up.'"

Parent, stand in the gap. Get your kid the help he needs if he's using drugs and alcohol. Do everything you can in your home to educate your child about drugs and alcohol—and their effects.

Drugs and alcohol are not molehills; they're mountains worthy of your time and intense effort. These are the kinds of things that will take a kid down, that will destroy your kid's motivation and ability to think and reason. And in these critical years, that is a critical situation indeed. A street-smart parent *always* pays attention to signs of drug and alcohol use. Nothing is a guarantee in life, but thinking the best of your kids, expecting the best of them, and speaking the best of them go a long way toward them behaving in an appropriate manner in every area of life.

LIFESAVER

As you do, they'll do.

Eye-Rolling

Kids are going to roll their eyes. It's not the end of the world.

I'd say, with a sense of humor, "Oooh, stop right there. Would you do that again? In slo-mo, not so fast? I want to show your mother.

You know, you're so much better-looking when you roll your eyes than when you don't. I think you ought to practice it more."

By that time, there will be a smile on your kid's face.

Rolling eyes are part of your teenager growing up.

Hopefully, by the time they're 30, they'll stop.

Don't make a mountain out of a molehill.

Facebook and Other Social Inventions

As a psychologist and author, I'm a little out-of-the-box. I do my own Facebook. I can tell you names of all kinds of folks who hire people to do their FB for them . . . but I won't. I enjoy parents throwing me a tough question, answering the bell when it goes *ding*, and helping that mom or dad turn their kid's life or family life around. As of this day, I have about 10,000 followers, and I love the back-and-forth of the technology and using it as a teaching tool for couples and parents. Plus my lastborn nature gets to do a little entertaining as well, since I make things fun for everyone on FB, including myself!

Parents read way more into this FB thing than they need to. Some parents feel that if their kid is on FB, some lecherous old person will come and kidnap them and maim them for life. But, as with all things, common sense needs to prevail. If your son or daughter has a FB account and they aren't giving away personal information to strangers (i.e., people they don't personally know and interact with), and they're taught not to "friend" anyone they don't know personally, then social inventions like FB are fairly innocuous. It can be a fun activity for your teenager to interact with her group of friends (and it might save you a whopper of a cell phone bill too, if you're not on a family plan).

However, kids need to be taught to be careful in who they "friend" on Facebook. So make sure you establish guidelines with your teenager (note I didn't say "pronounce guidelines upon them") for safe FB use. They shouldn't initiate friendships with strangers or even friends of friends they don't know. For instance, if your daughter gets a FB request from a friend of a friend in another state, you don't know if that person is really your daughter's friend's friend or not. So teach your kid how to be street-smart. She should decline to "friend" anyone she doesn't personally know.

> *Kids need to be taught to be careful in who they "friend" on Facebook.*

Clearly, FB and other social inventions are here to stay. Kids love cool, new gadgets. We live in a high-tech world. Just imagine what it's going to be like 25 years from now!

The key is to have balance (anybody who is on their FB account six hours a day needs to get a life and find other things to do) and to use common sense. You can teach your kid both.

LIFESAVER

Technology is here to stay, so be street-smart about it.

It Worked for Me

I'm about as non-techie as it gets. I haven't even figured out yet how to pay bills on my computer (yes, I know that's sad). So I was really freaked out when my brother bought my son an iPhone for a birthday/

Christmas gift. All the internet stuff and what I heard about the dangers made me nervous. I didn't want my 14-year-old son to have a Facebook account, and I didn't want him viewing images on the internet.

Then I heard you talk about how technology is here to stay, and how we parents need to get smarter and more knowledgeable about it. So I asked my son to show me how it all worked. He thought it was pretty cool that his "old" mom wanted to know and came to him for help in figuring it out. Now my son shows me things he discovers on the internet and even fun texts from his friends. The technology I feared has actually given us *more* to talk about.

Karyn, Minneapolis

Filthy Language

Talking dirty and cussing are cool things to do in a lot of teenage circles. So many teenagers use the F-word constantly as a given in their vocabulary. Sexually explicit, gross, and lewd language flies out of many mouths. And let's not forget taking the Lord's name in vain—that drives me right up the wall. Every time you use God's name as a curse word, you're getting God's attention—but not in the way you'd want to.

I hope you're not naive enough to think it's only boys who use filthy language, because girls can gross you out as good as any guy on a given day. Even teenagers who know better will fall prey to using bad language due to peer pressure. The drive to want to be like everybody else and fit in is intense during these critical junior high and senior high years. So when you stumble upon your son or daughter using gross language, don't be surprised.

Simply shoot it to them straight: "Honey, do you talk like that? I have to tell you that I'm surprised. In fact, I'm shocked you talk like that."

What are you really saying? "I think better of you than that. And I don't approve of it, nor do I appreciate it." You're raking some coals over the kid's head (and rightfully so). Many parents are reticent to call a spade a spade and tell kids how they feel. That's why so many kids get away with their bad language.

> *Kids don't like it when Mom or Dad is unhappy with what they've done.*

You don't have to demean your teenager when you catch him with filthy language. You don't need to say, "Hey, you no-good so-and-so, how dare you talk like that! Clean it up!" You simply need to reveal your disappointment.

The bottom line is that kids don't like it when Mom or Dad is unhappy with what they've done. They feel guilty—and they should, in this case, to turn around their behavior—and uncomfortable. And that discomfort will bring about change (at least within your hearing).

Can you stop filthy language from exiting your child's mouth? The reality is that kids will talk the way they want to talk. But don't forget that you're like a shepherd with a rod and staff. You help to curb the sheep and move them in a certain direction. But you don't have to whack them over the head and bruise them with the rod and staff.

A simple "I'm disappointed in what you just said" does more than any lecture ever could.

LIFESAVER

Tell the truth in love.

Grounding

"All right, young man, you're grounded!" a mom or dad announces out of anger and frustration. But what does that really mean? Does it mean that, when you're invited to Grandma's house for pot roast on the weekend, the 16-year-old who is in the doghouse won't get to go with you because he's grounded?

In my book, that's exactly what it means. If you're going to ground a kid for an infraction, ground him for 24 hours. If it's a major infraction, ground him for 48 hours. That's an eternity to a kid. But grounding means that he goes nowhere. That means not to Grandma's house for dinner, not to the concert he has a ticket for, not to youth group.

I'm not a huge grounder, but if you're going to use grounding as a discipline, don't use it like most parents use it. I call that "selective grounding"—in other words, grounding kids only from things they want to go to. If you're going to ground, get the maximum bang for your buck. Your kid goes no place. And that includes school. If the infraction happens on the weekend and necessitates your teenager being home from school on a Monday, he or she is fully capable of calling school, getting assignments, and doing the work at home. And if grounding him or her on a school day causes you all sorts of problems—you're a working-outside-the-home parent—then hey, don't do it. Don't ground at all. But if you do ground, target a specific time period and stick to it.

Nothing is sacred. Not even church. If your son gets ready to go out the door with you to church on a Sunday morning, turn to him and say, "Son, where are you going?"

"I'm going to church," he'll say.

"No, you're grounded; you're not going anywhere."

He might say, "All right!" but when you're all out the door without him, he'll feel that curveball you've thrown . . . especially when he doesn't get to go to his favorite restaurant with all of you afterward.

So knock the kid off the plate of life for a few seconds; let him know he's been dealt with.

Contrast that with the ridiculous time-out: "You go to your room!"

Why wouldn't he want to go to his room, when the average kid has every electronic gadget imaginable in there? That's certainly no hardship. The kid's most likely thinking, *All right! A whole night to myself with no hassles.*

So if you're going to ground your kid, don't fling words out in anger like, "You're grounded for life!" That's laughable, because you can't follow through, and your kid knows it. He's got your number.

Instead, ground him for 24 hours, and make sure he goes nowhere. Now *that* will make an impression.

LIFESAVER

Get the maximum bang for your buck.

It Worked for Me

Talk about a whole new perspective on grounding! When we grounded our son Adam after we caught him drinking again, we took your advice. He went nowhere—not to school, not to his job, not to his basketball practice or games—for two solid days. He lost his cell phone and computer privileges too, so he couldn't get in touch with his friends. By the time Friday and Saturday were over, he was a mess. When we handed his phone back to him Sunday morning, he said meekly, "Thank you," and that was it.

A week later, the guys he usually hangs out with were caught drinking behind the school and got suspended.

But guess where Adam was? At home, of his own free will, hanging out in the kitchen with me. You're right. This is the kind of tough love that works.

Nancie, Colorado

Guilt

Stop right there, parent. Did you know that guilt is the thing that propels you to make most of your lousy decisions as a parent?

Guilt runs the lives of too many of us, and kids are really good at heaping it our way. Moms especially fall into this trap. The pleading eyes, the "But, Mom" . . . and the cave-in begins.

> *Anybody can make easy decisions.*

But let's go back to the purposive nature of behavior, shall we? Your teenager knows your soft spot; he knows how to yank your chain, Mom or Dad. And if it worked last time, you can bet that he's going to give it a go again. He's not dumb.

You shouldn't be either. Anybody can make easy decisions. But telling your kid no when everyone else is telling him yes—or when everyone else is doing that thing you don't want him to do—isn't easy. Again, do you want your kid to be like everyone else? Not really. The best decisions you will make are often the difficult ones, but you must do what's right for both your teenager and your family.

Don't let your son or daughter's disappointment, failure, or anger because you're not doing life their way put you on a guilt trip—"Bad, bad Mom and Dad!"

Don't "guilt" yourself. Don't "should" on yourself. Be practical, pragmatic, and balanced.

Guilt only leads to caving in . . . and excuses for caving in . . . and those excuses just make the weak weaker.

So buck up. Do what's right. If you do, you and your son or daughter will win every time.

LIFESAVER

Don't let the guilties run your life.

Hair and Grooming

I bet the first thing you think of when I say "hair" is girls, isn't it? Hair and grooming are especially important to women, and it starts at a young age. Little boys don't walk around with bows in their hair, but little girls do, and they sometimes change the bows a couple of times a day to coordinate with their outfits. Now, boys? If their mom can manage to drag them away long enough from torturing the ants in the backyard, she might be able to get a single jab of a comb down their heads. Boys don't care about hair, grooming, or hygiene. That's why moms get good at the "sniff test" for boys before they go out the door. But then comes the magical day when boys start to notice the opposite sex, and everything changes. They might spend almost as much time as a girl does in front of the mirror, checking out their looks, their breath, their hair, etc.

In the world of hormones—where acne pops up, where the "perfect people" seem to be the popular ones—you need to be your child's cheerleader. No, not the over-the-top pom-pom-donning variety, but the kind who shows an interest in your teenager's world and cultivates her heart.

That means you as a parent need to slow down enough to observe your child—her moods, what she talks about. This is far more important than what she wears or how she looks in the long run.

Trends in clothing and hairstyles change every year. Right now in college basketball, the players' shorts are long, down to their knees, and huge. You sometimes wonder if they'll fall off right in the middle of the action, giving all a game to remember. Look back 20 years to professional basketball games, and you'll think it's weird to see kids playing in short shorts. But trust me, someday soon we'll revert back to that. And 20 years from today, your kids will be laughing at themselves for wearing such baggy shorts when they were in high school.

So styles change, but the heart—how a kid thinks, how he relates to others, how he behaves—stays. Don't lose your kid's heart in the midst of clothing, haircut, or hygiene battles.

It's rare that you have to tell a girl to take a shower because she smells. Often she's the one showering twice a day and changing clothes multiple times. Yet you may lift an eyebrow at the hairstyles she chooses to adopt. But, I ask you, does it really matter 10 years from now if, for a whole year, she wore her bangs so long you couldn't see her eyeballs? (When she eventually gets tired of peering through her bangs, she'll get them cut.) Or if, for a while, she insists on a lavish pink streak in her hair?

No one wants to be around a kid who smells like a dirty sweat sock.

With boys who haven't yet noticed girls (and even some who have but are clueless about what attracts girls), they might need some help. No one wants to be around a kid who smells like a dirty sweat sock. And he's not going to get a girl's attention if he looks like he hasn't combed his hair at least once this century. So if you have a son who loathes water and wouldn't wash his face for a month or shower if you didn't make him, you still need to be the parent. You know good hygiene is important. (Washing his face will likely mean less zits, which he *will* care about, and taking a shower might make him more aromatic to potential friends at school.) So you need to throw the parental flag up, stop the action, and say, "Okay, you need to take a shower." And life doesn't proceed until that shower is completed.

Because the noses of you moms are usually a little more fine-tuned than those of us dads, you are often the ones throwing the yellow flag for shower time. Bless you.

But even when you do have to throw that flag, learn to let some things go. Nothing is perfect in life. Cleanliness is good, but it really isn't next to godliness. Always stay balanced. The pink-streaked hair won't always be there, but your daughter will. So keep the focus on what's important in the long run—your relationship with each other—and let the little stuff go.

And for entertainment in the meanwhile, pull out the pictures of what you used to look like when you were a teenager. They'll be good for laughs . . . and some perspective.

Suddenly your daughter's bangs won't look so bad after all.

Styles are fleeting, but the heart keeps beating.

Homework Battles

Every quarter my youngest daughter's grades are transmitted to me via my computer. I just click on her report card, and *voila*! The grades appear. Yes, I'm the parent, so I understand why the school feels they have to send her report card to me. But the reality is, they're *Lauren's* grades. They're the result of *her* homework. They're not mine.

As God is my judge, I can't remember any of my kids ever asking me, "Dad, would you help me with my homework?" Now, they have asked me to run down to the store and get some poster board and other things like that to do a project. But the reality is that their homework is their homework. I already went through school and did mine. (Well, sort of. To say I was not a prize student is a grand understatement. But then, some of you already know that story if you've read my other books.)

Whose homework is it?

Here's what happens in many homes. Right after dinner, the homework battles start. And they don't end until 11 p.m., two hours after the 13-year-old's bedtime, with tears on Mom's part, slamming doors on the teenager's part, and a raised voice on Dad's part, with a few "Don't talk to your mother that way" comments thrown in.

Let me ask one thing: whose homework is it?

"Well, I'm just trying to help," you say. "After all, I have a degree in education. And I'm pretty good at math."

You don't belong there. It's not your job. It's your kid's job.

So let me ask this: why are you involved in your son or daughter's homework?

Is it because you believe your child has to have all A's to be successful? Or you need to get some psychological jollies yourself out of people patting you on the back to tell you how smart your kid is? But what if your kid is simply average? Every person has their likes and dislikes, their natural talents and areas they struggle in. So if you're overinvolved with your teenager's homework, it would be good to ask yourself why. Do you think she can't do it on her own? Are you afraid she'll fail? Are you striving for perfection?

Parent, you need to step out and let your teenager do her own work.

So where *can* you help?

- Clearly set a time for kids to do homework (for example, 6:00 to 8:00 p.m.), and create a space where they can concentrate without other distractions.

- Help teenagers who struggle with organization learn how to prioritize what they need to do. In today's schools, you can usually go to the computer and find out what your kid's assignments are.
- Consult with teachers when you see your son or daughter struggling.

If you look at the last school year, it's a good indication of what the coming year will be like. Chances are you'll go through the same hassles—only magnified. With that in mind, get your kid some help—but you stay out of it! Instead, hire a tutor to help your child—a college student or even a smart high school student who comes to your home and helps your kid on a regular basis. Places like the Sylvan Learning Center not only assist kids in learning the skills they need to build from in specific subjects, but they also offer study-skills programs that can make a lasting impact on kids' study habits.

Don't allow homework to become a power struggle. Don't allow your kids to needlessly engage you in a battle over homework.

Your kids' personalities resemble a seismograph during an earthquake in Southern California.

And don't allow your son or daughter to stay up late to finish homework. When teenagers don't get sleep, they're cranky with everybody (that includes you) the next day. So do yourself and everybody in your home a favor. Set the homework time, insist homework get done as much as possible during that time frame, and then declare it bedtime—for everyone's sake.

The priority is always responsibility to home, then to school-work, and then to other things like part-time jobs, music, sports, and time with friends. So A (home) comes before B (schoolwork), and then C (other activities, if there's time) can happen. If your son isn't able to accomplish his homework without frustration, he needs fewer outside activities so he can focus on it.

You're through with junior high; you're through with high school. It's your son or daughter's turn. Let it be so.

It's not your homework; it's your child's.

Hormone Changes

To quote my sweet wife, Sande, the worst age for a girl is 10 to 11. Psychologists call it "early adolescence." Girls are beginning their menstrual cycles earlier today than they did in past generations. Though hormones hit boys as well as girls, the impact of hormones seems more pronounced in young women. I always refer to teenagers affectionately as the *hormone group* since hormones dictate so much of what your kids do during these years. The hormone changes set up swift mood swings that pop out in phrases like, "You never let me do this" or "You always do that." Hormones set up the extremes from which teenagers operate.

During these critical years, your kids' personalities resemble a seismograph during an earthquake in Southern California. Your kids are not always in control of their emotions, which means that when they're engaged in battle, either with each other or with you, somebody's got to blow the psychological whistle. "All right! Everybody to neutral corners. Let's take a time-out and come back when everybody's calmed down. Then, whatever the issue is that started this family explosion, we'll get to it."

And when you come together again, talk rationally. Allow each person a chance to speak without being interrupted, and give each other a chance to clarify what was said so there is no misinterpretation. Letting a bit of air out of everyone's tires will help prevent minor irritations from becoming major blowouts. It also teaches your teenagers that the best decisions are made when everyone is calm and not in a state of upheaval.

Especially for Girls

Menstrual cycles set up all sorts of emotions in girls—they're crabby, overwhelmed, achy, hurting, overemotional. The smartest thing any mother can do is to prepare her daughter at a young age for the experience of menstruation (since girls can start their period as early as 9 or 10), so that the young girl isn't overwhelmed or surprised when it happens. If this stage is presented as a normal part of life and a step in becoming a young lady, just as is her development of breasts, pubic hair, and hair under her arms and on her legs, your daughter will be well-prepared. But don't stop with just preparing her for the physical changes and how to handle them. Also tell your daughter about the emotional changes she'll go through during that cycle. Some girls struggle greatly with PMS, feeling bloated and depressed. Other girls aren't affected at all. If you see your daughter struggling with these symptoms, talk to your local pharmacist or doctor. There are all kinds of products that can help during that critical week.

It's also important that your daughter feels like she can share any emotions with you—in a respectful way, of course—without being judged. Her changing hormones are also preparing her for interest in boys (to a greater or lesser extent) and for motherhood. All of a sudden your 12-year-old daughter, who didn't give babies a second look before, now thinks they're "cute." That change is a natural preparation for dating, marriage, and having children someday. Girls who know what to expect and can talk about those emotional changes with their mothers, and who have understanding fathers, navigate their growing-up years with far less intensity.

Especially for Boys

Trust me, there's not a man on this earth who couldn't tell you about a wet dream he had. For those who are ill-informed, a wet dream is one that culminates in a young kid experiencing an orgasm during his sleep, associated with a dream that would be far too graphic to describe in this book. For those of you ladies who are saying, "What is all this about? My son wouldn't have one of those!" pull aside your husband and ask him if he ever had a wet dream. Depending on his level of stupidity or his bravery, he might just share that with you.

You would be wise to prepare your boys, even at the age of 11 years old, about what will happen to them and why. You can say something like, "Someday you might wake up with semen in your underwear, some wild thoughts, and a racing heart, and be shocked, wondering what just happened. You might be tempted to find a match and burn your underwear. But don't waste a good pair of underwear—just throw them in the wash. Wet dreams are okay; they're normal. Girls get periods, you get wet dreams."

Then, when your son has his first wet dream, it will connect in his mind. *Hey, Mom and Dad aren't as out of it as I thought they were. I remember them telling me about this.* Even if you have the sweetest 11-year-old boy in the world, someday he will think (even if briefly) that you're an idiot walking around, merely because he's an adolescent and knows it all.

Preparation is the name of the game. Whether you have a son or daughter, you need to have a conversation with your kid that runs something like this:

"A lot of things are going to come up in your teenage years that you're not sure about. You might tell yourself, 'I could never talk to Mom or Dad about this stuff.' So let me tell you flat out that whatever it is you're thinking about, I'd consider it a privilege if you'd talk with me about it. And that means anything that comes into your head in the next few years. You'll have mean kids at school who will dis you. You'll feel out of it, like nobody cares. But you need to know that I care about you and everything about you. If you're ever in a situation that you shouldn't be in and don't want to be in, call me. I'll come get you, no questions asked.

"I'm not in charge of your life. I don't run your life. You do. But I want you to know that I have confidence in you to make good decisions in life. The temptation will always be there to be cool. 'Be like us, snort this, drink that, smoke this,' kids will say. But I believe you're strong enough to stand firm and stand for the things we believe in as a family. And I'm proud of you."

Preparing your teenagers for the normal hormone changes of adolescence, expecting the best of them, and having a healthy sense of humor are musts for living with the hormone group.

LIFESAVER

This too shall pass.

Hugging . . . or Not

I learned something a long time ago. In the adult population, there are huggers and non-huggers. Have you ever hugged a person who is as stiff and straight as a board? Clearly, it's not a behavior they're used to, nor are they comfortable with it. In the same way, you'll find teenagers who are huggers and comfortable with displaying affection in public. It's really nice to see a young man who will hug his mom in front of a peer group. Pretty cool, in fact. Okay, Mom, so some of the credit for that has to do with who you are, but even more has to do with who your son is.

Then there are other teenagers who are more comfortable keeping others at arm's length. They might also want you to walk five steps behind them. And they certainly don't want you to hug or kiss them in front of their friends. Some will even say, "Hey, drop me off here."

"Here?" you say, befuddled. "But we're a block from school."

"That's okay. Just drop me off."

What is your son really saying? "Sorry, Mom, but I don't want to be seen with you, and I don't want to risk you embarrassing me by saying, 'Bye, honey, have a good day' and blowing me a kiss in front of my friends."

> *Don't take it personally.*

Don't take it personally. Your teenager is groping to find his own way in life; he's trying to cut his own path.

And if you have more than one teenager, keep in mind that your kids are different. Your first son might hug a tree if you give him the opportunity. If that's the way he is, it's a good guess that your second son will be somewhat distant. Or if your firstborn is reserved and introspective—a kid of few words—your secondborn will have the warmth of Bill Cosby.

Welcome the differences rather than being offended by them.

LIFESAVER

Always treat your kids differently, because they are different.

It Worked for Me

Boy, am I glad I talked to you about hugging my teenage son. I'm a hugger; my son is not. I had no idea how much I was embarrassing him by trying to hug him in public. And I was taking it personally when he didn't want me to hug him or stick around at his school events. Now I know that's just part of growing up and becoming his own person. Thanks for helping me get my head on straight . . . and my son says to thank you too.

Denise, Florida

Internet Use

Go back five years, and you might find people like myself giving suggestions to a parent to make sure the computer is in a neutral place—a public place—in the home. You would hear experts say things like, "Don't let your kids have a computer in their bedroom. The idea is to be on top of what's going on, to be able to walk by and see the screen at any time."

Today I'd tell parents that's probably the least of your worries. Teenagers have phones and computers with internet access 24-7 if they wish. You can't know every site they are accessing. Yes, there are history buttons on computers, and yes, you can be the POS (Parent Over Shoulder) and take a peek at what your kids are up to every once in a while. But many families don't have just one computer today; they have multiple sources for internet use, including several computers and cell phones.

That means, for the most part, your 11- to 17-year-old kid can access anything on the internet that he wants to . . . with or without your permission. Not only that, kids hit the internet for everything from schoolwork, to downloading or listening to music, to searching out facts they're curious about, to interacting with friends. There are schools in Tucson, Arizona, and in other areas of the country where everything is done by computer. There are no textbooks, just the internet. Want to read chapter 5 in your social studies book? Go online and read it on the computer or your iPad.

Parents, here's where the hard work you've put into your kid pays off. Yes, you can give your kids guidelines, including not to divulge personal information or family information to strangers on the internet, and you'd be street-smart to do so. But having positive expectations and trusting your son or daughter to do what is right will go further than any rules when it comes to internet use. If you've instilled your family values in your kid—in a healthy, balanced way—and have lived out those values in front of your kid, he or she has a higher probability of absorbing them than if you pull them out of your back pocket and start lecturing your teenager (but secretly do the opposite in your own life).

Here's where the hard work you've put into your kid pays off.

Let me include a short note here about gaming (playing computer games on the internet with a group of people). I don't know much about this area myself since I don't play games on the internet, and none of our five kids were into gaming. But a good friend of ours is. He and his teenage daughter play games on the internet with a group of like-minded folks for two hours every Friday night. It's their "daddy and daughter time," and they play with a group of 10 other friends on a carefully monitored site where a select group of people has agreed on the rules, the type of language that can and cannot be used, and the comments and behavior that are and are not acceptable. If anyone steps out of bounds, they are banned from playing the game again.

Many internet-savvy teenagers who like the interactive world of games are drawn to gaming. It can be a complex, time-consuming world that's exhilarating to many kids. Like anything, if played on "safe sites," where the play is monitored and offenders are kicked off, it can be a fun, relaxing time (especially for kids who are loners and have difficulty making friends at school). But, as with all things, anything taken to an excess is not good. Gaming once or twice a week for a few hours of needed relaxation is a good thing. Gaming each night and entering the world of the game so much that you live there constantly in your head is not good. It can create an emotional rift in families and with friends and a psychological dependence on an unreal world.

The internet is here to stay. Teach your kid to be street-smart about it, encourage balance in all things, and realize you can't control everything in his or her life. Just remember that your words of encouragement, belief, and trust matter far more to your teenager than you think. Your son or daughter will rise to your expectations.

(LIFESAVER)

Balance is important—in all things.

Interruptions

You expect interruptions from a younger kid when you're talking on the phone, but what if your 14- or 17-year-old makes it difficult by getting in your face when you're on the phone?

Say to the person you're talking to, "Excuse me a minute," cover the phone, and say to your kid, "I'll talk with you in a few minutes." Go back to the conversation. When the conversation is over, tell your kid, "I was absolutely disappointed that you would come in and interrupt my phone conversation." Give your kid "the look."

> *Give your kid "the look."*

Remember, parent, that your teenager wants to please you, and he doesn't like you being disappointed with his behavior. Note that you're not cutting *him* down; you're telling him you're disappointed with *his behavior*—the words that came out of his mouth and his pushy demeanor.

Then let it go at that. Hopefully, your words of disappointment will bring forth an apology from the kid. Even if they don't, he'll think more the next time before he interrupts you.

205

If the behavior continues, I'd inflict some discipline on that teenager. If he has a cell phone, lock it up for a couple days so he can think about respecting others' phone time in the family.

LIFESAVER

Teach respect, restraint, and responsibility.

It Worked for Me

Our house is crazy. We have two dogs, a ferret, and two very loud teenage boys a year apart. I've never been able to have a phone conversation without being interrupted. One of the boys always bursts in and instantly "needs" something. As the only female in the house, I desperately need some girl time, so I gave your advice a try.

Within two minutes of me being on the phone, my older son came into the room and yelled, "Mom, I need . . . "

I said "Excuse me" to my girlfriend, covered the phone, and told him I'd talk with him when I was done.

A minute later, he interrupted me again. This time I ignored him, walked into another room, locked the door, and continued my conversation. The boys started fighting out in the hallway right in front of the door and kept it up. I could barely hear my girlfriend over the ruckus, but I filled her in on what I was doing.

"That explains it," she said. "I hope it works." And she laughed.

When I finished, I opened the door, caught them wrestling in the hallway, and gave them both "the look." I told them quietly how disappointed I was in both of them—that one had to interrupt me in the middle of my only girl time, and that both had to fight right outside the door where I was talking.

Then I turned and walked away.

The wrestling stopped. There was dead silence.

Usually I'd yell at them and tell them to cut it out. This time I stayed calm and went to the kitchen to do the dishes.

An hour later, I overheard the boys tell their dad, "Uh, is Mom sick or something? She's acting kinda weird."

The "kinda weird" stuck. I only had to play through that phone interruption scene one more time the next night before they got it: leave Mom alone if she's on the phone. What a relief. Thanks for the tip!

Annie, Seattle

Junk Food

I have one question: where is all that junk food in your cabinets coming from?

The answer seems pretty simple to me. Our society basically encourages people to eat poorly. (Though I do admit I see more people in grocery stores now reading the fine print on products.) Sugar and sodium are huge contributors to many of the diseases prevalent today. Parents and schools don't help. Most school districts publish their lunch on the internet, or it comes home on a monthly calendar. Take a quick peek at the menu, keeping in mind this is the *educational system*.

The professionals in education would tell you we feed our kids chicken nuggets, pizza, and hot dogs because those are the only things they'll eat. But the bad habits start with what we feed infants in our society. So many things you buy off the shelf for baby foods aren't exactly nutritious stuff; they give babies a taste for sugar. Most kids develop poor eating habits early in life. I even read about a lawsuit where someone sued McDonald's because McDonald's "made" them fat. Talk about passing the buck! But in our society, it's never anyone's fault. Taking personal responsibility has gone the way of the dodo bird. Parents believe in discipline until you discipline their kid at school, then they show up with an attorney in tow.

> *If you're the one bringing it home from the grocery store, stop. Find healthy alternatives.*

So if junk food is a big issue to you, let's not pass the buck. If you're the one bringing it home from the grocery store, stop. Find healthy alternatives for your diet. Yes, I realize it's a challenge to do so with hectic schedules and fast food so easily available. But if you have to pick fast food, go for the healthiest kind you can find, or pick one of the couple healthy items on the menu.

You as the parent and authority in the home have control over what's consumed in the home. Most likely you're buying it. So buy the good stuff! Eating too much junk food leads to all sorts of health problems, not to mention weight problems. People today are growing fatter and more out of shape than ever before in our history. You'd think with all the attention on health clubs that we'd be further down the line.

But then, if you take a look at my silhouette, you'd be thinking I ought to read my own book. Personally, I just have to tell ya, I always enjoy a bowl of fat grams or carbs. . . .

LIFESAVER

Garbage in, garbage out.

Know-It-Alls

Know-it-alls are extremely annoying, aren't they?

Even more, they've set up the greatest temptation for you to engage in battle with them. You know that what they've said isn't true, nor is it accurate. And you, being the parent, have that *need* to set the record straight. . . . But don't.

The reality is that the most teachable moments for Mr. or Miss Know-It-All will play out in a very natural way. Let's say you know your 13-year-old daughter's paper is due on Monday morning. Do you rag on her all weekend to get it done? No. I'll say it again: whose homework is it?

> *Let the natural consequences take care of themselves.*

Sunday night rolls around. She's sitting with her siblings in the family room, watching a movie. You know she hasn't done anything on it. Do you remind her? No.

The more prudent thing to do is to send an email to her teacher on Monday morning:

> To my knowledge, Annabelle hasn't done a lick on her paper due this morning. I thought it would be best if you would talk with her.

The street-smart parent enlists the help of a third person— someone who doesn't live with you. Then it's easier for those natural consequences to play out.

Let's say that your son is going out the door without a jacket. You've heard the weather forecast for rain and sleet starting in the afternoon. You tell your son, "Honey, your jacket . . ."

"Oh, Mom"—he rolls his eyes—"I don't need one. It's not gonna be that cold."

So be it.

After school, when it's sleeting, your son will probably wish he had a jacket. Maybe, just maybe, freezing a little might translate into listening to what Mom has to say . . . or at least being more open to it.

If your child has health issues, though, then your kid has you over the proverbial barrel, because the natural consequences of not wearing a jacket might have dire medical effects on a kid with asthma or low immunity. Then you pull out the parental ace and say, "I know you don't want to wear a jacket, but it's going to sleet this afternoon, and you're going to wear one."

Just remember: save your parental aces for where they count. Let the natural consequences take care of themselves. They'll be a better teacher than you can be at this stage in your son or daughter's life.

LIFESAVER

Know-it-alls won't know it all for long.

Lack of Motivation/Living Up to Potential

Most kids who lack motivation do so specifically for a reason. It goes back to purposive behavior. What's the purposive behavior of a kid not doing any homework? Of a kid who seemingly fails every subject he takes? The irony is that many times kids who aren't completing their homework, aren't participating in class, and are failing tests are actually really bright. They could do the work, and they could do it well. Then why are they so undermotivated?

You don't have to look too much further than you, parent, to find the answer. Ouch, that hurt, didn't it? But bear with me for a minute. If you're one of those parents who has pushed, who has high expectations for your kids, who is quick to point out every flaw, who says, "Hey, what's with the B on your report card?"

(when it's one B in a string of all A's), you're creating the kind of conditions in your home that will catapult your kids into an unmotivated state . . . and keep them there.

Kids who live with unrealistic expectations and perfectionism fear success.

"Wait a minute, Dr. Leman," you're saying, "you meant to say they fear *failure*, didn't you?"

No, I mean they fear *success*. They're doing failure pretty well.

Like John, a sophomore in high school who used to be a solid B student . . . until his freshman year, that is. Then he decided he could no longer compete with his brilliant older sister, who was a junior, or ever jump over the high bar of his parents' expectations for him. Now he's doing straight F work in just about every subject—even the ones he used to love and do well in.

> *Kids who live with unrealistic expectations and perfectionism fear success.*

Kids who feel pressure to always measure up, to do things perfectly right, are kids who are most likely to go down the path of choosing to do nothing. After all, if they're successful at all, they'll *always* have to be successful in their parents' eyes, and the stress is too great.

A watched late bloomer never blooms.

And there are late bloomers in life. I was one. I didn't bloom until I got thrown out of college, became a janitor, and was going literally nowhere in life. However, looking back, I now realize that the time I started blooming was when my brother, five years older than me, moved away, and so did my older sister. I was at home alone with my parents. It was the first time I didn't have Super Brother or Super Sister hanging over me. They'd gone on to their adult life, and I no longer lived with the weight of their successes every day.

Sometimes circumstances of life force a kid to reevaluate and get motivated. For me, that moment was when I was 17 and graduating from high school. All my friends were heading off to college, but no college would take me. That stark realization turned me around. I began to get serious about heading somewhere in life.

> *A watched late bloomer never blooms.*

When a kid lacks motivation, that behavior serves a purpose in his life. He might be getting negative attention from Mom or Dad, but at least he's getting attention. By lack of motivation, that kid is saying, "I can't measure up to what you think I ought to be, so I'm not even going to try."

So what can you as a parent do?

First, back off on your expectations. Encourage him in what he does well. Take the pressure off.

Second, if you have an eighth grader who is 12 or 13 and failing miserably at school, ask the school to hold the kid back. Let him repeat eighth grade. Give him a do-over so he can go into high school more prepared.

"But, Dr. Leman," you're saying, "what's that going to do to his psyche? It'll damage it tremendously."

Can anybody tell me what a psyche is?

Let's get past the psychobabble and realize, as Harry Truman once said, "The buck stops here." You may have to pound on an administrator's desk to get her to retain a kid in seventh or eighth grade. Most public schools have swallowed hook, line, and sinker the idea that "self-concept" (what a kid thinks of himself) is more important than academics (a kid's performance at school). After all, we wouldn't want to crush little Buford's self-esteem, now would we? However, if little Buford is flunking everything in school, he doesn't have much self-esteem to start with!

If you give your child another shot at the same grade, you are treating him in a respectful manner by saying, "I know you're struggling, so we're going to give you a do-over."

You might notice that I'm using a boy for an example in this scenario. That's because statistically and psychologically, there is much more credence to holding a boy back than a girl. Boys, by their nature, are about a year behind girls in their maturity.

But you also might want to be inventive. If you're retaining a kid in seventh or eighth grade, you might move that teenager to another school to make the do-over a little easier.

> *The do-over might change his life for the good.*

If you think holding your kid back is a tough call, then let me ask you: if you don't take that kind of decisive action, what's going to change your kid? When is the motivation light going to come on?

Kids today can slither through school and graduate near the bottom of their class, or not graduate and get a GED. They may mature and grow up, and the lightbulb goes on. Then they go to a community college, get good grades because they're motivated, and can transfer to most state schools on a basis of their work at the community college.

But wouldn't you rather your kid gain some proper motivation now?

It's time to take a careful look at your own expectations of your teenager . . . and to fire up some motivation in him. Repeating a grade won't hurt his psyche. The do-over might change his life for the good.

LIFESAVER

The buck stops here.

It Worked for Me

You hit the nail on the head when you talked about perfectionism and critical parents on your recent radio show. I didn't think I was perfectionistic or critical, but I was wrong. I had no idea my behavior was causing my daughter to flunk math. She'd stopped trying, and who could blame her? I'd always ask her why she got a B when I knew she was smarter than that. Then she started getting Ds and Fs, so we took away her privileges, but that didn't help.

Then I realized I was the one who needed to change first. I told my daughter that I knew math was hard for her, and I was sorry I had made it even worse. I asked her what I could do to help her. That little talk opened up our communication. Yesterday she came home with a C on a math paper. I could tell she was nervous showing it to me. But when I saw it, I told her, "Great job. I know you've been working hard, and it's paying off." She looked startled, but then she smiled.

You're right, Dr. Leman. The change in my kid had to start with me. I just wish I'd been smart enough to figure it out earlier.

Kurt, Tennessee

Loner

When you hear the term *loner*, usually it's said with a negative connotation, implying socially isolated people. Many times those who commit heinous crimes are described as loners. But a lot of well-adjusted people could be labeled as loners as well. They tend to be firstborn and only children. Books are some of their best friends. They have no problem entertaining themselves, they tend to be introspective, and they are often uncomfortable socially. After all, they were the first or only kid in the home, relating to adults most of the time instead of other children.

I can't tell you how many times in my practice as a psychologist that parents would bring me their child and describe her as a loner. They were concerned because she never invited other kids over to their house, and she didn't hang out with a peer group. Instead, she loved to read fantasy and sci-fi books and spent a lot of time writing her own music.

> *A lot of well-adjusted people could be labeled as loners.*

There are three types of people: people who love people, people who love data, and people who love things. A common thread for loners is that they tend to be people who love data and things. They're not people persons. In fact, being in large groups can tend to exhaust them.

So when parents bring me a child they describe as a loner, I ask, "Well, what about the other kids in the family?"

"Oh," the parents say, "she's an only child."

"Case dismissed," I say. "Go home and sin no more."

For the record, only children, though they might have some loner-like characteristics, do really well in life. Take, for instance, people like Anthony Hopkins, Robert DeNiro, Brooke Shields, Elvis Presley, Barack Obama (please spare me the emails about Barack Obama having a sister—she's a half sister, nine years removed from him; therefore he's a functional only child), and businessmen Carl Icahn and Thomas Boone Pickens, as well as Hall of Fame football players Joe Montana and Roger Staubach. Not everyone is social or into friendships. If your kid isn't, you ought to be jumping up and down right now. If your kid has some loner-like qualities, she won't be drawn into the destructive behavior that many teenagers get into in order to be accepted by their peer group.

Then again, if your loner seems depressed, is wearing nothing but black, isn't doing well in school, doesn't communicate with anyone (even you), or doesn't do much of anything, you've got a problem. It's time for a little visit to your local shrink.

Take a look around at the loners you know who are adults. They're quiet people—people of few words. But often they're brilliant. Why not let your kid get to know some of them? You could have them over to your home for dinner sometime.

The important thing is to realize that we're all different, and to respect those differences rather than trying to squeeze your kid into a mold of what you think she should be.

LIFESAVER

We all walk to the beat of a different drum.

Lying/Dishonesty

When kids lie, the ideal response is to have a calm dialogue about why they lied. Some teenagers may not even be aware of why they lied or be able to articulate the reason. But most kids who lie on a regular basis have parents they perceive to be too controlling, too authoritarian. The only way those kids think they can get any freedom in life is to lie. They're afraid that if they tell you the truth, they'll get in trouble.

But lying breaks down respect between the two of you. So if your son or daughter is lying to you, say, "The fact that you're lying to me is a problem, because it means I can't trust you. Now you tell me, would I be smart or stupid to hand the car keys over and to let you go on a weekend trip with your friends if I can't trust you?"

If your 11-year-old daughter continues to lie to you, give her vitamin No for *anything* she asks for until she comes to the realization that something is up. When she gets a clue about it, she'll likely protest, "Hey, what gives? You always let me do . . ."

Now's the teachable moment. "Well, we had that discussion about lying, and my trust level in what you say has dropped a lot because you're continuing to lie. So now I can't believe you about anything. That means you don't go anywhere until you learn that honesty is the best policy.

> *Give her vitamin No for anything she asks for.*

"In fact, life will work out better for you, and you'll have more freedom, if we can have honest dialogue. Even if it might be something you know I don't want to hear, I'll respect you for telling the truth. My vow to you is to always tell you the truth too, but I'll go a step further. I will always want to know how you feel about it because I want to be more respectful toward you."

Win your teenager's cooperation. As your son or daughter begins to see you as a partner—with each of you telling the truth to the other—the lying will stop. And when it does, your kid gains more freedom again.

LIFESAVER

Honesty is always the best policy.

It Worked for Me

I was shocked the first time I found out my 14-year-old son had lied to me about where he was after school. Then I found out through another mom that it wasn't the first time my son had lied. I took your advice and asked him straight-out why he'd lied. He got that "uh-oh, I'm caught" look. When he finally told me the truth—that he lied because he thought otherwise I wouldn't let him do anything or go anywhere—I realized just how much of a smother-mother I am.

I'm now learning to trust my son and let him go (still very hard, but I'm making progress). He's learning to tell me the truth, even when he knows I don't want to hear it. We're starting to develop a relationship based on trust.

Hannah, North Dakota

Me, Me, Me

The phrase "me, me, me" pegs our current generation. Most parents have brought up kids to think they're the center of the universe. With the slightest effort they make, today's kids are enthusiastically greeted with "attaboy" or "attagirl" and "I'm so proud of you!" Under the guise of the verbiage that positive statements will help our kids' self-esteem, we go overboard and lavish on the praise. But many times it's false, empty, and of no value.

For those of you who are people of faith, you'll find that nowhere in the Bible is there a reference to a person's "self-esteem." I'll just let it go at that.

Then again, maybe I won't. Be humble, be forgiving, be gentle. . . . Well, you get the idea.

Yet we're driven as a society by the whole false premise and concept of self-esteem. Think carefully for a minute. Is positive self-esteem an attitude you really want to strive toward? Talk about "me, me, me"—that's exactly what you'd get!

If you look at the teachings of Jesus, you don't hear about "me, me, me"; you hear about others. Jesus himself washed people's feet to prove a point.

Instead of worrying about your child's positive self-esteem, why not look for ways that you as a family, including your kids, can give to others without expecting anything in return? When you have a heart for people, you don't have to look far to find people in need. Your teenagers should be part of that. During holiday time you'll see a lot of people taking on projects as a family, but what about the rest of the year? It ought to be an ongoing project.

We Lemans sponsor a couple of kids through some programs in third-world countries. Could we do more? Absolutely! But at least the Leman kids learned early in life that others matter; life isn't all about them. They didn't go around every corner asking, "What's in it for me?"

Some people who know our family today think it's a miracle that we're all givers. But to me, the results are fairly predictable. The five Leman kids are givers—there's not a taker in the bunch—because in our home, we focused on giving to others.

It's also interesting that, opposed to their baby-of-the-family father who likes the limelight, our five kids actually shy away from it. They have a very humble attitude. I was intrigued some time ago, while looking at my son's Facebook page, to see what he said for his occupation. The job title he entered? "Helper." In reality, Kevin Leman II is the head writer of an Emmy Award–winning television show, the funniest one in daytime television. And he's hilarious. But he is as laid-back as a comedy writer could be, gets along with everybody, and is known for his honesty, integrity, and giving nature.

When you have a heart for people, you don't have to look far to find people in need.

If you think it's impossible for a teenager to think beyond her own skin, you're wrong. But in order for her to do so, it's important that you model giving—and that you consider others' ideas worthy of your time and attention.

As you do, thus will your kid do.

LIFESAVER

It is more blessed to give than receive.

Messy Room

This has been a problem for parents since time began. I'm sure even the caveman's son was reminded to pick up his furs from the family room. If I walked into my youngest daughter Lauren's room right now, I'd see stuff all over the floor, including a glue gun, paper, and sparkly items. Lauren is a detailed worker, and she's always making things. She spends hours crafting handmade gifts for family members, not only for birthdays and Christmas, but for other times too.

> *I'll come into her room sometimes, shake my head, and say, "This is a masterpiece."*

I'll come into her room sometimes, shake my head, and say, "*This* is a masterpiece." It's my way of saying, "Hey, Lauren, I notice your room."

Those of you who feel your teenager's room ought to be cleaned every day and be neat as a pin, well . . . you can go there, but it's probably not a good idea. In my estimation, that battle isn't worth it. If the mess really bothers you, close the door. But if it's a big thing to you to have your kid shovel out her room a couple times a week, then say, "I know this is your space, your room, but you are a member of this family, and your room is part of a house that we own in conjunction with the kind lender down the street. So we

220

respectfully ask that you clean it two times a week. You pick the days." Preferably one would be Saturday, when the kid is more likely to be home.

If your teenager disregards your instruction, then hire a sibling to go in and clean the room, and pay that sibling out of your teenager's allowance. Or hire a neighbor kid to go clean the room. Or even pay yourself a handsome salary out of your teenager's allowance to clean it. That will get the message across quickly (especially since teenagers don't like anyone else touching their stuff).

That simple solution also represents real life. You can either take your car to the car wash and pay nine bucks, or you can wash it yourself in your own driveway and keep the nine bucks. In the same way, your kid can either pay someone to clean her room or can clean it herself and keep the money.

No room for arguing there.

LIFESAVER

Let your home reflect the real world.

Money Matters and Jobs

If I listened to everybody who talked about me when I was a kid, I could certainly conclude that I wasn't going anywhere. I did poorly in life and in school. But, in looking back, I was actually quite an enterprising kid. I rescued golf balls that went into the creek from the local country club, and I had a fruit stand.

Times have changed since that fruit stand, though. Today the financial future not only of individuals and families but of our country is in jeopardy. Entire countries in Europe are on the brink of financial collapse.

What you think about money and how you treat it are big things that affect all of life. (Interestingly, money is mentioned well over 100 times in the Bible.) Money issues surround all of us: the huge debt our country is saddled with; the economy struggles; the high cost of college education; the failure of retirement, with cities coming out publicly and saying they can't pay the retirement checks of their workers. In such a milieu, it's critical that you teach your children to save money (and, if you are a person of faith, to tithe money) and to spend the money they do have wisely.

> *What you think about money and how you treat it are big things that affect all of life.*

Teach your kids about finances as early as possible. Purchase some stocks or bonds in your child's name; that's a great way to educate kids about the stock market and how it works. And by doing so, you're conveying, "You need to understand these things, because the government isn't going to take care of it for you."

Social security as we know it will be tremendously different 25 years from today. The retirement age will go up in order to make it easier for the government to deal with the massive numbers of baby boomers hitting that age. Your teenagers need to understand that they had better be in charge of their own financial wellness.

That's why, if your teenagers are willing to put five bucks into a savings account, match it with your own five. Let your kids see that money grows and creates interest. But the willingness has to start with them.

"But, Dr. Leman," some say, "money is the root of all evil. The Bible says so. Aren't you then putting too much focus on money?"

No, the Bible says that the *love* of money is the root of all evil. Check it out for yourself in 1 Timothy 6:10. You need to raise streetwise kids who realize that their financial security has more to do with their judicious choices regarding money than anything the federal government or an employer will do for them through a retirement fund.

Allowances

I heartily believe kids should have allowances.

I can hear some of you right now: "Dr. Leman, that's easy for you to say, but we're just eking by."

But you spend money on your kid anyway, right? You buy him school clothes; you give him money for lunch or buy groceries to make a lunch. Why not put some of that into allowance form? Give your kid some control over money and how it's spent. If you do, he'll learn the value of a buck, because it'll pass through his hand . . . all too quickly the first few times around. But as he gets more accustomed to handling money, he'll get smarter about managing it.

It also gives you some teachable moments and leverage in other situations in the home. If your teenager doesn't complete his expected chores and you have to ask his younger sister to do them, the next allowance he receives will be a little short. Whatever you had to pay your daughter to do your son's job has been deducted from his allowance.

Kids will learn quickly when you use that simple solution. I guarantee it.

Jobs

Should a teenager have a job outside the home?

It's healthy for kids to have part-time jobs. They can make a fortune babysitting. I always tell parents that the best babysitter you can get is a 12-year-old girl who has not yet discovered the wonder of boys. And they're cheap labor.

Kids can mow lawns, do yard cleanup, do housecleaning, etc., even before they're 15 or 16 years old. It's good for teenagers of any age to have to listen to what someone else—the boss—says about how a project needs to get done. It gives them a little taste of what life's about . . . and the working knowledge that they're not always in the driver's seat. They don't always get to take breaks when they want to; they take breaks when they're told to.

However, it's important that kids realize that work is a *privilege*, not a *right*. The priorities are always in this order: home, school, other things (including work). So your teenager should work only if she is contributing to home in a proper way, and if her performance at school is acceptable (note I didn't say *perfect*). Then work can become one of the "other things" she does. Working is a privilege to be earned if the other two main areas of life are taken care of.

If your teenager is working outside the home, but now you have problems at home because he's not doing what he ought to do around the house (for example, you've told him three times this week to take the garbage out, and that's three times too many), when do you pull the rug? If you're in that position, call the manager of the store and say, "My son has been working for you for seven months and enjoys it. From what I understand, you are satisfied with his work. But in all fairness to you, I wanted to give you a heads-up that he may not be able to work much longer. He's got responsibilities here at home that he's not taking care of, and we believe his first responsibility is to his home, then school, then other things, which includes his job. And by the way, this is not a confidential conversation—feel free to talk to my son and let him know I called you."

> *Working is a privilege to be earned.*

I can read your mind right now. You're thinking, *What do you mean, call the manager of the store? Shouldn't you talk to your kid and give him a warning first?*

Well, warnings aren't a part of this game plan. If you really want a new teenager by Friday, these are the kinds of actions that will get your kid's attention. Actions that will stop him in his tracks and make him say, *Whoa, my parents are really serious about this.*

Keep in mind that, in most homes, parents warn, coax, bribe, and threaten, yet no behavioral change occurs. Well, *Have a New Teenager by Friday* is no ordinary book. But I guarantee you that if you begin to do things differently, you *will* have a new teenager by Friday.

Parent, you're not helpless. You hold all the aces. Sometimes you have to pull one out and use it.

It Worked for Me

I've always been big on our kids working outside the home somehow once they reached the age of 13— whether it was mowing lawns or bagging groceries. I grew up working when I was a kid, and I wanted our boys to understand the value of hard work. Two of our boys have done well, juggling home and school with their work. Our middle son loves his job, but his grades started slipping and his attitude at home took a nose-dive. We took your advice and pulled him out of his job. He wasn't happy, but he didn't have a choice. You're right. Sometimes a parent does have to pull out that ace card and use it.

Jeff, Nevada

Savings/IRAs

When I was a 14-year-old, I was seen as a goofball. But this goofball was actually caddying at the Country Club of Buffalo, carrying two golf bags at a time (called a "double"). I was getting paychecks of 70 bucks a week—a lot of money in those days. Looking back, I realized I was making pretty close to what my father was making. I was also a careful saver. I worked hard and put money away.

Seeing how that mind-set paid off for me, I've encouraged my kids to do the same.

When our kids worked at summer camps and earned money, I would cash their check for them, acting as their bank. But what I actually did was put their check into an account for them. I would pay them the full amount of their paycheck so they'd get the money they'd earned as a result of their hard work, and then I would deposit that paycheck in their account, thus matching what they earned. It showed them that saving a little at a time could add up faster than they thought. All our kids had IRA accounts to give them a nice start. With many banks and even some stocks and bonds, all it takes is a hundred bucks to kick off the savings. Why not give it a try?

College/University

Have an honest discussion with your son or daughter about scholarships, grants, and borrowing money for college. I personally know some young people who are coming out of colleges being $240,000 in debt! For parents in modest income ranges who have kids who do well in school, wow, are you blessed. Your kid will apply for financial aid or grant money, and they won't have to pay it back. But for those of you who don't fit into that category, let me ask you: is it really worth your kid going four years to a school and feeling weighed down by that much debt, unless he or she has a very specific goal in mind, such as becoming a medical doctor? Why not be creative? Have your kid go to community college first for general classes, figure out what he wants to do, and then transfer to a school with a major that holds his particular interest. Also, there's nothing wrong with your teenager working a year or two or after high school if he isn't sure what he wants to do.

And let me make a personal plea here. If you are able financially to pay for your kids' college or a portion of it, do so. Don't let your kids leave college or university with an insurmountable weight of debt to start life just because of the "principle" that they should pay their own way. Help however you are able to. But also keep honest communication between you and your college student so you know your investment is being made wisely (i.e., your student is going somewhere—toward a real degree and a job potential, instead of just checking things out—with all that money you're spending).

LIFESAVER

Money does matter . . . greatly.

Mouthy

When your kid gets mouthy, your first instinctive reaction is what? You want to throw him under the bus. But don't retaliate. In fact, I'd suggest that you get quiet, stay quiet, and show some distance in your demeanor (your body language, your tone of voice).

Inevitably your son will approach you because he needs something. "Mom, do you know where my sweater is?"

Just say quietly, "No."

"Can I run over to Jack's house and shoot some hoops?" he asks.

"Uh, no, you can't."

Use as few words as possible. Then wait for the teachable moment—that time when your teenager will come to you and say, "Hey, what's with you?"

Now the spotlight is turned on. It's your time to shine. What are you going to say?

"Do you really want to know what's with me?" you ask in a calm tone. The kid nods. "Then I'll tell you. I'm very unhappy about the conversation we had two hours ago."

Notice that's all you say. You don't belabor the point. You end the conversation there. You put the tennis ball on your kid's side of the court.

Now it's his call—whether he wants to continue the conversation or not.

He might say, "What's the big deal?"

If so, he's not ready to hear the truth. Some kids are slow learners. So let it go . . . for now. You need to deal with the situation, but trying to deal with it like you would a puppy who has gone potty on the rug—by rubbing his nose in it—won't work.

> *Wait for the teachable moment—that time when your teenager will come to you and say, "Hey, what's with you?"*

Continue your quiet, distanced demeanor. Your son will see your different behavior, your attitude, your lack of action. Eventually he will come back and will usually say, "Sorry, Mom, for what I said."

You accept that apology. You affirm that you love him. Life goes on.

But now's the *real* teachable moment. No doubt your kid is going to ask for a favor.

"No, Jake," you'll say, "we're not going to do that."

You don't explain why; you just state the facts and let him draw the conclusion of why. *Oh, I can't go to my friend's house now because of what I did this morning.* Your kid will figure it out; trust me.

But parent, you can't afford to back down. If you want a new teenager by Friday, there must still be consequences for his earlier behavior. You can't do things the same old way that got you into your current position. You have to do things differently. That means making a decision and sticking with it.

God didn't put you on this earth to be run over by your kid. When you throw your kid an emotional curveball—something he doesn't expect to happen—you teach a lesson.

Throw 'em an emotional curveball.

Music

Every generation has their music. When Elvis first appeared, TV pioneer Ed Sullivan made it clear that they would only film Elvis from the chest up. He wasn't sure America was ready for those gyrations. In 1964, the Beatles were considered "outrageous" for the way they wore their hair. Now think about the content of artists today like Eminem, 50 Cent, Snoop Dogg, and Lil Wayne.

Music has changed with every generation. Not many parents in recorded history have said, "Wow, I love my kid's music." But the smart parent will find something good to say about that music— whether it's the beat, the singer's voice, or the subject of the music.

When you and your teenager are listening to music in the car, say, "Honey, can you turn that up a little bit?" If the lyrics are crappy, your son or daughter will likely be embarrassed. But no matter what the lyrics are, listening to them together gives you the opportunity to discuss them with your kid.

There is some music—if you can call it that—from rappers that is downright disgusting, filthy, and demeaning to women. You have to draw the line on those things. But you also need to realize that your teenager may have no idea what she's really singing.

I sang along with songs for years before I connected the dots of what the lyrics were really saying. I have the peppy song called "Oh, What a Night"—made popular by Frankie Valli and the Four Seasons—on a 45 in my jukebox; I sang along with those lyrics for many years as an adult before I figured out what they really meant: they were describing a guy's first night with a prostitute.

A lot of teenagers don't connect the dots with the music they're listening to either. If they turn up the car radio and are singing along happily, with no embarrassment about some of those kinds of lyrics, you'll have a good hint that your child is clueless about the true meaning of the song. If they get embarrassed, *voila*—they are caught in the act and know that you know that they know what they're listening to. And they're less likely to listen to that song again . . . at least in your hearing.

> *Not many parents in recorded history have said, "Wow, I love my kid's music."*

You may not like the beat, etc., of your teenager's music, but there is value in talking with your son or daughter about the lyrics of songs and why some lyrics are acceptable and some aren't.

Music is such a huge part of our lives; it's pervasive in our society. Even in a restaurant, there's always a "musak" background.

I wish I could live long enough to see some of the teenagers today dancing at their fiftieth high school reunion to the music they grew up with. That would be entertaining, wouldn't it?

And now a quick word about music lessons. If music lessons are *your* dream for your teenager, not hers, don't go there. All you're asking for is trouble. Go take lessons yourself instead.

Some kids have an inclination for music. If so, furthering their curiosity, letting them experience an instrument and practice it, and paying for music lessons can encourage that natural interest. But what if your teenager starts an instrument and, a few weeks later, wants to quit? The Leman rule is always this: you can pick one activity per semester, but once you pick it, you have to stick with it for that semester.

But let's say your teenager has taken music lessons since she was eight. Maybe she does need a break for a year. It wouldn't be the end of the world to take a pass and give her a breather.

On the other hand, there are a lot of musical adults today who say, "I'm so glad Mom and Dad didn't let me quit, even when things got hard." If that's part of your concern, then get an honest appraisal of your son or daughter's talent in the musical field. If your kid has a gift in music, he or she should be encouraged to allow it to flourish. But would I force a kid to continue lessons? No. If your son or daughter loves music, he or she will come back around after the break. If not, you'll know that too.

The long and short of it is, don't go to war over your teenager's music, whether he or she is listening to it or creating it.

LIFESAVER

Every generation has its music.

It Worked for Me

Your talk about kids and their music put things in a completely different light for me. I grew up in a very conservative home, where "you don't drink, don't dance, and don't go with girls who do," and I've had a difficult time handling my kids' music. It just seemed so vulgar. But your tip to listen to the lyrics instead of the beat was a good one. I was amazed to realize that many of the lyrics my son and daughter were listening to were actually positive ones. And it gave me a chance to discuss the few negative ones I heard.

When I told my son the other day in the car, "Hey, turn that up; I want to hear it too," he looked at me and grinned. "You're all right, Dad," he said. Just goes to show that even an old dog can learn new tricks.

Randall, Kentucky

Name-Calling

When teenagers name-call, they normally do it to their brother or sister. To me, it's reminiscent of two otters playing by the side of the river. They slap each other, run away, and circle back, and then, when the slapping gets too intense, one or both of them takes a little swim break.

What's the purposive nature of name-calling? Do they do it because they really don't like their brother or their sister? That could be. But it's probably more likely that they don't like their brother or sister all the time. Being around anyone 24-7 can be wearing.

But the crux of the issue is the competition. Name-calling is a competitive sport. Your kids are all about going back and forth with each other enough to try to get you involved in their competition. That means their fighting and name-calling really is an act of cooperation.

The smart parent removes the name-calling siblings from the scene into a room by themselves or, even better, outside, if you live in a moderate climate. Why is outside the best? Because it dramatically shows your kids that name-calling is not allowed in your house. If they want to name-call each other, they can do it outside the house and out of your hearing. (Which, of course, ruins the fun of it.)

So after you usher them out the back door, say, "I'm so disappointed that you, at 15 and 16 years old, act like little kids going after each other. It's getting old. It's time for the two of you to grow up. You need to solve this. If you continue to name-call each other and fight about the Xbox, I'll step in and take care of it. But you won't like my solution."

Then you firmly shut the door. Taking the battle outside your hearing can take down the temperature in your home. You don't get ticked off because you don't have to listen to it. Your kids are less likely to name-call each other if they think they'll be put outside the door for doing it.

Let the peace reign.

LIFESAVER

Fighting is an act of cooperation.

Oversleeping the Alarm

"Oh, I know what you're going to say on this one, Leman. You're going to say, 'Hey, he slept through his alarm, so the little sucker can get his tail out of bed and walk himself to school.'"

Wrong. My advice is that you offer to *drive* your son or daughter to school.

With that in mind, let's change the scene a bit. This is the third time in a week that your teenager has failed to get up for school on time. Now you're talking about a horse of a different color.

Every kid on the planet has forgotten their lunch or a homework paper at one time or another. So if you're going to drive by the school an hour later, there's nothing wrong with dropping your kid's lunch or homework off. That's a kind thing to do. We all forget things. Every step in life doesn't have to be a teachable moment. Parenting should be tempered with grace, kindness, and affirmation of the fact that we're all imperfect.

Some kids who are heavy sleepers will sleep through their alarm clocks. But I'm talking about a kid who is chronically not getting up. This is a kid who, even when you wake him up and try to get him going, won't get up. So on to Plan B: tell the administrator of the school that your teenager has no reason to be late. Ask the attendance person to call your kid in once he does get to school and have him explain why he's late. It's almost always better to have this pressure coming from a third party.

On to Plan B.

If your kid has to walk to school for one reason or another, so be it. If you end up being the driver, notice that your teenager may try to pick a fight with you on the way to school. After all, somehow this is your fault because he didn't get up. When that happens, just smile. As he exits the car, say, "Have a great day, honey."

And life will go on. Don't get suckered in; don't engage in battle. Don't get on your high horse: "I don't understand why you, a 15-year-old, can't be responsible enough to get to school."

Save your breath. Let the principal, the dean of students, the attendance person, and the teachers do the work for you.

It'll stick more.

LIFESAVER

Save your breath.

Overwhelmed by Life

All of life doesn't have to be scheduled, nor should it be. Constant activity is not good for anyone. So why is your kid running full speed on a conveyor belt? Is it because her mantra in life is "I only count when I'm doing something"?

Every kid needs some downtime, including yours. Even though some kids seem to measure up to all the stress of their activities, all that busyness won't be good for them in the long run. So the next time your kid's soccer coach approaches you and says, "Hey, your son's really good. I want him to be in city soccer—the all-star traveling group. It'll be every weekend for several months, traveling to play soccer against other teams," think for a minute.

You can have the greatest Diehard battery in the world, but if you leave the lights on, eventually the battery will wear down.

Most parents would say, "Hey, what a wonderful opportunity! That's better than selling drugs on the corner, isn't it?"

Well, let me think about that for a minute. Yeah, I guess it is better than selling drugs on the corner, but being on the traveling team means your kid will miss family pizza night, won't worship together with you, and won't have any break between Friday and Monday. It'll be go, go, go, with no downtime.

You can have the greatest Diehard battery in the world, but if you leave the lights on, eventually the battery will wear down.

Hans Selye, one of the first psychologists to write about how the body reacts to stress, made the point that each of us has *adaptive energy*. Adaptive energy is that reserve—that extra battery—that kicks in and gets us through the next day, the next week, the next month, when our original battery runs down. However, we've all read stories about entertainers, performers, and actors collapsing on stage. What were they hospitalized for? Exhaustion. Exhaustion is the last stage Selye wrote about—basically you can burn the candle only so much until you get to a point of exhaustion, whether physical or mental or emotional. Teenagers should never even be close to that brink. They need to be kids and to spend time doing things they want to do, without constantly being evaluated or having a grade or performance review at the end.

And by the way, parents, take a look at your own schedule. Are you running flat out? If so, it's time to make a change. We all are given the same 24 hours a day. The question is, how do we choose to spend that time? When people say, "I can't change that," what they really mean is, "I'm unwilling to change that." Parents who schedule their kids' lives full of activities often get a psychological boost out of knowing that their kids are successful in so many areas of life. It gives them something to talk about to their friends. Many parents vicariously relive their own lives through their kids, placing their own unfulfilled desires and wishes on them. But is it healthy for either the parent or the child? No.

Everyone needs the opportunity to breathe, without something or someone breathing over them.

LIFESAVER

It's time to chill.

It Worked for Me

You caught me. After I heard you speak last week, I went home and took an ax to my schedule (well, not literally, but you know what I mean). The next day I showed my two teenage daughters what I'd done and said that I wanted to see what we could trim from their schedules too. I was amazed by their response. They seemed relieved. One was happy to give up the speech meets she'd been doing for years. In fact, she said she was kind of tired of them. My other daughter cut two activities. We decided we'd make the change at the end of the semester, two weeks away. Not only will we save ourselves money, but we'll save ourselves a lot of stress too. Thanks for the kick in the seat of the pants that I needed to get proactive, instead of sitting back and just letting life happen and getting overwhelmed.

Annemarie, Ohio

Parties

There are parties that are harmless, and then there are parties that are dangerous. When your teenager is talking about going to a party, the first couple questions you ask are:

1. Whose home are you going to?
2. Will an adult be there?

Parents, be careful about what home your kid visits for any reason. Best-case scenario: if your teenager is going to spend time in someone's home, know the parents well and visit the place yourself to know whether it's a safe environment for your kid or not.

But let's face it. There are going to be parties your teenager attends that you won't know about, especially since such events tend to happen spontaneously. Teenagers usually aren't the most planned-in-advance individuals. And most parties are held in places where adults are not around. They consist of drugs, alcohol, music, and sex, and kids are getting wasted, throwing up, and engaging in all sorts of under-the-cover activities that I need not describe in this book.

By and large, most parties are not good for teenagers . . . ever. Once kids hit the 15- to 17-year mark, the parties they're having are not the fun, innocuous ones they had at nine years old, when they were pinning the tail on the donkey. The stakes have been raised big-time.

When parents go away for a weekend and leave a 15-year-old home, they're certainly rolling the dice.

Even good kids do stupid things. Take, for instance, some friends of mine who left their 17-year-old—a very responsible, good kid—home when they were away for a weekend. Adam was certainly the kind of kid you didn't have to worry about. His parents decided he could have a buddy spend the night with him to keep him company.

> *With parties, you can expect the unexpected . . . even with good kids.*

Well, it turned out that Adam and his friend decided they wanted to have a few people over. Word spread that Adam's parents were gone for the weekend. Soon the whole school showed up, brought six-packs, and started drinking. A few hours later, the boy was stunned to see the damage done to his home and his mother's prized rug, and to find out that some items had even been stolen from the house.

Recently, my son, who is over 30 years old, ran into a friend of his at Disneyland. His friend introduced him to the young woman by his side.

"Kevin Leman," the woman said. "Oh, right, you live in Tucson. I was at a party at your house."

Kevin, who grew up with the Leman stance on no parties, said, "I don't think so."

"Did you have a house that steps down to a big family room on the bottom floor?"

Kevin was startled. "Well, yeah."

"Then I was at a party at your house."

Now Kevin was intrigued. "Oh, really, when?"

"When my friend Jake was watching your house for your parents."

We found out 13 years later that, unbeknownst to us, the young man we had stay in our house to take care of our pets had a huge party while we were gone!

It all goes to show that, with parties, you can expect the unexpected . . . even with good kids.

Knowing that someday your teenager will end up at a party where he doesn't want to be, it's important for you to have an upfront pact with your kid so that if he's ever in that situation, he can call you and you'll come get him, no questions asked. If it's a spontaneous party happening at your own house and he doesn't want it to be that way, you'll call in trusted neighbors . . . or the police.

You see, it's a matter of safety.

Your teenagers also need to know some basic party rules:

- If you are ever at a party where a kid is drinking profusely—for example, chugging down a fifth of bourbon—there's a high probability he will kill himself. It happened when I was a dean of students at the University of Arizona. If you see things like that, you need to call 911 immediately.

- Say no to drugs or alcohol of any kind. Don't even start down that road. Just say, "I'm a Smith, and we Smiths don't drink or do drugs."

- Never put your beverage down; keep it in your hand and in front of your eyes. If you forget to keep your eye on it, throw it out and get a new one when you need it. Not everybody is like your mom or dad or your sweet aunt who makes apple pie for you. There are people in life who will abuse you, rape you, use you, and kill you.

- Call Mom or Dad immediately, no questions asked, if the party is starting to get out of control in any way.

Kids will want to get together. But it's important to know who is supervising, where your teenager is, and that your son or daughter knows basic party ground rules.

Even better, if your teenager is dying to go to a party, have it on your own turf, where you can set the rules and be the ever-present watchdog, ready to blow the whistle if anything is heading south.

Still better, help your teenager find healthy activities where he or she can interact with like-minded kids one-on-one or in smaller groups in more controlled, less potentially dangerous settings.

LIFESAVER

Trust your kid, but cut the cards.

Peer Pressure

Peer pressure, like sibling rivalry, has been around since the days of Cain and Abel, and will continue to be around. It is a major influence in any teenager's life. However, the *degree* to which peer pressure influences your kids depends on how secure they feel in your home. Your home is a safeguard that allows your teenagers to be able to resist the temptations out there in the peer group. Kids will be more easily able to resist peer pressure when they are reared in homes where:

- values are lived out instead of being crammed down their throats;
- they are accountable for their actions and had to own up to mistakes they made;
- Mom and Dad are readily available to discuss topics of concern, attend events their kids are involved in, and make family fun and family dinners a priority

Your son will shake his head and say about the partiers in his class, "Those guys are jerks. They're messing up their lives."

Does that mean you isolate your kids to protect them from what's out there? No. Nobody wants to be a pheasant under glass—most particularly the pheasant. You need to make your teenagers aware of the pressures and temptations around them—drugs, alcohol, sex, bad-mouthing, gossip, etc. But if you partner with them, sharing in their victories and in their defeats, and expect the best of them, you'll be amazed at what your kids can stand against, even in tough times.

Your kids want to please you.

If your kids had to pick between parental expectation and peer pressure, the hands-down winner every time would be parental expectation. That's because, at their core, your kids want to please you. And they're not happy when Mama's not happy and Daddy's not happy.

You have a larger impact on your teenager than you think.

LIFESAVER

Don't sell your parental power short.

Physical Development (or Lack Thereof)

Physical development is a difficult issue for both sexes. Kids always speak from extremes: the short kid always wishes he was three inches taller; the tall kid always wishes she was three inches shorter. Sure, from a parent's perspective, "You are who you are. One of a kind. Not like anybody else." But in a world where it's tough to stick out in any way, kids who are "different" (ahead of or behind in physical development) can have it rough. How can you help? Affirm your son or daughter for who he or she is, pay attention to your kid's heart, and make your home a safe haven. But also use your head in realizing how your kid could be treated in his or her peer group as a result of physical development (or lack of it).

Boys

Boys who are *behind* the curveball in growth get the toughest rap of all. First of all, boys usually are a year behind girls in their maturation. That means if you're a little slow in physical development, there will be girls in your class four inches taller than you. You might have a squeaky voice, while the other boys in class have hairy armpits and every marking of a man. When you're trying hard to be macho and compete with other guys, being shorter or smaller can be very emasculating.

> *When you're trying hard to be macho and compete with other guys, being shorter or smaller can be very emasculating.*

Take Randy, for instance, a technically brilliant kid who is 14 but looks like he's 10. All his athletic classmates are stretching toward the basketball hoop and look like junior highers or even beginning high schoolers. But Randy? A playground monitor recently assumed he was in a much younger grade (worse, she said that in front of his classmates). That same day a girl in his class decided to give him two new nicknames: "Girly Boy" and "Short." How do you think Randy felt when he went home that day? And why do you think he played sick the next day so he didn't have to go to school?

Feeling not big enough to compete in a big-boy world can have a lot of emotional and psychological effects on boys. That's why I tell parents they are wise to hold boys back a year from kindergarten—especially if they don't seem ready and are close to the cut-off age. If you give your boy the head start of a year to mature, he'll be less likely to lag behind the pack in physical development.

How can you help? Giving that boy the opportunity to talk through his feelings and the events that happen during his day is very important. Maybe it can happen at night as you're sitting on the edge of his bed. Tell him stories about buddies of yours (or maybe even you) who got picked on for being short or small; then at their 10-year high school reunions, they were bigger than the other guys who picked on them. For instance, I know a guy who's now 5'11" but who was 4'10" in high school—he looked like a sixth grader with a chemistry book! And then he grew 10 inches in one summer. Such stories don't help with all the flak in the interim, but it might help your kid gain some perspective.

Since competition is the name of the game for boys by their very nature, when you're the runt of the litter, you're the one who's going to get picked on. I remember one party when I was 16—in those days the parties were pretty tame, but there was usually somebody sneaking a beer out back—and I was hanging out with some boys in a rec room. Next thing I knew, out of the blue, I caught a fist on my jaw and went sprawling. Somebody had dared a guy to slug me, and he did! For no reason! That's the world of boys. All kids do dumb things, especially boys.

But here's what else happens in the world of boys. At the end of one school year, he might look like an 11-year-old kid. But when he comes back to school, he has shot up five inches, has a deep voice, and looks 14.

Boys who develop quickly seem to get all the perks: they look like men, sound like men, and can even get older girls' attention. They also have the competitive edge in sports. What's not to like? But their lack of maturity can sometimes get them into situations where they shouldn't be. For example, they might look old enough to pass for 18 years old, which means they can start running with an older crowd. At a young age, they can get themselves into some dangerous partying, drinking, or illegal drug situations. Also, older girls assume they're older and can take advantage of them. Males aren't the only sexual predators in this day and age.

Girls

The biggest difficulty for girls are those who are *ahead* of the curveball in physical development. Girls generally mature a year earlier than boys. If your daughter is 13 years old and put together in a nice little package (including a 36-inch bust) that makes her pass for a 17- or 18-year-old, that's trouble in a bottle. Even though her emotional maturity is just 13, her physical maturity will certainly attract older guys. And because she looks more mature, she'll likely see her school-age peer group as very immature. Her natural migration will be to older groups . . . and that can have consequences. The difference between an early developing girl and an early developing boy is that the girl will be noticed by males; most males who develop early get only a passing look from girls. That's why the stakes are higher for early developing girls.

> *Girls generally mature a year earlier than boys.*

If your girl has a figure that will catch a male's interest, make sure you discuss with her why it's important that the type of clothing she wears is carefully monitored.

What can a parent do for a daughter who looks older than she is? Be watchful that she doesn't fall into an older peer group. You definitely don't want her dating early. Encourage interactions with girls her own age.

Girls who are underdeveloped have similar kinds of issues to boys who are underdeveloped, except for one thing: it's more acceptable in our society for a girl to be underdeveloped than for a boy to be. For parents of girls who are underdeveloped, I have some important advice. If your daughter is 11 and all the other kids in the class have a training bra (or more), get your daughter a training bra too—even if she has nothing to train (and I mean *nothing!*). Gym locker rooms are a cruel world for both boys and girls.

———

All kids want to be in the middle; no teenager wants to stick out on either side. The middle school world in particular is all about not being different—about being one of the crowd. If a kid has acne, develops early or late, has a disability, or has a big nose or ears, he or she could become an insecure kid's punching bag. Whoever is different will be pounced on and ridiculed. And that never feels good.

That's why the degree to which your kid feels positive about herself going into the teenage years will make all the difference in helping her navigate the many mazes of adolescence. Every day where she is different can be excruciating and seem never-ending. A parent needs to be aware of how painful it is. (This is a good time to look back on your own adolescent years and a time you were picked on for being different, and to relive those emotions.)

Am I saying that you should coddle and feel sorry for your kid who is different in some way? No, you should reassure him that, before long, he'll change. Partner with your kid to listen to his woes, encourage him in all the things he's good at, and help him focus on who he is—on the inside.

LIFESAVER

You are the psychological blankie for your teenager.

Piercings

One night my 15-year-old son, Kevin—reminiscent of many a teenager—blurted out during dinner, with no warning, "I'm gonna get an earring."

Well, I wish you could have seen Mrs. Uppington's face. I mean, she came unglued. With an expression of horror, she gave me "the look" (we husbands know all about what that means), then pointed to her ear. All as if to say, "Leemie, say something. Did you hear what your son just said? He wants to get an *earring*!"

> *All kids want to be in the middle; no teenager wants to stick out on either side.*

You would have thought Kevin II said, "I love Satan."

The kid simply wanted an earring.

After dinner was over, sweet Mrs. Uppington was in my face, reminding me again as if I could forget: "Kevin Leman, I want you to talk to your son."

Notice: it's "*your* son."

She continues. "You tell him he is not going to have an earring!"

After about three days of Mrs. Uppington chewing on my ear (and not in an affectionate way), I took matters in my own hands.

I showed up at dinner with an earring in my ear.

Much to my dismay, as I sat waiting for his response, Kevin II didn't notice the thing. He was a teenager, eating like a pig at a trough.

Then I moved and got myself in a little better position for viewing.

He caught a glimmer out of the corner of his eye and looked at me. Narrowing his eyes, he said, "You look absolutely ridiculous."

"Really?" I said. "Your mom likes it."

Now Kevin Leman II is past 30. I think it's a safe bet that he's not going to get an earring.

Some of you reading this book have body piercings. Some of you have tattoos. You paid a good buck for them, and you love them. Well, call me old-fashioned, but my advice to parents in regard to body piercings is this: body piercings are okay once your son or daughter is of age and they're paying for them.

You can heartily disagree with me on this issue, and that's fine. If you do, let me say this right now: anything you see in this book that you don't like, you can cross out. In fact, you might run across a page or two that you vehemently disagree with. You have my advice to shred those couple pages. Tear them right out of this book. No two people will agree on everything, so much about life is a judgment call. All I'm saying is that if you want to be a street-smart parent, there will be times you reach in your back pocket and throw the orange flag.

Right now I'm reaching in my back pocket for that orange flag and making the judgment call about piercings.

If you want your kid to look like a pierced something-or-other creature, and that's okay with you, then so be it. In some cultures, it's common to pierce a baby's ear. I don't have problems with ear piercings, but anything else pierced is an extreme measure.

You have to remember something else. Teenagers live in their own world, not an adult world, and don't really care about the adult world. Teenagers look at each other and say, "That is so cool. I want one!" But your son or daughter won't stop to think, *Hmm, I wonder what my potential boss will think about my nose ring and lip ring when I apply for that accounting job someday.*

> *Your son or daughter won't stop to think,* Hmm, I wonder what my potential boss will think about my nose ring and lip ring when I apply for that accounting job someday.

The hormone group has a different culture, a different language, and a different perception of what reality is. This group isn't savvy about thinking ahead, to how the body piercing might affect their life someday.

Kids grow up too quickly in society. Why else do you see a four-year-old with a Mohawk? What do you think when you see that?

I think, *What is wrong with those parents? Did they really want a Mohawk for their kid? Is that the parents' way of saying, "Hey, I want to make sure my kid is cool"? Or did the kid say, in a moment of impulse, "Hey, I want a Mohawk," and the parents were stupid enough to agree?* Either way, those parents are dumb as a rock.

Oh, I love my judgmental self!

You, the parent and authority figure, need to draw the line on some things. My line is, okay, if you want a pierced ear (note: one hole in each ear), that's all right by me. But when you start piercing other body parts or your ear multiple times, and there's more metal on you than an ultralight aircraft, and you can barely lisp out words because of your tongue ring, there's something wrong.

Parents, don't forget that, to others, body piercings imply an attitude. It's amazing how quickly jewelry that calls attention to itself gets removed when college graduates start job hunting and receive their first few rejections based on their looks.

LIFESAVER

Appearance counts.

Place of Worship

Does your teenager have to go to your place of worship with you? (If you're not a person of faith, you can skip this section and go on to the next.) There are two schools of thought on this.

First Perspective

When your kid gets to the point that she says, "I don't want to go with you," what do you say?

"Okay, honey, talk to me. Why don't you want to go?"

Let your adolescent tell you specifically why she doesn't want to go:

- "The pastor is boring."
- "I get nothing out of the messages."
- "The kids there are a bunch of geeks."
- (You fill in the blank, because you've probably heard a bunch more reasons.)

Be honest. "I have to agree with you," you tell your adolescent. "The preacher has a long way to go. Some days I find myself dozing off. And yes, some of the kids are geeks. But you know what? We worship together because we have a deep faith in God as a family, and we've agreed that worshiping together is a healthy thing for all of us.

"I was thinking the other day that there aren't many things we tell you that you must do on a weekly basis. So considering your negative feelings about it right now, I want you to know how much I'll appreciate you getting dressed this morning and going with us. I'll know as I see you sitting two seats down from me that even though you really don't want to be there, you respect and love this family enough to go with us."

In my book, that's probably the best way to handle the situation.

Second Perspective

Some places of worship have youth groups that are terribly boring . . . and others have ones that are downright fun, and the with-it youth pastors tune in to youth culture. Worship becomes, at that youth group, a fun experience with music and topics kids can relate to, as well as great group activities. If your adolescent is involved in such a group, fabulous! But a lot of parents get upset because their kid insists on going to a different place of worship than them because he wants to go there for the youth group.

Parent, if this is your situation, be thankful to God that you have a kid who wants to go at all. So lay off! Do everything you can to allow your teenager to get to the other place as often as he wants. Visit the gathering yourself and make it a point to tell the youth pastor, "We go to [name of the place of worship], but our son really loves your youth group. You must have great things going on, because he always wants to come. Thanks for providing such a place for him."

A good, active youth group is a wonderful support and encouragement for an adolescent. It's that healthy "third party" from which your teenager can gain wisdom and guidance. So do everything you can to keep your kid in the flow.

May I remind you that 90 percent of Americans *say* they are Christians? But what they really mean is: "Well, it says on the coin, 'In God We Trust.'" Wouldn't you rather your adolescent grow up with a developing, healthy, personal relationship with God? The place where it happens doesn't matter; it's the experience that counts.

So win the cooperation of your teenager by allowing her to make some of her own decisions, like where she wants to go to youth group. Allowing her to choose will help her to "own" her faith and make decisions about how to carry it out, even before she's out of your nest.

Win the cooperation of your teenager.

Pornography

Last week you, Mom, found your 13-year-old son ogling a porn site. What do you say? Where do you start? Especially for a mom who has lived a somewhat modest, fairly straight life and finds her son viewing some of the most disgusting pornography you could imagine? Most moms would change their son's name to Isaac and try to kill him on the spot. But that's not a good idea.

Pornography is one of the most highly addictive behaviors that anyone can engage in. Personally, I think it has the strength of the addictive powers of crack cocaine. The images that your teenager sees can't be easily erased from his mind.

People define *porn* in a lot of different ways. Some people think the *Victoria's Secret* catalog is pornography. But the pornography I'm talking about are the sites that your kids access on their phone and on their laptops, which display women in indecent attire (or no attire) and in lewd positions with men, other women, or solo.

> *Pornography is one of the most highly addictive behaviors that anyone can engage in.*

Sadly, pornography on the internet isn't going away. So what do you do if you find your son engaging in it?

First, be honest about how disappointed you are to find him on that site. "I have to tell you the truth. I really thought you were above that. Now I see clearly that isn't true—you're not above that. And I'm greatly disappointed."

Let that sink in for a minute, then continue. "I'm glad to see you have an interest in the opposite sex. But this sex isn't as God created it to be. This is a perverted form of one of the greatest gifts God has given us."

Notice I've chosen Mom to talk to her son, not Dad, because who better than a woman to talk to a boy about how women want to be treated? Not a woman on this earth wants to be compared to some porn site. Not a woman on this earth enjoys being used or abused.

A kid who is most likely to visit porn sites in great regularity is usually the teenager who feels inept in relationships with the opposite sex. It's also the kid who has begun having wet dreams and doesn't know what to do with them. This is a kid who is just beginning to experience the fact that certain parts of his body are more pleasurable than others. In all probability, he's probably masturbating on a regular basis.

If your son wants to learn about sex, he needs to learn about it from you. There are lots of books available, including one of my favorites: *A Chicken's Guide to Talking Turkey with Your Kids about Sex.* (I've already mentioned it, but it bears repeating here.)

To call a spade a spade, sexual sin is a life-changing decision you make that can affect your entire life—it's another part of why I call these the critical years.

That's why it's so important for dialogue to take place between mom and son regarding what a healthy sex life is and how girls want to be viewed and treated. There's not a kid on the planet who wants to hear about his parents' sex life, though. If you don't believe that to be true, just put down this book for a second. Hold this place with your thumb. Now, think about your mom and dad having sex. . . .

"Ugh, Leman, did you really have to write that? You just ruined my day."

The other day, at one of my seminars, a woman looked me in the eye and said, "My mother wouldn't do a thing like that."

I couldn't help but think, *Then how did you get on this earth?*

So, Mom, when you discover your son's interest in porn, take advantage of this rough spot in life to teach him what's special about sex. (Girls aren't immune to porn either, but it's less likely to happen with them; however, when it does, you're in the hot seat, Dad.)

Call me a dinosaur—"a hunka hunka burnin' love" dinosaur—but this is what I believe: the best sex is sex that occurs within the safe confines of marriage, with two people who really love each other, have committed to each other, and know each other intimately.

Tough talks end up being the best talk.

It Worked for Me

I never thought pornography would touch our family until Jason, my 14-year-old, started accessing porn sites on his iPhone. His sister caught him at it and told me, even though he begged her not to. I was sick that my son had willingly seen such images. I took away his iPhone and made him sit at the kitchen table and write a five-page paper, using my computer for research, on what seeing pornography does to your mind and heart.

When it was time for his play practice, I took your advice. He didn't go anywhere. In fact, I had him call the director and explain why he wouldn't be there. He got an earful from the director as well, since he had a lead role in the play. But I told Jason that life wouldn't continue until the paper was done and we'd had a chance to discuss it. (I've never seen my son write a paper so fast.)

That was one of the best discussions Jason and I have ever had in his teenage years, because he had to face up to what he did and how it will affect him from now on. He lost his computer privileges for a week, had to explain to his teachers why he couldn't get his papers done, and lost the use of his iPhone completely for a month. During that month I had a phone expert delete all the porn links from his phone and clear out the previous history. That way I could tell, going into the future, if Jason was continuing to access those sites.

Six months later, I'm still really watchful since I know porn is addictive. From time to time, I check out the history buttons on his computer . . . without him knowing. But I'm so glad we caught it as early as we did.

Linda, New York

Power Struggles

Here's the guarantee: if you engage in a power struggle with your teenager, you lose. Every time. And for one specific reason. You have much more to lose in a power struggle than your kid does. When you're slugging it out (figuratively speaking, of course), and you have an audience of either strangers or friends, yeah, they might be looking at your kid. They're saying to each other, "Whoa, that kid is over the top. A real piece of work." But trust me, they're mainly looking at you, saying, "What the heck kind of parent would let a kid get away with acting like that?"

> *No one wins in a power struggle.*

Socially you have much more to lose than does your adolescent, who lives life moment by moment anyway. (You deal with the embarrassment a lot longer.) No one wins in a power struggle.

Previously in this book I mentioned how important it is to remove your sails from your child's wind. Let the winds blow, then retreat and get quiet. Go into silent mode and wait. It won't be too long before that hormone-group kid needs or wants something. When she does, give her vitamin N (No). Again, remain quiet and wait.

Sooner or later, she's going to come back with, "Hey, what's going on? You haven't let me do anything. Everything I ask for, you say no."

"I'll tell you the truth," you say calmly. "I'm blown away by what you said earlier this morning. I didn't like the words you chose to use with me, or your attitude. And I didn't like the look on your face."

Then turn your back and walk away, because at that point there's another opportunity for a major blowout.

What you really want is for your teenager to "get in touch with her feelings" and realize that what she said was hurtful, irresponsible, and highly disrespectful. She owes you an apology. Now you need to stick to your guns without shooting yourself in the foot. Do not let life go on for that teenager until an apology comes.

However, resist the temptation to say, "You owe me an apology." Think about it for a moment. Do you really want her to apologize to you because you've told her that she owes you one? Nothing is accomplished if that happens. The apology is simply too easy.

> *Resist the temptation to say, "You owe me an apology."*

However, if the kid comes to her senses and apologizes of her own free will, at least you have the satisfaction of knowing that she is capable of apologizing and has done it with some degree of sincerity.

Now let's address boys for a minute. They are much like their counterparts—grown men. When a grown man has a disagreement with his wife over something, then they have sex, the problem is solved in the man's mind. However, for the woman, the problem still remains. In the same way, if a boy smoothes over a disagreement with his mom, once the apology is given, life is clear sailing again. So of course he'll come back after the apology and ask for a privilege. However, for the mom, the problem still remains in her mind.

What can a mom do to bridge that gender gap? The same thing she does with her daughter. Say, "Not today, honey. Let's revisit that idea tomorrow."

It's a gentle way of saying, "There are boundaries and guidelines in this family. When you step over the line, there are consequences. And you're experiencing those consequences right now."

LIFESAVER

Stick to your guns
without shooting yourself in the foot.

Pregnancy

Chances are, by the time you hear about your daughter's pregnancy or your son's girlfriend's pregnancy, she's going to be at least three or four months along. After you get over the initial shock, the question floods in: "Now what do we do?"

Recently I was asked by two sets of parents in that position to sit down with them and the young parents-to-be and be a part of their discussion. The young woman was adamant about not having an abortion, which I applauded. However, as the discussion progressed, it became very clear what this young woman and her family had in mind. The 15-year-old would give birth, and the child would be raised in her home with her mom and dad.

Whose child is this?

I thought, *Whose child is this? Who is going to raise the child? Who is the child's mom? We're talking about a 15-year-old girl. She's not old enough to drive a car, yet she's the mom.*

At that moment I could tell you what was going to happen. That child was going to be raised by Grandma and Grandpa. The 15-year-old would go through life like the baby was her brother or sister, not her son or daughter. The young woman would finish out the year by correspondence or transfer to another school to finish high school. Then she'd be off to the university. With her child in tow? No, the child would remain with Grandma and Grandpa.

Some people would say, "Well, what's wrong with that? You yourself applauded the girl's decision not to abort the child."

Yes, but there's a primary question that's missing: what is best for that child growing in the 15-year-old's womb?

Secondly, what is best for the young man and young woman, the parents of the child?

As I brought up these things to the two families and the parents-to-be, I could see in the young man's eyes that he agreed. He wasn't happy about the direction the conversation was going.

Before I left the room that day, I pointed my finger at each individual and said the same thing to each of them: "You're selfish."

Let's just say their expressions didn't mirror gratitude. In fact, the look in the eyes of Grandma (the mother of the pregnant girl) was about as close to pure venom as I've seen.

But then again, the family had asked me to sit in and give input. So even if you, reader, disagree with me, I'll give my input.

The best place for any child to grow up is in a home with a mature couple—a mom and dad who love each other.

Grandparents today are rearing kids in huge numbers because their kids have been irresponsible in their lifestyles. But let's go back to the primary question: is that really the best thing for the *child*?

I believe the best thing any pregnant-out-of-wedlock girl can do is to find a loving couple who shares the same faith, basic principles, and values she holds dear, and then give the gift of a lifetime—adoption—to that baby and the adoptive family. It is a wonderful act of love for a couple to bring someone else's child into their home and raise that child as their own. And so many worthy couples are waiting in the trenches for just that opportunity.

A year later I talked to the father of the baby. "How are things going?" I asked him.

He looked down. "Not very well. They don't want me to see the child. They want me completely out of the picture."

"You remember that day we sat down?" I asked him.

He glanced up with troubled eyes. "I remember it well."

"Remember when we went around and asked everybody what they thought we should do, and you went along with it? I could see in your eyes you didn't agree with that, did you?"

"No."

"Why didn't you speak up and say that?"

He hung his head. "I was just scared. I didn't know what to do. But I knew in my heart what you said was right."

Now before you crank out those hate letters to send me, let me state a couple things. I know that within many societies in the United States, it is countercultural to offer a child for adoption, and there are many grandparents who have successfully reared their grandchildren. But the reality is that grandparents are not designed to be parents. They should be grandparents. There's a significant difference in those roles.

Many grandparents have physical limitations in energy and may be less likely to discipline the children. They ought to enjoy their grandparenting years. All grandparents want to spoil their grandchildren just a little. But when a grandparent is acting in the parent's role, that spoiling "just a little" can lead to a selfish child who thinks only, "Me, me, me." Grandparents have already served their time rearing their own children; they shouldn't be put in the role of rearing grandchildren just because their kids have decided to bail out and be irresponsible. But again, whose child is it? And why is that child's welfare not being factored into the mix?

We live in a society where giving birth to a child out of wedlock isn't a big thing. Actresses in Hollywood call their publicist and tell them to prepare a statement: "I'm with child." It's delivered without a shred of shame or concern. Many women today have the idea, *Why would I need a husband?*

Anybody who understands human behavior realizes that every kid needs a good dose of femininity and a good dose of masculinity. That concept is as old as time itself.

But in all of this seeking after "my rights," it's the unborn babies themselves who get shuffled to last place on the priority list, when their needs should be first.

LIFESAVER

Do the right thing . . . always.

Privacy

Everybody needs privacy. Parents do; kids do.

To your teenager, her room is her domain. It's the castle within the castle. Some parents go to great extremes to make the kids feel this is their space—the kids can even paint the walls. That's a little overkill in my book, but the point remains. Your kid's room is her room, which means she needs to be responsible for maintaining it—cleaning it and putting laundry in the appropriate bin at least often enough that the health department doesn't have to be called in to condemn the room.

"Should I snoop?"

Within the confines of that privacy, your teenager will do schoolwork, write notes and emails, and access the internet.

Parents often ask me at seminars, "Is it okay to snoop in my teenager's room, computer, or journal, to see what he's thinking?"

Basically, my answer is no. Your teenager needs his privacy.

However, if your 17-year-old all of a sudden has a lot of cash and is buying things you know you didn't give him money for and he doesn't have a job, your suspicion he might be dealing in drugs could be right on target. Plus, you can't help but notice one of the drawings on the side of his school notebook is a marijuana leaf. You don't need a PhD to figure that one out.

Should you snoop then?

Absolutely!

"If I fear my teenager is involved in any illegal activity, should I snoop?" you ask.

Yes, I would.

"But doesn't snooping destroy relationships?"

Yes, it can, but so does getting arrested, having your education interrupted, and having to serve jail time. Do you really want your son or daughter to have a criminal record? And do you want to spend the thousands of dollars it will take to defend someone who is arrested for possessing or selling drugs?

So trust your kids, give them privacy, and respect that privacy. Sometimes kids just need a place to chill out, to ponder life's meaning, to text, to talk on the phone, and to do homework without interruption. But there are times when your parental nose will tell you that something is wrong. During such times, you need to be like a bloodhound: sniffing out where the trouble lies. And that sometimes means violating the basic trust and privacy boundaries you've set up in your own home.

LIFESAVER

Trust your gut feeling.

Procrastination

Back in 1985 I published a book called *The Birth Order Book*. It took me a while to convince the publisher that people would be interested in such a thing as birth order. I'd been speaking and talking about it since 1966, and I got my doctorate degree in 1974, 11 years before I published that book. Well, back in 1985, I was a guest on the *Phil Donahue Show*. Okay, so you have to be old to remember Phil, but he was pre-Oprah. Back then, if you got a segment on *Donahue*, it was like getting a segment on *Oprah* today. And not only was I on Donahue, but I was the entire show—a slot usually reserved for famous actors, actresses, and entertainers. My appearance on that show is what jettisoned the book to a top 10 bestseller.

Interestingly, the part of the book that drew more attention from readers than any other part was procrastination. We talked about the purposive nature of the behavior—that it exists for a reason—and I offered a couple of explanations. One was growing up with a critical-eyed parent—one of those people who knows specifically how life ought to be . . . and especially how *your life* ought to be. The kind of parent who is never satisfied with your performance. No matter how high you leap, it's always an inch short of their expectations. And they never pass up an opportunity to tell you that you could have done better. As a result, the critical nature of the parent gets incorporated into your life in how you see yourself—you're never good enough.

When I explained that, adults all over the country reading my book and hearing me talk had a light go on in their brains. *Whoa, that's me. I start a lot of projects and don't finish them. When I'm hot, I'm hot, but when I'm cold, I'm near worthless. I'll start on a project, get 90 percent done in record time, and do well, but then I'll stop and not complete the task. Why?*

I explained. "It's because you fear being evaluated and, more specifically, you fear getting criticized. So your thought process is, 'If I don't complete the task, I can't get criticized. I can tell myself the lie that if I had more time or energy—or whatever—then I could do this.'"

Well, I got thousands of responses from readers and listeners on that one part of the book alone. That spoke volumes to me about how many of us live with critical parents.

> *We're all flawed, so it isn't difficult to pick out one of your kid's flaws.*

So, parent, if you have a teenager who's a procrastinator, and you have to push that kid to do everything, it might have an awful lot to do with your ability to find the flaw.

Trust me, we're all flawed, so it isn't difficult to pick out one of your kid's flaws.

But if your kid is paying the price for your flaw-picking—through their nonachievement, underachievement, or procrastination on a daily basis—it's time for a change . . . on *your* part.

Otherwise those teenagers will grow up to be the adults who are always going to hit the home run but never do. The people who migrate from one job to another, at each point telling themselves the lie, *This time I'm going to hit the jackpot.* But they never hit the jackpot, and they continue to suffer from negative thoughts.

That's why the words you choose to use—or don't choose to use—with your teenager make all the difference in the world.

LIFESAVER

Your words make all the difference.

Rebellion

In order to be rebellious, you have to have someone to rebel from. Teenagers tend to rebel when they are trapped in environments that are extremes—either too authoritarian or too permissive.

The chances of a kid turning rebellious in a home where balance reigns; where there is good, healthy discussion between family members; and where kids are listened to, respected, and held accountable, is practically zero.

What spurs rebellion in a kid's mind is his environment. If a parent is always telling his teenager what to do, that's the antecedent to rebellious behavior. After all, how would you like to be told what to do all the time? You'd probably rebel too!

One of my favorite stories of all time is that of the prodigal son in the Bible. I love it because it mimics family relationships, and I've always liked stories with happy endings—even if they do start out a little rough.

> *How would you like to be told what to do all the time? You'd probably rebel too!*

The story starts out with the younger brother being fed up with working hard every day in the fields on his father's estate. He says, "You know what? I'm sick of this place. I'm sick of being told what to do. It's so mundane. I'm so outta here. I'm going to go and ask Father right now for my share of his estate."

Surprisingly, the father gives his younger son his due. (Can you imagine what that father was thinking when he heard all the complaints from his son? How heartbroken he was?)

The son takes off for a faraway land. That meant this prodigal, who was Jewish, went to a place that was occupied by Gentiles, not Jews. In other words, he wanted to get as far away from home as he possibly could. That's how repugnant home was to this kid.

Well, he went off half-cocked, didn't he? That's part of why I love this story, because it's so reflective of today's society. My dad used to say, "There's no fool like an old fool." Gosh, I think in many cases it should be, "There's no fool like a young fool." Fools come in all different shapes and sizes.

So here's this kid who's a know-it-all, and he's got money to burn. He's going to go and live life in a big way. He parties and has a great time. I'm assuming he lived a life of wine, women, and song in abundance.

But then his party lifestyle comes to a screeching halt one day when he runs out of funds. He figures out that his father's farm hands are better off than he is. At the time he is feeding pigs, and he's so hungry that even the slop he's feeding the pigs looks good.

> *Here is this kid acting cooler than cool, but as the saying goes, "All good things come to an end."*

Here is this kid acting cooler than cool, but as the saying goes, "All good things come to an end." And the prodigal son was indeed at his end. He'd squandered everything. So he decides, *I'm going to go home and ask for my father's forgiveness.*

Another thing I love about this story is what happens when the father sees his kid from afar. Does he say, "Well, I can't believe my eyes. Look what the cat dragged in! Had enough of the city life there, big boy, did you?"

No, that's not what the story says. It says that the father ran to his son—he saw him from afar and ran to him. Not only that, but he embraced his son, called for the servants to put a robe on him and a ring on his finger, and ordered a feast in his honor. When he brought out the fatted calf, he celebrated the fact that his son had come home.

When you think about it, isn't that real love?

That parent had every right to say, "Well, smarty pants, you learned your lesson out in the real world, didn't you?" He could easily have rubbed his kid's nose in the dust.

But he didn't. He welcomed his son home with open arms.

Then in comes the other brother, who has been working feverishly on the farm and in the field, doing what he's supposed to do. When he finds out his father is throwing a shindig in his brother's honor, he has a fit. "My father is throwing a party for that no-good

264

brother of mine? The one who shirked his responsibilities and left me here holding the bag? You've gotta be kidding! How come I never get a party?"

Ah, doesn't that reflect families today too?

A note for you biblical scholars out there. No, I'm not stupid. I realize the primary purpose of this story isn't to teach us about family relationships. It's really a description of a person coming back to Almighty God after straying from the narrow path and then receiving forgiveness and a place in heaven with God himself.

Before I leave this section, though, I need to speak to the parents who have done everything right . . . and who still ended up with a prodigal. A kid who, despite everything he was taught in the home, decided in his heart and mind to reject those values. I've run into these heartbroken parents in every town I've visited. They are sweet people who did life as they should, yet their kid had a wire crossed somewhere. That kid decided, like the prodigal son, "I'm outta here."

Friends, that choice is called free will. God made everybody in such a way that, as we come into this world, we have free will. Without sounding like some TV preacher, I think that affirms how much God really loves us: to give us the wonderful gift of choosing for ourselves whether to accept or reject him.

In the same way, your teenager has free will. It's up to her to decide whether to accept what you teach her or to reject your values. That is not within your control.

But it is within your control to choose to love the prodigal— whether she's near or in a faraway land. Forgiveness is a wonderful thing . . . for both of you.

LIFESAVER

Love them despite what they do.

It Worked for Me

When you talked about prodigals at a recent event, I couldn't believe it. It was like you were talking directly to me. Our daughter had run away from home when she was 16 and had returned to us a year later. But I was struggling to accept her back in our home after all she'd done and the grief and pain she'd caused us—especially my wife. I've heard the prodigal son story dozens of times, but this time it hit home. Instead of being the father—so happy to welcome my daughter back—I was acting like I was the brother, who held a grudge. And this was my *daughter*—I was her *father*! After asking God to forgive me, I went straight to my daughter and told her how sorry I was for the way I'd treated her.

That was a month ago now. Nothing easy is accomplished overnight, I know that. Our relationship is still cautious—we have a lot of years of a bad relationship to work through—but now we are starting to trust each other. Thanks for your straight talk that hit home. I really, really needed that.

Evan, Vermont

Refusing to Help at Home

If your kid refuses to do anything at home, he shouldn't receive any benefits of being a family member either. Give him the bread-and-water treatment, I say.

If he's not doing anything at home, there's also a good chance he's not doing much at school. So as far as school lunches go, he shouldn't get a dime. And you shouldn't make his sack lunch either. Let him rustle up his own grub in the refrigerator to take to school.

Take your teenager back to the basics. He gets no allowance since he's not fulfilling his role as a member of the family. If he has a TV in his room, it is removed. If he has a laptop, it is stashed away. If you bought him a cell phone, or if you're paying his monthly bill, those go bye-bye. If he has driving privileges, the family car is off limits for him.

He has nothing but electricity, cold water, hot water, dinner (if he shows up on time for it; if not, it's removed and isn't available), and a place to lay his head at night.

> *Give him the bread-and-water treatment, I say.*

Even better, you don't discuss the removal of any of these items with him beforehand. All of a sudden they're just not there.

If your kid has any brains at all, it won't take long before he questions what's happening.

Now's the beginning of the teachable moment. "From where I sit, I can see you don't give a lick about anything happening at home, and I feel that's disrespectful to all of us. So until you decide to contribute to this family, you'll have only a place to bunk, water for a shower, and meals to eat with us . . . if you show up on time. And no, you won't be driving the family car."

Everything settles down to the basics. If your kid is stubborn, he'll think, *Well, let's see how long this lasts. I'll just live with it for a while and wait for Mom and Dad to give up. There's no way I'm taking out the garbage or doing any of that stuff.*

There are kids who will play that game for a long time because they're stubborn or downright lazy. Other kids will do so because they're hiding out from life, feeling defeated, or becoming mentally ill. If you suspect any of those three might be happening with your son or daughter, get professional help. Sometimes you have to have an intervention.

If the kid is just stubborn or lazy, sooner or later the motivation will build to do something other than sit around the house and make his own lunch for school.

When the opportunity arises, talk with your son or daughter. "If you'd like to talk about it, I'm all ears. I can't do life for you, but I want to help."

Again, keep the ball in your teenager's court. Don't become the constant nag or the one who pushes from behind. And you certainly shouldn't be the person who leans over him with a watering can, urging, "Bloom, baby, bloom."

Someday your kid will figure out, *Hey, doing nothing really isn't working for me. Maybe I better get off my tail and start doing some things around here.*

So be patient and wait (as much as it's killing you inside). Your child needs to see some kind of plus or payoff before he or she is willing to become a contributing member of the family.

Sometimes a no-fringe existence is just what they need to see the point.

LIFESAVER

It's a home, not a hotel.

Responsibility

I have news for you. If your child isn't responsible at 5, 8, or 10 years old, she's not going to be responsible at 14 or 16 years old either. A kid who isn't taught to be responsible won't be responsible.

This one, parent, is strongly in your court. If you've looked the other way, made excuses, or snowplowed your child's roads of life and now you and your teenager are paying for it, you need to step up to the plate. Time is short, especially if your kid is 15 to 17 years old.

Life has a way of holding your teenager accountable—and that includes the state your family lives in, the Department of Motor Vehicles, police officers, your kid's teachers or professors, the principal of his school, his supervisor, and anyone else who is in authority over him. All will react negatively to your teenager's irresponsibility.

I never go out of my way to make any parent feel guilty, but if there ever was a case for it, it's in this area. So take a tablespoon of guilt; you deserve it if you've allowed your child to be irresponsible.

Responsibility is a huge thing in life. If your kid has told lies, pointed fingers, thrown tantrums, and done all sorts of shenanigans to avoid owning up to her responsibility in different situations, it's time for things to change. If your teenager doesn't learn responsibility now, when will she learn it?

The younger your kids are, the more malleable they'll be. The older they are, the tougher your job will be. But, parent, you have to do it. There's no alternative. You, your kids, and the world around them will pay for it if you don't.

(LIFESAVER)

You reap what you sow.

School (Doing Poorly)

Kids don't suddenly start doing poorly in school; it usually goes back to the elementary years. That's often where things start to go astray. For example, when kids aren't learning fourth-grade principles, but no one ever stopped and said, "Hey, you need to hang out in the fourth grade again for another year," there's a cumulative effect of such neglect. It's like adults who never have their teeth cleaned. In all probability they're going to end up with gum disease. Some of the disease might be reversible, but usually it will mean some delicate surgeries that are expensive and time consuming.

Some kids are not academically oriented at all, but they are very good at working with their hands. However, we live in a society that says the winners in life are the academic types. So what about the mechanical kids who haven't had success in their first 11 years of public school? Do we expect them to turn around as a junior in high school? It's doubtful that will happen.

> *A nostalgic feeling shivered up my spine, and I thought,* What am I gonna do now?

But that doesn't mean you shouldn't try to help a teenager who really wants to make a change through tutoring, special instruction, extra visits to the school on vacations, or after-school work with a teacher. The school system usually has a plan in place to deal with kids who don't achieve.

I remember back in my growing-up years, I always loved sports and played sports every season. But I only played the first six weeks of every season because after that point, eligibility slips needed to be signed by all the teachers, and I was never eligible. So even though I was a sports nut, it wasn't sufficient motivation for me to do better. I just assumed I'd play for the first six weeks of every season.

It didn't hit me that I was going nowhere until my class was standing up as a group on "Moving-Up Day," when each class would move from their spot in the auditorium to their new class spot. We seniors sang a song about "our golden days coming to an end." It was sorta weird . . . but a serendipity I'll never forget. A nostalgic feeling shivered up my spine, and I thought, *What am I gonna do now?*

That moment was when everything was set in motion for my future.

It turned out I didn't get accepted to college until nine days before the semester started. And then my acceptance was conditional on taking only a 12-credit load. That's when this boy, who did poorly at school, finally started to get serious.

When a kid doesn't care about school, it can be hard to motivate him. But I guarantee that when the motivation does kick in, he'll work hard to make something of himself.

I ought to know.

When I look back at my life, one thing remained constant. I had two parents who loved me, two parents who believed in me. Keep in mind they had no reason to believe in me. After all, getting thrown out of Cub Scouts isn't really a sign of greatness, nor is picking off heirloom Christmas tree ornaments with a pellet gun and blaming the cat. That's why I've always tried to pay a special tribute to my parents, now both in heaven, because they deserved it. I'm so thankful they were able to live long enough to see their younger son receive his doctorate degree.

No matter what, parent, don't let your belief in your teenager waver.

LIFESAVER

Late bloomers still bloom.

Self-Worth

It's good for teenagers to feel capable—confident in themselves and what they can accomplish. All kids should grow up with a healthy self-appraisal, knowing the pluses and minuses of their personality and talents, and being secure in their place in the world. After all, knowing our strengths and weaknesses is very

271

important. Good marriages have a great balance—one spouse is strong in one area, the other spouse is strong in another area. If they both had the same skills, then one of them wouldn't be needed. Variety is what makes the world go round.

Your teenager needs to know that he will excel in some areas . . . and not in others. His natural gifts will rise to the top in some areas . . . and not in others. But if he is grounded at his core—strong in his understanding of himself—his failures won't get him down; they'll motivate him.

> *We're producing kids who view reward as their right.*

However, I also want to say clearly that I believe this whole issue of self-worth is overplayed in our society. As a result, we're producing kids who view reward as their right. Now there's a repugnant thought, because your rights only go as far as not interfering with someone else's rights. Mutual respect is the key, and that respect is sadly lacking in our world today. Instead, we've raised a generation of kids whose general attitude toward life is, "You owe me."

If you want your teenager to leave home with respect for others and their ideas, and to see themselves on the same plane as others, no matter their gender, race, age, or size, then model a healthy self-worth. Show respect for others. Work hard. Admit your failures; laugh about them. If you put things in perspective, so will your teenager.

Keeping a healthy perspective means you stay grounded so your teenager will stay grounded. When your kid does something well, encourage him: "Wow, you got a B! I know you studied hard for that science test. You've got to be really happy with yourself. Those are great results." But don't overly praise him: "Oh, Johnny, you are just the best in soccer *ever!*" Your teenager will know you're blowing smoke; he's seen for himself that others are better . . . in just about every area.

It's important for your teenager to realize that she is *one person* in the world. Her role is important, yes, but so is everybody else's. And she's part of your family, where nobody is above the work it takes to run your home. Everybody pitches in, everybody helps.

LIFESAVER

Balance is the name of the game.

Sex

I was once invited to a wedding where the first time the bride and groom kissed was at the altar. Personally, I'm not into that. If my wife-to-be had chronic halitosis, I'd want to know about it long before I hit the altar.

Where there are people, there will always be different opinions, and there will be extremes. In our world today, there are still arranged marriages. Yet in the Western world—the United States and Canada—kids often grow up too fast and are rushed into dating when they're not emotionally ready for the relationship . . . or the consequences. I know parents who think it's fine if their teenagers have sex, as long as they have "protection." I know other parents who won't allow their children to date until they're in college or out on their own.

Let's be blunt. The form of dating has changed a lot since the era when I dated my wife-to-be, Sande, and our idea of a date was sharing a 39-cent hamburger. I still remember when we had to have a blood test before we got married. My lovely wife was so naive, she asked the person drawing her blood, "Why exactly do we have to do this anyway?"

"Oh," the technician responded, "because we have to see if you have syphilis or gonorrhea."

My wife-to-be's eyes batted 20 times rapidly in shock, and then she managed, "Oh, oh, well . . . I can just tell you I don't have those." In January 2011, the Alan Guttmacher Institute reported:

Although only 13% of teens have ever had vaginal sex by age 15, sexual activity is common by the late teen years. By their 19th birthday, seven in 10 teens of both sexes have had intercourse. On average, young people have sex for the first time at about age 17, but they do not marry until their mid-20s. This means that young adults are at increased risk of unwanted pregnancy and sexually transmitted infections (STIs) for nearly a decade.[7]

NewsStrategist.com reports that the average age of sexual initiation is about the same for men and women. But here are a few interesting notes they provide as well:

- People who lived with both parents at age 14 waited longer to engage in sex for the first time than did those in other family situations.
- For most women, sexual initiation occurs with a slightly older man, while most men first have intercourse with a woman their own age or younger.
- Among teenage girls, the younger the girl was at first intercourse, the more likely it was that her partner was considerably older. Eleven percent of girls who were age 15 at first sexual intercourse, and 10 percent of those under age 15, lost their virginity to men who were aged 20 or older.[8]

Okay, parents of daughters, I doubt you'd want your 14-year-old girl to become a sexual receptacle for some horny 17-year-old boy. But basically that's what's happening in our society. And, of course, all the pleasures of sex include venereal diseases, such as syphilis (which is making its way back in good numbers), chlamydia, and herpes simplex.

The very language of teenagers today—"Oh, he's so hot"—further pushes the envelope of sex and what is socially acceptable. And today it's no longer boys who are the aggressors; females can be just as aggressive. It is also not uncommon today for teenagers to engage in oral sex and tell themselves that they haven't had sex; they've just hooked up with each other. I've even heard accounts of kids giving oral sex to each other on school buses!

Clearly, parent, all parameters on sex in society have been removed, and movies, music, TV, and many other images bombard our kids with sensual entertainment, pushing them to grow up way too fast.

The numbers are speaking loudly. Just how sexually active are today's teenagers? Perhaps the most reliable source is the US Government's Centers for Disease Control and Prevention. They report that, in 2001 (the latest year for which data has been released), over a third of the males and females in grades 9 through 12 had experienced sexual intercourse.[9]

> *I doubt you'd want your 14-year-old girl to become a sexual receptacle for some horny 17-year-old boy. But basically that's what's happening in our society.*

The numbers of different studies don't always agree, but the principle is clear. Your teenager *will* face pressure to have sex . . . and it will be intense. So how will you prepare him or her for that moment when it arrives?

If you haven't already talked to your child about sex before he or she is age nine, that discussion probably isn't likely to happen now. Or, if it does, it'll be handled in a cumbersome, embarrassing way. For some great material to get your own head around the subject, read my book *A Chicken's Guide to Talking Turkey with Your Kids about Sex.* (Okay, I know saying this for the third time sounds like a shameless plug, but it's a good, basic book that parents and kids can profit from.)

Parent, you can't walk around with your teenager 24-7, especially after they have access to autos at age 16. (Note when sexual activity kicks in as well—age 17. The age of freedom—more money, access to a car and remote parking areas . . .) Nothing will prevent your teenager from parking and doing the Watusi unless something permanent has been imprinted on his mind that says, *This is wrong. It's not good for me.*

> *Nothing will prevent your teenager from parking and doing the Watusi unless something permanent has been imprinted on his mind that says, This is wrong. It's not good for me.*

But how can you get your kid there? Especially in a world where sex is expected on the first or second date—even in the adult population? And when teenagers graduating from high school as virgins are now the exception?

Expose your son or daughter to good information about why it's best not to have sex with anyone outside the bounds of marriage. Besides the high risks of venereal disease, your teenager risks great emotional pain from someone who may just want another notch in his or her belt. Love is only love if it's committed, within the bounds of marriage, and between two people for a lifetime. Then, and only then, is sex "safe."

Make sure you tell your teenager how great sex is—how exhilarating. He needs to know the truth from you, but also the reality. If he doesn't, and he hears from a friend about how great his "score" was on Friday night, he might think, *Hey, my parents were lying.* But if you tell your son or daughter, "Wow, sex is great. It's worth waiting for!" then you're showing your teenager you're not really from the Dark Ages, and you do understand the emotions and the urge to have sex. But it's all about the right time, the right place, and the right man or woman—in a marriage of a lifetime.

Again, it's all about partnering with your teenager—being *for* them rather than *against* them. Give the facts to them straight—no guesswork, no embarrassment. Dads need to talk to daughters; moms need to talk to sons. Who better than someone of the opposite sex who loves you to shoot it to you straight about what the opposite sex is looking at and thinking about?

I've always said that the best sex organ we have is our mind, and I truly believe that. As you grow in real love, in a committed relationship, it is the mind where you connect.

Teach your teenager to use the brain God gave her to think her way through life so she ends up on her feet—not damaged and pummeled by people whose mission in life is to use and abuse others.

> *"How far should we allow our kids to go on dates?" Here's a quick answer that makes it easy: keep your clothes on at all times.*

Sex is sacred, and it should be treated as such. Treating it any other way is truly playing with fire.

Often when I'm in seminars with parents, they ask me, "How far should we allow our kids to go on dates?" Here's a quick answer that makes it easy: keep your clothes on at all times. What's private stays private and shouldn't be seen by anybody else except your medical doctor.

That simple solution takes care of a lot of problems.

Make sure your teenager believes that sex is worth waiting for. "Scoring" outside of marriage leads only to guilt, betrayal, broken relationships, and being a notch in somebody's belt instead of the star in your someday-to-be spouse's eye.

LIFESAVER

What's private stays private.

It Worked for Me

I grew up in a home where you just didn't talk about sex or anything "private," and I'm uncomfortable talking about it. So I was a really good candidate for your book *A Chicken's Guide to Talking Turkey with Your Kids about Sex*. When my son turned 11, a girlfriend passed it to me and said, "You need to read this." She was right. Since I'd grown up with the view that sex is private, it took all the courage I had to talk with my son about sex, what girls want (and don't want), and why sex is worth waiting for. But I knew you were right—I couldn't pass the buck to my husband. Who better than a girl to talk to guys about girls?

It took two days for me to recover after the experience, but my son seemed to take it all in stride. I knew the message had gotten through when I heard him talking with his nine-year-old brother. "Yeah, Mom just gave me the sex talk. But she said a lot of stuff that surprised me too. Like how hot sex is, and why it's worth waiting for until you get married." It evidently intrigued his brother too, because the next day Alec came to me and said, "Uh, Mom, I was thinking it might be time that we have, uh, you know, that sex talk. . . ." Now this mom isn't quite so chicken. On to round two!

Marlene, Idaho

Shoplifting

Here's what you have to understand about shoplifting. The police, the retail executives of stores, and judges have a simple way of dealing with shoplifters. So if you get a call from the police station that your daughter is in custody because she shoplifted, and the evidence is clear, ask to talk to your teenager (if she's not the one who called). Tell her, "Honey, I feel so bad for you; this is such a terrible predicament that you got yourself into."

I know you want to bail her out, but don't right away. If she has to sit in that jail for a while, then so be it. In fact, the longer she sits, the better. A lot of learning and thinking about the consequences will take place during that intense time.

If your daughter ends up going to court—and in all probability she will—here's my suggestion. See if you can reach the judge and find out if you can be in the room, but at the *back* of the room. Certainly you shouldn't be sitting next to your teenager. After all, are you the one who shoplifted? Let the kid face the music on her own.

Let the kid face the music on her own.

What are you saying to that judge with your actions? "Judge, my daughter is the one who shoplifted, not me, so I would like you to communicate with her and deal with her without my interference. If you need me, I'm in the back of the courtroom."

Will it be an emotionally disturbing experience for both you and your daughter? Of course. And it should be, to drive the point home.

But will it have a happy ending? Ah, yes, it'll have a great ending. If a teenager has to face the music on her own, chances are it's the last time she'll shoplift.

LIFESAVER

A little reality can be a big wake-up call.

Sibling Rivalry

Way back in 1985, I handed in a manuscript to my publisher with this title: *Abel Had It Coming.* "Kevin," the publisher said, "you can't have a title like that."

"Why not?" I said. "It's got a nice family flavor . . . and it's true."

"Well, you can't," the publisher said.

"Okay, *fine*," I said in my true baby-of-the-family frump, "then you name the book."

So they came up with a very provocative title: *The Birth Order Book*.

> *Your kids will needlessly engage you in their battles.*

Congrats to all you creative firstborn and only children.

But my point remains. Sibling rivalry has been around since Eve birthed the brothers Cain and Abel. The two were as different as night and day, and they didn't make it easy for Eve to try to keep peace in the household. They were rivals up to the very last, bitter moment . . . when one killed the other out of jealousy.

Sibling rivalry is based on competition. It reeks of "I'm bigger than you are," "I'm better than you are," and "I'll show you." And it gains furor when a parent is watching.

Sibling battles will erupt. The question isn't *if*, it's *when*. And when it happens, what's a parent to do?

- Don't get involved in the hassle. Put the ball back in the court of the feuding siblings.
- As quickly as you can, isolate the squabblers in another room or, in warm climates, outside your house.
- Tell them, "I want you to solve the problem yourselves. I'm sick of hearing about it."
- Tell them, "If you don't solve it, I'll solve it in a way that makes sure neither party will like the results."

Your kids will needlessly engage you in their battles. The nature of their purposive behavior is to draw you in and air their side of the case before you, Judge Judy or Judge Wapner.

Don't do that. Don't go there, parent.

Instead, move them to a room where they can take care of the argument all on their own. Then sit back and watch the predictable results. They'll be out of there in one minute, trying hard to get you back into the fray.

Send them back into the room. Ignore the stomping, loud voices, and name-calling. Realize that a lot of it is for your benefit, to see if Mama Bear (especially) or Papa Bear will step in. When you don't, it's amazing how much quieter the whole environment gets.

Just watch and see.

LIFESAVER

Don't play the "judge and jury" game.

Sleeping Constantly

No doubt, the hormone-group years are tiring. The medical community could tell you that teenagers who are going through growth spurts need to sleep longer; their bodies require it. In addition, teenage life can be very emotional, and sleep also helps the mind regroup and awake refreshed.

Complicating those real-life issues, though, is that many teenagers tend to take on raccoon-like qualities—i.e., they'll be up half the night, especially in the summer, when school is not a part of their life.

Last week, Lauren was home from school because she had a cold and didn't feel well. At 2:30 p.m., I finally heard her stirring in her bedroom, so I knocked on the door and opened it, and there she was, still in bed, propped up on her elbows and looking at something on her computer screen.

"Lauren," I said, "can I get you some breakfast? Would you like breakfast in bed? And by the way, the bank called and said you were a few hours late. . . ."

This was my way to gently, and with humor, tell my daughter, "Holy crow. It's after two in the afternoon, and you're still in the rack?"

Note that I didn't go in there and say, "How come you didn't go to school today if you feel good enough to lay in bed and stare at your computer?"

> *The hormone-group years are tiring.*

Humor is the way we Lemans do life. You might not be great at humor. But my point is that you have to find some way to communicate to your teenager that you love and care about her without coming across as a judgmental jerk. If your kid doesn't feel loved, she might give you lip service (since there will be other consequences if she doesn't), but her words won't connect with her heart.

So when your teenager is sleeping a lot, ask yourself, *Could the kid be growing? Are his pants getting shorter? Is his voice getting deeper?*

If so, let the kid sleep when he needs to. Streamline his activities so he can get a bit more rest.

But then there are those kids for whom sleeping constantly is a result of laziness, a way to escape a life that can be overwhelming, or the beginning signs of depression. If you have concerns, ask yourself, *Is he still accomplishing what he needs to get done around the house—pulling his weight in the family? Is he acting discouraged or depressed? Like life is too much to handle?*

That's when Mom or Dad needs to step in to address the situation. Take him to your medical doctor for a checkup to see if anything else might be going on. Otherwise, let him sleep, and interact with him when he's fully alert.

Again, navigating the hormone-group years is all about partnering with your son or daughter and capturing his or her heart.

(LIFESAVER)

Sleep does a body good . . .
unless the body's dead.

Sleepovers/Overnights

If you know the teenagers your kid is hanging out with, and their parents have a healthy back-and-forth trust relationship with them, and you visit each other's houses frequently, overnights are no big deal. However, an excess of anything (for example, two sleepovers in a row) is rarely good and can further exhaust your growing, needing-extra-sleep teenager. Of course, they make the most sense on a Friday or Saturday night, when the kids don't have school the next day, since during *sleepovers*, they won't get any *sleep*. However, cross-gender sleepovers are never a good idea in the teenage years, since these are the hormone years where things that "shouldn't happen" can happen.

The smartest move on the chess board is always the one that's done with forethought and caution.

So when your daughter approaches you about a sleepover, your first question should be, "Where?" Is the sleepover being held at a home where your kid frequently is, where she's comfortable, and where you know the parents and the environment where she would be hanging out and sleeping?

Your second question should be, "With whom?" If you don't know the friend well or the parents or siblings of the friend, now would be a good time to take a pass . . . unless the overnight with the new friend is at your home, and the other parents are willing for their kid to be there.

Don't just take your kid's word or her friend's word for it, though; make the call yourself. If your teenager is away at a sleepover, be a street-smart parent and always phone the home to check in. That call gives you the lay of the land: Are the parents truly there? Is everything going as planned? Did any extra sleepover residents arrive that your daughter or son wasn't aware would be there?

The smartest move on the chess board is always the one that's done with forethought and caution. In the Leman home, sleepovers were perks, not givens. And they were always carefully checked out.

LIFESAVER

Know where your kid is bedding down.

It Worked for Me

I loved your advice regarding sleepovers. We decided that our daughter wouldn't do any sleepovers until she turned 12. Then we'd think about it. We turned down several offers for sleepovers because we didn't know the other kids or the families very well. And we're glad we did. Now our daughter is 14, and she's found a great group of girls who are all from similar backgrounds, and we parents hang out together a couple times a week too when the girls get together. After two years, we've visited each other's houses and shared hard stuff, work woes, and our dreams.

Just last week, the girls had their first sleepover at our house, and they all had a ball. Interestingly, they all called to check in with their parents before going to sleep . . . even without me nagging them to do so. My daughter says not having sleepovers was worth the wait, because this group of girls is just the best!

Amanda, Illinois

Smoking

It amazes me when I see teenagers smoking today. The kids of my generation smoked, but then, we were stupid and didn't have all the information about smoking that's so readily available today—like how it leads to lung cancer and emphysema and shortens your life span. That ought to be enough to make anybody stop, but I also know firsthand that such habits die hard.

When I was a teenager, I used to sneak my father's cigarette butts—he smoked Lucky Strikes, a strong, unfiltered cigarette—from wherever he left them. I'd stash them in my pocket and smoke them on the way to school. To make things easier, several of the parents of kids I ran with allowed their teenagers to smoke in the house . . . at 15 years of age!

> *Guys like me who once smoked and quit are probably the biggest crusaders against smoking.*

So I've been there—I was a smoker. But guys like me who once smoked and quit are probably the biggest crusaders against smoking.

If I had a kid who was smoking, I'd certainly want to nip it in the bud right away. It's a bad habit—very unhealthy not only for your son or daughter, but also for all those who have to endure the secondhand smoke. However, now that your child is a teenager and anything you say can be used against you, harping about the evils of smoking probably won't accomplish your purpose of getting your kid to quit. But a friendly visit to your family practitioner (whom you've tipped off, of course, that your teenager is smoking) would help to set the stage, or a dinner out with some other third party that your kid respects.

There's another way to cut off the flow too. Cigarettes cost a lot of money. Where is your teenager getting the money for his smoking habit? Is it from you? From his allowance? From his job? If so, cut off the flow. And yes, even if that means informing his employer that he no longer has your permission to work. Remember, parent, this is all about having a new teenager by Friday. If you want change, you have to stick to the plan, with no warnings and threats. You simply act.

Your teenager can only bum a free smoke off his buddies for a short while before they'll get sick of it. Without the money, the habit will fizzle.

Don't sit this one out, parent. The long-term health repercussions are too large for you to do otherwise. You need to act now.

If you don't like it, cut off the flow.

Spaceyness

Let's be honest. Some kids have more space between their ears than others. They have a hard time staying on task and don't tend to follow through on their responsibilities because their thought life is elsewhere.

But I'm convinced that kids who seem spacey have been taught to be spacey. When they couldn't find something, Mom, Dad, or another sibling found it for them.

"Oh, your shirt isn't hanging in your closet? Are you sure?" Mom asks.

The kid nods. "Sure, I'm sure."

So even though Mom knows she just did the laundry and hung that shirt in there, guess who goes to his closet to check it out? No, not the son. Mom does. She walks away from the middle of *her* project to go see what's up with *his* project, which all of a sudden has become finding his favorite shirt.

"Oh, honey, it's right here in the middle of your other clothes," she announces.

Spacey-Boy has won again. Not only did he get her to find it for him—something he could easily have done for himself if he'd looked more than a second in his closet— but he got her to divert her attention from her task. In other words, Mama jumped right at Spacey-Boy's beck and call. Boy, does life get any better than that? No wonder Spacey-Boy continues to be spacey. He's got it made in the shade.

> *If your child is spacey, why is he spacey? Does it get him out of responsibility?*

Many kids are spacey because they have decided it's easier to have other people do things for them. It's a way to duck out of responsibility, and it's very manipulative.

It's never good to do things for kids that they can do for themselves. Does that mean you never get up and get your child a drink? No, doing so shows love, kindness, and grace. However, doing your kid's homework, always rescuing him from tight places, or not sending him back to look for that "lost" shirt isn't doing him any favors. Instead, it's enabling him to be spacey and not own up to his responsibilities. And that's not doing anybody any good—you, him, the rest of your family members, his teachers at school, his friends, or anyone else he interacts with.

Some kids are spacey because they have ADD (attention deficit disorder) or ADHD (attention deficit/hyperactivity disorder).

However, I am of the professional opinion—after years of counseling children, teenagers, and their parents—that people slap these labels on too quickly instead of working with the purposive nature of the behavior. If your child is spacey, *why* is he spacey? Does it get him out of responsibility? Does his sister get disgusted when he forgets, and she does his job for him? Or is he held accountable to do his own job, even when it's not convenient for him? So before you visit your local medical doctor and shrink, do some sleuth work of your own. Is your child spacey, disorganized, and unable to focus all the time, or just when something is required of him?

A lot of kids are walking around on ADD or ADHD medicine when what they need instead—or in conjunction with the medicine for the short term—is someone to teach them responsibility, accountability, and how to focus on a project. Because some kids have been diagnosed with ADD or ADHD, some parents take license with that and excuse their own kid's inappropriate behavior as, "Oh, he has ADHD; he can't help himself." No, he can, and he needs to. If he doesn't learn how to control his behavior now, God help him—and those around him—when he becomes an adult.

Now is the time to give your teenagers the tools they need to live as healthy adults who give back to home and community, rather than acting as takers.

Never do for them what they can do for themselves.

Stubbornness

If your teenager is stubborn, what is the purposive nature of that behavior? Many kids are good at being stubborn when their parent is pushing them to do things. But why would a kid want to be stubborn instead of giving up and making it easy on herself? Because the purposive nature of being stubborn ensures that she will get attention from her parent, even if it's negative attention. And all kids thrive on attention—of one kind or another.

A kid who is stubborn is, by her behavior, loudly saying, "I am not going to be who you want me to be. No way, no how."

For every kid who is stubborn, let me assure you that someone else who lives under the same roof is also stubborn. Could that person be you? When you see a powerful, stubborn child, there is always a powerful, stubborn parent behind the scene. The child learned the behavior from

> *All kids thrive on attention—of one kind or another.*

someone, and she continues to use it because she's getting results.

If you have a stubborn, powerful child, you won't get anywhere by being stubborn and powerful back. You will never win, because you have too much to lose and she doesn't. So don't paint yourself into a corner. In the heat of battle, too many things fly from our mouths that should never see the light of day. Instead, stay calm. Don't think revenge. Think, *Oh, an opportunity.*

Let's say that your son refuses to clean the garage once a month, and that's one of the ways he is supposed to help around the house. Don't say a word. Instead, have his sister do the job, and pay her out of his allowance.

For the daughter who refuses to let someone know she won't be at an event, let her take the phone call from the perturbed supervisor of the event. In fact, work a little behind the scenes by calling the supervisor first, letting him know that your daughter refuses to call but won't be there, and ask him to call her directly and ask her to explain herself. Do the same thing with your son, who was supposed to drive straight from school to the dentist's office and decided to hang out with his girlfriend instead. When you get the call from the dentist, tell the receptionist, "Could you call back in about an hour when my son is home, explain who you are, and tell him exactly how much you didn't appreciate him blowing off his appointment?" As an added teachable moment, deduct the no-show penalty fee that the dentist charges from your teenager's allowance that week.

Invoke a third party's help behind the scenes, and then let reality do the talking.

It works . . . every time.

Don't paint yourself into a corner.

Suicide

Suicide has become much more common in children and teenagers than it used to be. It is now the fourth leading cause of death for children ages 10 to 14 and the third leading cause of death for teenagers 15 to 19. For children in the United States under age 15:

> About 1–2 out of every 100,000 children will commit suicide. For those 15–19, about 11 out of 100,000 will commit suicide. . . .
>
> In any one year, 2–6% of children will try to kill themselves. . . . About 15–50% of children who are attempting suicide have tried it before. That means that for every 300 suicide attempts, there is one completed suicide.
>
> If a child has major depressive disorder, he or she is seven times more likely to try suicide. About 22% of depressed children will try suicide. Looking at it another way, children and teenagers who attempt suicide are 8 times more likely to have a mood disorder, three times more likely to have an anxiety disorder, and 6 times more likely to have a substance abuse problem. A family history of suicidal behavior and guns that are available also increase the risk.[10]

A suicide attempt, or a warning that a teenager is thinking about committing suicide, is a cry for help. It's an attention-getting device, a call that says, "Things are not going well in my life, and I can't handle it myself." Often teenagers who attempt suicide have had a recent loss or crisis, experienced bullying, or had a family member or classmate who committed suicide. Some teenagers who try to commit suicide make the attempt in a very public manner, so others find out about it. Do they really want to die? Often, no. But they are reaching out for help in the only way they know how. By their actions, they are screaming out, "Please pay attention to me. Help me!"

> Most teens interviewed after making a suicide attempt say that they did it because they were trying to escape from a situation that seemed impossible to deal with or to get relief from really bad thoughts or feelings. . . .
>
> Some people who end their lives or attempt suicide might be trying to escape feelings of rejection, hurt, or loss. Others might be angry, ashamed, or guilty about something. Some people may be worried about disappointing friends or family members. And some may feel unwanted, unloved, victimized, or like they're a burden to others.[11]

In my professional experience, the teenagers who really want to kill themselves—whose goal is to end it all—*will* kill themselves. They won't necessarily give a public warning but will carry out their plans in a quiet, private place, with no one looking on and no hope of anyone interfering with their plans. Sadly, these teenagers who do indeed take their lives are most often firstborn and only children—the perfectionists of life.

I talk a lot about the dangers of perfectionism, because it is slow suicide. If you have a perfectionistic teenager, there is a huge chasm between his ideal self and his real self that causes dissonance in his life. He can never do enough or be enough to meet the expectations of this "ideal self." If the dissonance grows too great, the teenager may feel the chasm can never be spanned, and depression can kick in.

There are lots of reasons for suicide attempts—for both those that fail and those that succeed. So what can you as a parent do to protect your child? Be aware of changes in your teenager—no, not the traditional, hormone-laden, minute-to-minute changes, but the growing signs of depression, mental illness, and withdrawal from friends, family, and activities that your teenager used to love. If you suspect that your teenager may be contemplating suicide, do not let him or her be alone at any time. Take immediate action and get professional help from your medical doctor, who may refer you to a psychologist.

But the best antidote of all is your parental involvement and communication with your child. Kids who try to commit suicide feel that they aren't listened to, that no one cares, and that they're disconnected from their families and friends. No matter how difficult it is to hear what your teenager wants to say, keep the communication lines open. Stay calm. Listen more than you talk. Your keen observation skills can truly be the difference between life and death for your son or daughter.

LIFESAVER

Be observant—always.

Texting/Sexting

Texting is here to stay. It's part of the growing technology world that your teenagers know and love. But it's also important that your teenager know when it's appropriate to text and when it's not.

Thomas L. Friedman was disturbed when he read an article in the *New York Times* about a teenage girl's use of digital devices—she sends and receives "27,000 texts in a month . . . carries on as many as seven text conversations at a time . . . texts between classes . . . and, often, while studying." Her grades, as a result, are slipping. "We need better students who come to school ready to learn, not to text . . . [and] an all-society effort . . . to nurture a culture of achievement and excellence."[12]

Wilkes University professors report that texting is now the number one distraction in class. "Nine in 10 admit to sending text messages during class—and nearly half say it's easy to do so undetected. Even more troubling, 10 percent say they have sent or received texts during exams, and 3 percent admit to using their phone to cheat." Psychology professor Deborah Tindell says, "Students these days are so used to multitasking. . . . They believe they are able to process information just as effectively when they are texting as when they are not." She now tells students that if she even sees a cell phone during a test, that person will get an automatic zero.[13]

Some schools have a policy of no cell phone use during the school day. Others make rules for when it's appropriate to use a cell phone—for example, during study hall and in between classes, but not during class or tests. If she chooses not to adhere to the rules, take action. Having no cell phone for a school week is an eternity to a teenager who lives by texting.

Also, it's increasingly important in today's world to realize the significance of the types of messages your son or daughter is sending and receiving.

In 2008, high schooler Jessie Logan sent nude pictures of herself to her boyfriend. When they broke up, he sent those pictures to other high school girls, who began harassing Jessie. Miserable and depressed, Jessie was afraid to even go to school. Her mother had no idea what was going on until much later. Jessie agreed to tell her story on a Cincinnati TV station so that no one else would be caught by the dangers of sexting. Two months later, unable to cope with the continued harassment, she hanged herself in her bedroom. Now her mother, Cynthia Logan, grieves her loss and has taken on the battle to make Jessie's story public and warn kids about the dangers of sending sexually charged pictures and messages.

> [Sexting] is a growing problem that has resulted in child pornography charges being filed against some teens across the nation. But for Cynthia Logan, "sexting" is about more than possibly criminal activity: It's about life and death.
>
> Last fall, the National Campaign to Prevent Teen and Unplanned Pregnancy surveyed teens and young adults about sexting—sending sexually charged material via cell phone text messages—or posting such materials online. The results revealed that 39 percent of teens are sending or posting sexually suggestive messages, and 48 percent reported receiving such messages.[14]

Parents, do you see those stats? Thirty-nine percent of teenagers are sexting, and 48 percent report receiving them! That means it is highly likely your teenager has already been involved in sexting—from one side or another. So have a lot of other folks—those who ought to know better, I might add.

Take a look around. Adults lose their careers (an ESPN sports guy was fired for sexting), professional athletes (including Hall of Famers) have suits filed against them for inappropriate language in texting, and marriages have broken up over sexting.

> *Kids need to know that, no matter how private a conversation might seem, it's not.*

Before you allow your kids to have a cell phone (I always say that every teenager needs a cell phone when beginning to drive), or even if they have one now, impress upon them how to handle that phone with care. Kids need to know that, no matter how private a conversation might seem, it's not.

That means you need to teach your teenagers to have common sense and to stay within the guidelines for texting. If it's something that should not be said or shown in person, it shouldn't be said or shown on a text message either. And if they receive messages that are inappropriate, they should be deleted. If that person is a friend, he or she should be told that such language is unacceptable, and if it happens again, your son or daughter will no longer be texting that person.

Teenagers live to text. Just watch one sitting with her family in a restaurant, ignoring them and texting her friends like crazy. Then again, if a kid is sitting at dinner with her family, texting shouldn't be allowed. There is a time for texting and a time to put the cell phone away. And if they're texting all day instead of interacting with others in person, something is wrong. Everything in life is about balance.

Texting will be a part of your kids' lives. So make sure they know the guidelines for safe texting:

1. Never text while driving.
2. Sexual text messages or images are never acceptable.
3. Realize that any message you send might become public.
4. There's a time to put the cell phone away.

LIFESAVER

Think before you text.

Withdrawing

Why do teenagers retreat to the haven of their bedrooms? Everybody needs privacy; everybody needs a break and some alone time. You do, and so does your son or daughter. Quiet time upon arriving home from school or work is a good thing for everyone.

But there's a difference between quiet time and withdrawing from life.

When kids withdraw from the family, it's usually the result of having a home where they are just talked at and told what to do.

Invite participation.

If you were bossed around all the time, how might you respond? You'd probably retreat too.

A street-smart parent draws her teenager into the mainstream of family life by saying things like, "Hey, honey, I'm stuck. I need some help. I don't know what to do. I'd love your insight into this situation. Would you be willing to help? Here's my problem. . . ."

What is that parent saying to her son or daughter? "Hey, I think you're a smart kid, and you're really talented. Your contribution to me and to this family is important. I don't know what we'd do without you."

If you have a teenager who tends to withdraw, ask him questions like, "What do you think we ought to do? We're planning a family trip, and I'm wondering where we should go. What are your thoughts?"

Statements like that invite participation. They give the kid a reason to jump into the conversation. And when your kid opens the door and becomes involved, keep your mouth shut. Don't shoot his ideas down. Welcome them, even if you think they're stupid.

Say, "Wow, that's interesting. Tell me more." Or, "You know, I never thought of that. Good job." Or, "What an intriguing idea. I'm going to come back to you again for more thoughts on that, and you don't even charge a consulting fee, do you?"

Encourage your son or daughter to talk, to settle into the mainstream of your family life.

Part of growing up and being a teenager means needing time to sort out thoughts and emotions, to daydream, and to be alone. So experiment with ways to draw your teenager out of her shell without draining her.

LIFESAVER

Invite your teenager to the party called life.

Epilogue

I love college football. So much so that when I'm in town, I go to the University of Arizona's football practice two to three times a week. Going to a practice means watching the players run routes and drills. It's certainly not the most exciting thing in the world, so you have to be a pretty over-the-top fan to enjoy practice. But that's me—I'm a football nut. So today, I literally dragged my sweet wife there with me (okay, so she reluctantly agreed to go).

There's one thing you have to understand about Sande. She's a woman who would much rather watch the food channel or sit in her favorite chair, looking through recipes in magazines. In fact, the Leman household boasts, on last count, over 4,000 pages of recipes that have been pulled out of magazines.

But Sande agreed to go along with me this time. On the way home, because of the heavy traffic at five o'clock in the afternoon, I had to do a little zipping around on side streets to get to a major thoroughfare. It just so happened that in our circuitous route, Sande and I drove by the small house where I lived with my parents when I first moved to Arizona as a 19-year-old.

All of a sudden, a memory of my mom, who is now in heaven, flooded back. My mom, I'm convinced, was a saint. How she handled a son she thought would never get out of high school (she went to school more than I did—to talk to the principal and teachers about me) was nothing short of amazing. She always loved me, believed in me (in spite of all I did), communicated with me, and had good expectations of me. Even when I was a junior higher and high schooler who drove teachers out of teaching, I could talk to my mother. We had a great relationship.

When I was 19 years old, I announced at dinner one night, "Mom, I'm engaged!"

My mother also had the corner on staying calm in the midst of my critical years. And this steady facet of her character was especially important for a son like me who was filled with great ideas (some of which weren't always smart).

So now, with that background, back to my flashback that day as I was driving past the old house. . . .

When I was 19 years old, I announced at dinner one night, "Mom, I'm engaged!"

My mom, God love her, didn't pass out. She simply said, "Well, oh, that's good. Would you like some more green beans, honey?"

I was a punk—a directionless 19-year-old with a cigarette hanging out of his mouth—and working as a janitor at the time, making less than 49 bucks a week. I had no real life plans; I was coasting along after high school. I'd been dating a girl for a short while, had shopped for a $200 ring at Montgomery Ward, and had managed somehow to put a $20 deposit down on it. I was engaged . . . for about a week or two.

The way my mother handled that little crisis made all the difference in the path my life took. Mom could have blown me out of the water with a few choice words. (I'm sure you could think of some if your son or daughter pulled what I did.) But what would that have gained? I might have married the girl just to prove I could do it.

Instead, my mother knew that I merely needed time to figure out life and the decision for myself. She continued to believe in me—that I'd do the right thing, in the right timing.

Now when I look back, I realize it would have been terrible—for the girl and for me—if we had married. The good news is, I got my 20 bucks back from Montgomery Ward!

Parent, the way you respond during these critical years makes all the difference. You need to think, talk, and communicate differently. If you do, and you focus on your teenagers' hearts instead of on their appearance and actions, you'll capture their heart for a lifetime.

I ought to know. I have five children, and each of them is unique and special. So is our relationship.

But I'll never forget the day my dear wife, Sande, told me the rabbit had died . . . for the fifth time. In all honesty, *pleased* wasn't the first emotion that came to my heart. It was more like, "Say WHAT?" (And yes, I do realize that I had something to do with the results, but in that moment, shock took control of my 50-year-old body.) Three of our children, Holly, Krissy, and Kevin II, were navigating or already had successfully navigated their teenage years. Our fourth child, Hannah, was five years old. And now we were to have a fifth child when I was starting to consider applying for my AARP card. I could just see myself in a walker, hobbling up the aisle at this baby's high school graduation, and folks asking, "Oh, is your grandchild graduating this year?" That baby's and my own high school graduations will be exactly 50 years apart.

> **4 Things You Never Want to Forget**
>
> - Your belief in your teenager matters.
> - What you *don't* say is just as important as what you *do* say.
> - You count far more than you know in your teenager's world.
> - What you put in your teenagers' bags sets them up for a lifetime.

But that baby, Lauren, now in high school, is truly a gift. I can't imagine the world without her in it. Or our family without her in it. A few months ago, she was in the play *Brigadoon*.

When she asked me, "Daddy, what night are you going to come watch the play?" I said, "Every night!" (Five performances.) Then I followed it with, "Lauren, I'm so proud of you."

Her response? She just smiled and said, "I know you are, Dad."

> *I'll never forget the day my dear wife, Sande, told me the rabbit had died . . . for the fifth time.*

Her confident response makes me smile all over, for it tells me I've done something right in rearing my kids. I know it further when I hear, "Dad, I love you," every time I see or talk to one of my five children. I know it again when my five children go out of their way to spend time with each other; keep family events as a priority; migrate back to the family turf for fun, relaxation, and stimulating conversation; and actually *like* each other (for those of you in the trenches right now, just realize that sibling rivalry won't always be the grueling experience it might be right now).

But with Lauren, hearing "I love you" chokes me up every time. In all likelihood, just doing the math, I know that I may not be around when she's 38 years old, as my oldest child, Holly, is now. After all, I'm already 68, and Lauren is only 18.

But I have no doubt that Sande and I have packed Lauren's bags full of what she needs to succeed in life—and that Lauren will indeed do well.

A lot of it has to do with the fact that we have respected each of our kids, partnered with them, and allowed them to be who they are—with their own unique talents and gifts. We didn't expect them to be "normal" or to keep up or compete with anybody else. We just enjoyed them for who they were—and are now.

> ## Great Resources You Can't Afford to Miss
>
> - *Teen-Proofing* by John Rosemond
>   A practical, doable management plan for mentoring teenagers toward responsible adulthood. www.rosemond.com
> - *Parenting by the Book* by John Rosemond
>   A foundational book that paints the big picture of child rearing. Indispensable, no matter the ages of your children. www.rosemond.com
> - *How to Really Love Your Teen* by D. Ross Campbell
>   A classic that helps parents relate to their emerging teenagers, communicate unconditional love, handle anger, and encourage spiritual and intellectual growth.
> - *Running the Rapids* by Kevin Leman
>   A practical, insightful book for parents to guide teenagers through the turbulent waters of adolescence.
> - *Have a New Kid by Friday* by Kevin Leman
>   A practical, real-life, tested resource for changing your younger child's attitude, behavior, and character in five days.
> - *Making Children Mind without Losing Yours* by Kevin Leman
>   A bestseller of sure-fire techniques for developing a loving, no-nonsense approach for rearing children.
> - *The Birth Order Book* by Kevin Leman
>   A classic that unlocks the secrets of birth order, which powerfully influences who you are, whom you marry, the job you choose, and the kind of parent you become.

Parent, what you do right now counts. *You* count. Every minute you spend with your teenagers counts. What you put in their life luggage will pay off. So don't fill their bags with the fluff of busyness, activities, and what everybody else thinks you should be doing. As one old geezer fisherman told me, "Don't just hand people fish. Teach them how to fish."

This morning I dropped Lauren off at high school and she said, "Bye-bye, Daddy, I love you."

"No, honey," I said softly, "I love you."

When I drove off, I knew that she would be just fine—no matter what life throws her way.

Just as the rest of my children will be.

And just as yours will be too.

★ THE WINNING PLAY ★

And the winner is . . .
both you and your teenager.

The Top 10 Countdown to Having a New Teenager by Friday

10. Think the best, expect the best, speak the best.
 9. Establish equality, but varying roles.
 8. Keep the ball in the right court.
 7. Prioritize—home, school, and other things, in that order.
 6. Speak the truth in love.
 5. Be a partner, but don't intrude.
 4. Let reality do the work so you don't have to.
 3. Lather on the encouragement.
 2. Focus on the relationship and your teenager's heart.
 1. Realize: this too shall pass.

Notes

Monday: He Used to Be Normal. What Happened?

1. Stephen R. Covey, "Business Mission Statements," The Community, accessed April 11, 2011, https://www.stephencovey.com/mission-statements.php.

2. GoodReads, "Louis Pasteur Quotes," accessed April 11, 2011, http://www.goodreads.com/author/quotes/692216.Louis_Pasteur.

Tuesday: Talking to the "Whatever" Generation

1. Sharon Jayson, "Young People Prefer Praise to Sex, Money," USAToday.com, January 10, 2011, http://www.usatoday.com/yourlife/parenting-family/teen-ya/2011-01-08-selfesteem08_ST.

Wednesday: Belonging Matters More than You Think

1. Cynthia Tudor, David Petersen, and Kirk Elifson, "An Examination of the Relationship between Peer and Parental Influences and Adolescent Drug Use," *Adolescence*, Winter 1980, 795.

2. US Department of Health and Human Services, *Mental Health: A Report of the Surgeon General*, 1999.

3. Ibid.

Friday: *Ka-ching, Ka-ching,* Dividends on the Way

1. Binyamin Appelbaum, David S. Hilzenrath, and Amit R. Paley, "All Just One Big Lie," *The Washington Post*, December 13, 2008, http://www.washingtonpost.com/wp-dyn/content/article/2008/12/12/AR2008121203970.html?hpid=topnews.

2. Proverbs 3:21; 4:5–6; 3:30–31; 3:13–15.

3. Ephesians 6:1, 3–4.

4. Jonnelle Marte, "How to Give Children the Gift of Investing," *Arizona Daily Star*, November 28, 2010.

5. Terry Cater, news release, February 3, 2011, taken from Dr. Louann Brizendine, *The Male Brain: A Breakthrough Understanding of How Men and Boys Think* (New York: Three Rivers Press, 2010).

Ask Dr. Leman

1. David P. Parker, "Bulimia," E Medicine Health, accessed February 1, 2011, http://www.emedicinehealth.com/bulimia/article_em.htm.

2. Craig Wilson, "Parents Worry about Toddlers' Tiny Fingers Itching for iPhones," *USA Today*, November 8, 2010.

3. Ibid.

4. Mayo Clinic Staff, "Self-Injury/Cutting: Definition," Mayo Clinic, August 3, 2010, http://www.mayoclinic.com/health/self-injury/DS00775.

5. Ibid., http://www.mayoclinic.com/health/self-injury/DS00775/SECTION+symptoms.

6. Donald J. Franklin, PhD, "What Is a Depressive Disorder?" Psychology Information Online, 2003, http://www.psychologyinfo.com/depression/description.html.

7. "Facts on American Teens' Sexual and Reproductive Health," The Guttmacher Institute, January 2011, http://www.guttmacher.org/pubs/FB-ATSRH.html.

8. "Seventeen Is the Average Age at First Sexual Intercourse," NewsStrategist.com, http://www.newstrategist.com/productdetails/Sex.SamplePgs.pdf.

9. Centers for Disease Control and Prevention, "Trends in Sexual Risk Behaviors among High School Students—United States, 1991–2001," *MMWR Weekly*, September 27, 2002, 856–59, accessed April 12, 2011, http://www.cdc.gov/mmwr/preview/mmwrhtml/mm5138a2.htm.

10. "Suicide and Children," Healthy Place: America's Mental Health Channel, January 7, 2009, http://www.healthyplace.com/depression/children/suicide-and-children/menu-id-68/.

11. "Suicide," Teens Health, November 2010, http://kidshealth.org/teen/your_mind/feeling_sad/suicide.html.

12. Thomas L. Friedman, "We Need Students Ready to Learn, Not to Text," *Arizona Daily Star*, November 27, 2010.

13. "Pa. College Profs Report Texting Is Now No. 1 Distraction in Class," *Arizona Daily Star*, November 27, 2010.

14. Mike Celizic, "Her Teen Committed Suicide over 'Sexting,'" TODAYshow.com, March 6, 2009, http://today.msnbc.msn.com/id/29546030/ns/today-parenting/.

Index of A to Z Topics

acne, 126
anger, 128
anorexia, 132
arguing, 134
attitude, 137
authority figures, 138

bad-mouthing others, 140
body language, 142
bossy, 144
boyfriends/girlfriends, 145
bulimia, 150

car key wars, 152
cell phone, 155
chip on shoulder, 157
chores, 160
clothing, 162
curfew/staying out late, 164
cutting/self-injury, 165

death, 167
depression, 169
divorce, 171
doesn't fit in with peers, 174

door slamming, 176
driving privileges, 178
drugs and alcohol, 180

eye-rolling, 185

Facebook and other social inventions, 186
filthy language, 188

grounding, 190
guilt, 192

hair and grooming, 193
homework battles, 195
hormone changes, 198
hugging . . . or not, 201

internet use, 203
interruptions, 205

junk food, 207

know-it-alls, 209

lack of motivation/living up to potential, 210

loner, 214
lying/dishonesty, 216

me, me, me, 218
messy room, 220
money matters and jobs, 221
mouthy, 227
music, 229

name-calling, 232

oversleeping the alarm, 233
overwhelmed by life, 234

parties, 237
peer pressure, 240
physical development (or lack thereof), 241
piercings, 245
place of worship, 248
pornography, 250
power struggles, 254
pregnancy, 256
privacy, 259
procrastination, 260

rebellion, 262
refusing to help at home, 266
responsibility, 268

school (doing poorly), 269
self-worth, 271

sex, 273
shoplifting, 278
sibling rivalry, 279
sleeping constantly, 281
sleepovers/overnights, 283
smoking, 285

spaceyness, 286
stubbornness, 288
suicide, 290

texting/sexting, 292

withdrawing, 295

About Dr. Kevin Leman

An internationally known psychologist, radio and television personality, and speaker, Dr. Kevin Leman has taught and entertained audiences worldwide with his wit and commonsense psychology.

The *New York Times* bestselling and award-winning author of *Have a New Kid by Friday, Have a New Husband by Friday, Have a New You by Friday, Sheet Music,* and *The Birth Order Book* has made thousands of house calls for radio and television programs, including *Fox & Friends, The View,* Fox's *The Morning Show, Today, Oprah,* CBS's *The Early Show, In the Market with Janet Parshall, Live with Regis Philbin,* CNN's *American Morning,* and *Focus on the Family.* Dr. Leman has also served as a contributing family psychologist to *Good Morning America.*

Dr. Leman is the founder and president of Couples of Promise, an organization designed and committed to help couples remain happily married. His professional affiliations include the American Psychological Association, the American Federation of Television and Radio Artists, and the North American Society of Adlerian Psychology.

In 1993, North Park University in Chicago awarded Dr. Leman the Distinguished Alumnus Award and, in 2010, an honorary Doctorate of Humane Letters. In 2003, he received from the University of Arizona the highest award that a university can extend to its own: the Alumni Achievement Award.

Dr. Leman received his bachelor's degree in psychology from the University of Arizona, where he later earned his master's and doctorate degrees. Originally from Williamsville, New York, he and his wife, Sande, live in Tucson, Arizona. They have five children and two grandchildren.

For information regarding speaking availability, business consultations, seminars, or the annual Couples of Promise cruise, please contact:

Dr. Kevin Leman
P.O. Box 35370
Tucson, Arizona 85740
Phone: (520) 797-3830
Fax: (520) 797-3809
www.drleman.com

Resources by Dr. Kevin Leman

Books for Adults

Have a New Kid by Friday
Have a New Husband by Friday
Have a New You by Friday
The Birth Order Book
It's Your Kid, Not a Gerbil
Under the Sheets
Sheet Music
Making Children Mind without Losing Yours
Born to Win
Sex Begins in the Kitchen
7 Things He'll Never Tell You . . . But You Need to Know
What Your Childhood Memories Say about You
Running the Rapids
What a Difference a Daddy Makes
The Way of the Shepherd (written with William Pentak)

Becoming the Parent God Wants You to Be

Becoming a Couple of Promise

A Chicken's Guide to Talking Turkey with Your Kids about Sex
(written with Kathy Flores Bell)

First-Time Mom

Step-parenting 101

Living in a Stepfamily without Getting Stepped On

The Perfect Match

Be Your Own Shrink

Stopping Stress Before It Stops You

Single Parenting That Works

Why Your Best Is Good Enough

Smart Women Know When to Say No

Books for Children, with Kevin Leman II

My Firstborn, There's No One Like You

My Middle Child, There's No One Like You

My Youngest, There's No One Like You

My Only Child, There's No One Like You

My Adopted Child, There's No One Like You

My Grandchild, There's No One Like You

DVD/Video Series for Group Use

Have a New Kid by Friday

Making Children Mind without Losing Yours (Christian—
parenting edition)

Making Children Mind without Losing Yours (Mainstream—
   public school teacher edition)

Value-Packed Parenting

Making the Most of Marriage

Running the Rapids

Single Parenting That Works!

Bringing Peace and Harmony to the Blended Family

DVDs for Home Use

Straight Talk on Parenting

Why You Are the Way You Are

Have a New Husband by Friday

Have a New You by Friday

Available at 1-800-770-3830 or www.drleman.com

Take the
5-Day Challenge

Family expert Dr. Kevin Leman reveals in this *New York Times* bestseller why your kids do what they do, and what you can do about it—in just five days!